School of American Research
Advanced Seminar Series

DOUGLAS W. SCHWARTZ, GENERAL EDITOR

SCHOOL OF AMERICAN RESEARCH
ADVANCED SEMINAR SERIES

Simulations in Archaeology

ATLANTIC RICHFIELD FOUNDATION
is gratefully acknowledged
for its support of the
School of American Research
Advanced Seminars.

SIMULATIONS IN ARCHAEOLOGY

EDITED BY
JEREMY A. SABLOFF

A SCHOOL OF AMERICAN RESEARCH BOOK
UNIVERSITY OF NEW MEXICO PRESS • Albuquerque

Library of Congress Cataloging in Publication Data

Main entry under title:

Simulations in archaeology

    (School of American Research advanced seminar series)
    Based on the School of American Research Advanced
Seminar on "The Use of Systems Models and Computer
Simulations in Archaeological Research," held in
Santa Fe, N.M., Oct. 9–13, 1978.
    "A School of American Research book."
    Bibliography: p.
    Includes index.
    1. Archaeology—Data processing—Congresses.
I. Sabloff, Jeremy A. II. School of American Research
Advanced Seminar on "The Use of Systems Models and
Computer Simulations in Archaeological Research" (1978:
Santa Fe, N.M.) III. Series.
CC80.4.S58   930.1'028'5   80-54568
ISBN 0-8263-0576-8   AACR2

To the memory of our colleague
Gilbert W. Low
(1939 – 1979)

Foreword

There is an exciting prospect that archaeological data and ideas will soon be examined regularly by fitting together sets of conceptions into computerized models that imitate the real world and simulate the dynamic operations of past cultural systems. Few such computer simulations have yet been presented in the archaeological literature because few archaeologists are familiar with the time-consuming and complex routine required in their construction or have available the necessary specific data. But computer simulations may well be the next profitable direction in our search for explanations of the past, for they grow so logically out of the steps taken by archaeology in the past century: from random data collection to cultural description, proceeding through chronological ordering to interest in process, and finally to systems construction. Now, with the opportunity conceptually to manipulate systems through simulation, we can anticipate that the past will be made understandable to a degree of elegance hardly imagined only a few years ago. Even the construction stages in computer simulation can provide ancillary benefits by exposing deficiencies in the data and weaknesses in the structure of models, by encouraging the amalgamation of apparently conflicting theories, and by allowing us to examine the trajectory and consequences of past cultural and environmental changes.

The exploration of this new research direction served as the focus of a stimulating interdisciplinary School of American Research seminar that included not only archaeologists but also a philosopher, an economist, a mathematician, and a systems analyst. This volume, an outgrowth of the seminar, begins with a comprehensive introduction: Sabloff's presentation of computer simulation of the context of contemporary archaeology, Aldenderfer's "primer" of basic principles for simulation, and Bell's focus on the formulation of testable computer simulation models and on the scientific methodology from which they are developed.

Part 2 presents the details and discusses the implications of four increasingly complex case studies. Aldenderfer begins with an assemblage simulation, carefully leading the reader from definition of problem and system through all steps of the simulation to an analysis of the final product. Cordell describes a site abandonment simulation for Wetherill Mesa, Colorado, critically examining the variables as a means of exposing the nature of simulation construction. Zubrow uses Forrester's model of urban growth and decay to simulate the organizational dynamics of ancient Rome and highlights the heuristic insights one may obtain from the simulation process. In the fourth case, Day examines epochal changes such as the transition from hunting and gathering to agriculture and from feudalism to capitalism, tying the examples together in a discussion of adapting economic systems.

In Part 3, three commentary papers reveal something of the lively, cross-disciplinary interaction that characterized the seminar. From Cooke's evaluation during the seminar emerged a concern for the paucity of sophisticated mathematics used in archaeological research. In his chapter, therefore, he introduces critical mathematical tools and concepts useful in describing cultural processes and in constructing and evaluating simulation models. Low assesses the explanatory purposes of modeling, using data from the Pueblo abandonment of the Colorado Plateau for illustration. In the final chapter, Renfrew discusses each of the papers thoughtfully, focusing on the nature of systems thinking and the great potential for the use of archaeology's unique data in the study of long-term culture change.

Judging from the insights foreshadowed in this volume and from the enthusiasm of the seminar participants, it is clear that computer simulation of past cultural systems will become a strong component in the archaeologist's kit of intellectual tools. Undoubtedly, one of the major contributions of this technique will be its pursuit simultaneously of detailed data and of broad theoretical constructs. The approach offers a greatly needed, internally reinforcing impetus for the growth of the discipline. In providing a comprehensive and informative appraisal of the current status and future prospects of computer simulation, this volume promises to become a landmark in the growth of archaeological research.

Douglas W. Schwartz

School of American Research

SIMULATION n   1: The act or process of simulating: feigning   2: a sham object: counterfeit   3a: The imitative representation of the functioning of one system or process by means of the functioning of another < a computer simulation of an industrial process > b: examination of a problem often not subject to direct experimentation by means of a simulating device

—*Webster's New Collegiate Dictionary*

Preface

The School of American Research Advanced Seminar on "The Use of Systems Models and Computer Simulations in Archaeological Research" was held in Santa Fe, October 9–13, 1978. The participants included Jeremy A. Sabloff (University of New Mexico), Chairman; Mark Aldenderfer (SUNY, Buffalo); James A. Bell (University of South Florida); Kenneth Cooke (Pomona College); Linda Cordell (University of New Mexico); Richard Day (University of Southern California); Gilbert Low (Massachusetts Institute of Technology); Colin Renfrew (University of Southampton, England); and Ezra Zubrow (SUNY, Buffalo).

Background papers by Sabloff and Bell were circulated prior to the seminar. The case studies by Aldenderfer, Cordell, Day, and Zubrow formed the focus of the seminar's discussions in Santa Fe. The oral commentaries by Cooke, Low, and Renfrew were written after the conclusion of the seminar, as was the final version of Bell's introductory paper. The case studies also were revised on the basis of the discussions at the seminar. Finally, Aldenderfer was asked to prepare a general introductory paper that would provide definitions and a general orientation for the case studies. Sabloff wrote the brief background paper included in this volume after he had received all the final contributions.

The original idea for the seminar was hatched in Cambridge, Massachusetts, in conversations with Richard Day and the late Dale Runge, both of whom thought it would be useful and productive to bring together archaeologists, systems analysts, economists, and other scholars to discuss the role of systems modelling and simulations in the study of the past. It is our great loss that Dale did not live to participate in the Advanced Seminar.

The unfailing support of Douglas W. Schwartz before, during, and after the seminar has been instrumental in the preparation of this volume. His willingness to take a gamble on a seminar whose results were hard to predict is much appreciated. The aid of the excellent staff of the School of American Research also is greatly appreciated. As always, Ella Schroeder and her staff, with their cooking and general support, made the stay of the participants at the School a highly enjoyable one indeed.

Finally, the tragic and untimely death of Gil Low in an auto accident in July 1979 is a huge loss to us all. We will miss his stimulating intellect and engaging personality. We dedicate this book to his memory.

Jeremy A. Sabloff

Contents

PART I

Introduction

1
Background

JEREMY A. SABLOFF

University of New Mexico

"The System is the Solution"
—Bell Telephone Company Advertisement

With the rise of the "new archaeology" in the past two decades, many archaeologists have come to believe that systems models can and will play a crucial role in the study of culture change.[1] Optimism about the role of systems analysis in archaeology generally has been unbounded, and systems models and computer simulations are clearly in vogue. Charles L. Redman (1973:16) has stated, for example:

> Insights into basic systems that have been derived from and tested on other bodies of data by general-systems theorists can be applied usefully to the archaeologist's study of prehistoric cultural systems. The systems approach will enable archaeologists to infer the full complexity of the interacting phenomena of cultural processes. This approach basically assumes that the great complexity of these systems and processes is systemically organized and potentially understandable.

Archaeological knowledge about the past has grown at a tremendous rate, and the archaeologist's ability to synthesize and utilize new data has become correspondingly difficult. It has become increasingly clear that new models must be employed to prevent archaeologists from drowning in a welter of detail and from being blocked from testing hypotheses about how cultures change.

3

In hindsight, it appears natural that archaeologists should have turned to systems theory as a means of coping with the increasing complexity of their data. In recent years, the use of systems models has grown rapidly, and systems terminology permeates the literature. Clearly, this rise of systems thinking in archaeology is closely allied with the development of the "new archaeology" in the past two decades. Although a systemic view of culture, through the use of functionalist approaches, has a long tradition in archaeology, it has only been through the recent writings of Lewis R. Binford and his colleagues that a normative view of culture has been transformed into a systemic, diachronic, evolutionary perspective. The contrasting systems and normative views of the Hopewell "culture," as illustrated by Struever and Houart (1972), are good examples of the potential of the systems view. Many of the cases developed by Binford in *An Archaeological Perspective* (1972a) also provide instructive examples.

In particular, the new archaeology's stress on the variability of the archaeological record and on the primacy of the goal of understanding the process of culture change has buttressed the growth of systems thinking in archaeology. Also, the growing importance of ecologically oriented studies has been closely correlated with the rise of systems thinking. The ecological emphasis on a holistic view of culture and the environment has been especially significant in this regard (see Willey and Sabloff 1980 for further discussion).

The trend toward a more "scientific" archaeology also has reinforced the emergence of the systems approach in archaeological studies since the use of systems models and precepts allies archaeology with other scientific disciplines. Moreover, systems theory provides a number of ready-made hypotheses which can be tested against the archaeological record.

The development of more sophisticated mathematical models in archaeological research has provided an additional reinforcement for systems thinking. Multivariate approaches to the analysis of area data can be assimilated most comfortably within systems models of culture process. The roles that computer simulations of partially known, ancient cultural systems might play in fleshing out systems models and providing means of testing alternative models also have enhanced the potential strength of systems analysis in archaeology.

It has been stated that "methodologically, the use of a systems perspective will ultimately force us to use simulation" (Hole and Heizer

1973:465). But how closely are computer simulations allied with particular systems approaches? Can computer simulations help solve some of the partial-data problems facing archaeologists? Will simulations simply serve as another aspect of archaeological model building, or can they be used fruitfully to test hypotheses generated by systems theory? Will their value lie simply in their use as heuristic devices for clearly ordering archaeological data? Or can computer simulations guide the archaeologist in his/her selection of the quantifiable data necessary for systems analysis to be undertaken (see Hosler, Sabloff, and Runge 1977)? Questions like these must be grappled with if archaeologists are to be successful in using simulations in their quest for understanding the past.

The School of American Research Advanced Seminar on "The Use of Systems Models and Computer Simulations in Archaeological Research" was designed to explore the utility of systems modelling and computer simulations, particularly the latter, in building explanations of past cultural processes. There has been much polemic in the archaeological literature concerning the potentially crucial roles that systems thinking and computer simulations can play in future archaeological research. But the exact nature of such roles is not yet clear, nor are the practical directions archaeologists should take in order for systems thinking and computer simulations to begin playing productive roles.

In planning a seminar on simulation, I felt that it would be useful to bring archaeologists together with scholars from other fields who use systems modelling and computer simulations in their research. In talking only among themselves, archaeologists often quickly lost sight of the limits of some of their approaches, and it was hoped that the seminar discussions would provide a useful antidote to such thinking. But the purpose of the seminar was not simply to bring archaeologists back to reality from their theoretical or methodological reveries. Rather it was hoped that the discussions might offer some pragmatic evaluations of just how archaeologists might employ systems thinking and simulations. Also, the seminar was conceived to see if there might be a basis for productive collaborations between archaeologists and systems analysts or archaeologists and economists or archaeologists and mathematicians. Moreover, it was not envisaged that the discussions would necessarily be a one-way street with the various specialists solely responding to archaeological concerns; it was hoped that the interests of archaeologists and the archaeological data base with its long sequences of cultural development might prove to be relevant to the interests and research of systems analysts, mathematicians, or economists. Initial observations at the seminar indicate that this hope may turn out to be a reality.

By the end of the seminar, the participants were in complete agreement about the productive role which systems modelling and computer simulations can play in archaeology (although there were some disagreements about specifics, as can be seen in the following chapters). It is hoped that this book conveys some of the optimism and, through its critical analyses of the use of computer simulations in archaeological research, indicates some of the paths scholars may follow in the future.

In addition, there was a great sense of intellectual excitement throughout the seminar sessions. Although a proper sense of caution kept the participants from going overboard in their optimism about the potential uses of systems modelling and computer simulations, they agreed that they could particularly have a significant role in archaeological theory building. Although systems thinking, especially the utility of General Systems Theory, has recently come under attack (Salmon 1978; Berlinski 1976), most archaeologists would probably agree that a systems perspective has much to offer archaeological research (see the review by F. Plog 1975). Moreover, there is a rapidly growing professional interest in the application of computer simulations to archaeological concerns, as attested by this seminar, the recent volume edited by Hodder (1978), the monograph by Zimmerman (1977), and a host of recently published articles (most of which are referenced in the following chapters). However, archaeologists are just beginning to realize the potential of simulations, and it remains to be seen how significant a role simulations will play in future studies.

Given the directions which archaeological theory and method seem to have taken in the past few years, the role might well prove to be important indeed. As the initial glow of the "new archaeology" has worn off, archaeologists have come to realize that although the goals of the discipline—centering around understanding the processes of culture change—have been clarified, the means of reaching such understanding are far from clear, and if the extravagant claims of the 1960s are to be realized, much hard work will be needed. In particular, archaeologists are beginning to see that in order to understand how the archaeological record is formed (Schiffer 1976), they must build bridging theory to link past remains with behavior. In turn, they can then use such middle-range theory to confirm theories of culture change (Willey and Sabloff 1980: Chapter 8; also see Binford 1977; Goodyear, Raab, and Klinger 1978). But most important of all, archaeologists must develop methods that will provide the data relevant to the creation and testing of middle-range theory and ultimately the confirmation or rejection of general archaeological theories. The seminar participants seemed to agree that as new methodologies appropriately linked to searches for middle-range theories are created in coming years, good systems modelling in general and computer simulation in particular will prove to be very useful parts of such methodologies.

Although many archaeologists would agree with Doran (1970:298) that minimally "simulations will certainly encourage that clarity, precision and objectivity of thought which so many are seeking," the seminar participants all felt that simulations can do much more. As F. Plog (1975:218) has pointed out: "Simulation will undoubtedly continue to grow in importance in archaeology as a technique for generating hypotheses, for testing alternative models, and for evaluating alternative archaeological methodologies." The chapters in this volume illustrate a wide range of these possibilities.

Four case studies (Chapters 4–7) form the central focus of this book. These case studies, which also were the foci of the seminar's discussions, are quite varied in substance, ranging from hunter-gatherer societies and village agriculturalists to complex urban systems and modern economic entities. There also was great diversity in content and goals, with emphases ranging from the study of the formation of the archaeological record to the testing of an archaeological hypothesis about site abandonment and to the evaluation of a system dynamics theory. In addition, the potential applicability of systems modelling in economics to understanding cultural processes is productively explored. In general, there was much interest in the nuts and bolts of the case studies. Concentration was not on the computer models themselves but on verbal descriptions of why the system was designed to work the way it did. Many discussions consisted of long "walk-throughs" of each model, the more concrete the better. Everyone showed a great deal of interest in how each of the case studies worked and why the investigator had developed the particular conception of the situation modelled.

The participants also wanted to understand each other's theoretical assumptions as these related to model construction. The archaeologists, for example, found the perspective (paradigm) from which the economist and the systems dynamicist viewed human and institutional behavior difficult to understand at the beginning of the seminar. When coupled with the differing vocabularies (just compare the language in Day's case study with that in the three other case studies) and concepts, these varying perspectives made *initial* discussion difficult. However, the effort to overcome these barriers turned out to be quite worthwhile as the participants soon found much more common ground in understanding cultural processes than they might have been willing to concede at the start of the seminar. For this reason, archaeological readers, for instance, should not be put off by the difficulties of reading Day's chapter, since a careful reading (or rereading) of his examples will show many ideas of potential relevance to archaeological attempts at grappling with the processes of culture change.

The important introductory chapter by Aldenderfer makes the telling point, which the case studies forcefully illustrate as well, that the application of computer simulations to archaeological problems is far from a simple procedure and does not produce results by magic. Moreover, careful thought must go into the decision to utilize simulation as part of a particular research strategy.

The second introductory chapter, by Bell, makes a strong argument that when it comes to testing explanations, a refutationist strategy makes most sense, particularly when hypotheses are couched in systems terms. Given the recent controversies in archaeology about various philosophical stances useful to the archaeologist, Bell's clear and forceful statement has much to recommend it.

Two of the commentaries, by Cooke and Low, examine the implications of specific mathematical formulations for systems modelling and the great flexibility and utility of the system dynamics approach to processual problems. Cooke's and Low's perceptions turned out to be very important for the archaeologists because the concrete illustration of how someone from another discipline would approach a question of archaeological concern was more easily grasped than the more general discussions that were concerned with basic philosophy and vocabulary. The concluding chapter, in Renfrew's inimitable and insightful style, fittingly evaluates the seminar discussions in terms of the place of systems thinking and simulations in future archaeological scholarship.

Finally, it should be stressed that most of the seminar participants began with the assumption that explaining culture change was a major goal of research. Thus, instead of spending time debating goals, the seminar participants focused on strategies that would allow scholars to define the mechanics of change in a meaningful way and use such knowledge to construct falsifiable, not ad hoc, explanations. What was of special note (and gratification) to the archaeologists at the seminar was that the nonarchaeologists came to believe that the archaeological data base, with its sequences of long time depth, as well as the general anthropological archaeological perspective, was of interest to them in their efforts to model and ultimately explain change. To archaeologists who have become used to their growing dependence on a variety of disciplines for new techniques, methods, and ideas, it was welcome news to hear that their own expertise might be useful or interesting to economists, system dynamicists, or mathematicians.

NOTE

1. I wish to thank Professor Cordell for her helpful comments and suggestions regarding the directions this introductory statement might take.

2

Computer Simulation for Archaeology:
An Introductory Essay

MARK S. ALDENDERFER

State University of New York at Buffalo

A happy man and wise is he
By others harmes can warned be.
             —John Florio, *Second Frutes*, 103, 1591

Despite considerable discussion and debate, computer simulation in archaeology is still in its infancy. Simulation, like a human being, will have a long, slow, difficult, and often painful period of growth and development before reaching maturity. Every discipline that has eventually adopted simulation has done so only after a lengthy period of testing and evaluation. Many other disciplines have abandoned the technique, finding it far more trouble than it was worth.

Archaeology is now in this position: the discipline must decide whether or not to continue to devote research and development effort to the technique, or to turn instead to more profitable methods. Until recently, archaeological opinion on simulation has been blissfully ignorant. Enthusiasm has been the rule, and many scholars have predicted that simulation would revolutionize the study of many hitherto insoluble archaeological problems. But as the number of attempts to build simulation models begins to increase, greater numbers of archaeologists are beginning to realize that simulation is not a panacea that can provide quick insight into intractable problems, and that,

11

contrary to expectation, the use of simulation often leads to the appearance of a whole series of epistemological and methodological problems which are equally intractable and often less interesting. Beginning to grow is the opinion that simulation is an expensive albatross weighing down the collective neck of the discipline, draining off ever-scarce resources from substantive research. Perhaps more benignly, some archaeologists have come to feel that simulation is an interesting excursion into the methodological frontiers of archaeology which now must be abandoned to return to the real problems facing the discipline. It is probably safe to assume that a majority of archaeologists consider simulation mildly interesting but on the whole not particularly useful in the conduct of archaeological research.

Current disillusionment and bewilderment about computer simulation stem from a misunderstanding about what simulation is and what it can and cannot do. In this regard, simulation has suffered the same fate as systems theory in archaeology. F. Plog (1974) has shown how a selective reading and use of the vast literature on systems theory has led to claim and counterclaim over its proper role in archaeological research. Much of this debate and confusion could have been avoided had more archaeologists realized that systems theory had been used and developed in many different disciplines, and that each of these disciplines has imparted its own emphasis and interpretation to theoretical systems concepts in order to make them applicable to a specific field.

Archaeology must now adapt computer simulation to its particular needs. Perhaps this can be accomplished with less confusion than that which attended the introduction of systems theory to the discipline. Although simulation has been discussed in archaeology since 1970 (Doran 1970), relatively few simulations have been presented in the archaeological literature despite the fact that it was perceived as important. Because of this, and because the majority of published simulations in archaeology have been rather unsophisticated compared to most other scientific fields, no single terminology or approach to the technique has yet had time to become ingrained in the discipline. The most effective strategy to counter any possible trend to fragmentation in the use of simulation in archaeology is to *consolidate* the more important features of simulation. Consolidation, the process of summarizing what is known of a particular concept, methodology, technique, or problem, is especially important when dealing with techniques such as simulation which have grown rapidly and spread across a number of scientific disciplines. In a study of cluster analysis, Blashfield and Aldenderfer (1978) demonstrated how consolidation tends to (a) reduce the unfortunate effects of borrowing idiosyncratic jargon, (b) prevent redundancy of effort, and (c) prevent premature closure of opinion on a technique newly introduced into a discipline.

This chapter is offered as an early attempt at the consolidation of information on computer simulation in archaeology. In form, it adopts the guise of a primer, or an introduction to the basic principles of a subject. The literature on computer simulation is vast, and it would be sheer folly to claim that any review of the subject is comprehensive. However, I have attempted to pinpoint the most important features of computer simulation modelling as performed in many disciplines; the chapter should be seen as a guide to the literature rather than a manual on how to use simulation.

SOME DEFINITIONS

The following definitions are offered as a first attempt at the refinement of the current state of knowledge about simulation technique in archaeology. They are not intended to be complete or authoritative, but instead are to serve only as useful approximations which can help to guide further inquiry into simulation methods by others. They also provide a common base for the use of these terms throughout the remainder of this chapter. Many other terms not included here are defined in the appropriate sections of the chapter.

Simulation is a difficult term to define. To some authors, such as House and McLeod (1977:22), simulation refers to the process of model building and model use on a computer. Other authors see simulation as a technique for solving problems. Naylor et al. (1966:3) define simulation as "a numerical technique for conducting experiments on a digital computer which involves certain types of mathematical and logical models that describe the behavior of a . . . system . . . over extended periods of time." Similarly, Kiviat (1967) notes that simulation "is a technique for reproducing the dynamic behavior of a system as it operates through time." Others prefer to recognize a simulation as a model. Martin (1968:5) defines a computer simulation model as "a logical-mathematical representation of a concept, system, or operation programmed for solution on a high-speed electronic computer." Despite inevitable differences in emphasis, most definitions of simulation recognize that (a) a simulation involves experimentation with a model of a system on a computer, (b) the model is generally a mathematical, logical, or "quantitive" representation of a system or process, and (c) the analysis of the model is dynamic—that is, the behavior of the model is explored over time. A fourth meaning must be added to this list: a simulation is often identified as a *simulation model*—the actual computer program that is used to implement the logical or mathematical model on a computer for experimentation. In this chapter, the terms *simulation* and *simulation model* are used interchangeably to refer to both the overall process and concept of experimenting with dynamic models on a computer and the actual computer program (with the implied mathematical model behind it) used in the experimental process.[1]

The term *Monte Carlo* is often associated with simulation, and the combination *Monte Carlo simulation* is common in the literature. Although it will make little difference in practice, many authors consider the combination of the terms to be inaccurate. The Monte Carlo concept was introduced in the late 1940s by von Neumann and Ulam to describe a process for the solution of deterministic sets of equations with the aid of random numbers used as stochastic variables. Later, the concept was extended to include problems in distribution sampling commonly encountered in mathematical statistics (Morgenthaler 1961: 368–70). To purists, these are the only two real uses of the Monte Carlo technique. However, common usage has extended its meaning to include any method or technique, such as simulation, which uses random numbers for the solution of a problem (Kleijnen 1974:9–11; Hammersley and Handscomb 1964:2).

Another common term is *simuland*, which according to Mihram (1972a:216) is "the system being mimed by a simulation model." A *system*, of course, is some set of interrelated entities defined for a particular purpose. In this paper, I use the term *real-world system* as an equivalent of *simuland*. Although I realize that most systems are not completely observable and, in the case of archaeology, no longer living, the term clearly specifies the entity which has been the subject of the modelling enterprise.

Various definitions of the term *model* are found in the simulation literature. Unfortunately, the precise definition of the term is no longer

14

possible or even desirable because it means many different things. However, the terms *mathematical model, analytical model, numerical model, feedback model,* and *conceptual model* are commonly found in the simulation literature, and it is important to distinguish these model types. Mathematical models simply use some form of mathematics to represent the structure and operation of some system. Mathematical models offer conciseness of representation, relative ease of manipulation, and a large number of theorems which can be used to explain and describe systems (Bender 1978:1).

Analytical models are those which describe systems using that branch of mathematics known as differential and integral calculus (Kleijnen 1974:5; Hall and Day 1977:9; Shoemaker 1977). Analytical models, then, are one subset of mathematical models. A numerical model of a system attempts to solve equations by the substitution of "numbers for the independent variables and parameters of the model and manipulates these numbers" (Kleijnen 1974:5). This type of model only provides approximate solutions to problems, whereas analytical models, if they can be solved, provide exact solutions. Sometimes simulation models are called numerical models (Hall and Day 1977:10– 12), but this is confusing, and the practice should be discontinued. In some cases, numerical methods are used to solve differential equations which defy exact (or analytical) solution because of their form or number of variables. A simulation model can have both numerical and analytical components at the same time. The exact form of the model depends entirely on the definition of the system and the type (if any) of mathematics used to represent that system (see below).

A feedback model is a special type of model which has been made popular by the success of the systems dynamics school of simulation modelling (Forrester 1968, 1969, 1971). Briefly, a feedback loop is the basic unit of any system dynamics model, and it represents a closed chain of causal relationships between the state of a system and some decision, action, or change in the model. Both positive and negative feedback loops are possible, and the interaction of these loops combined with other systems' properties can express very elaborate detail. It is likely that most models, especially those in the social sciences, can be easily expressed by a set of feedback loops. Forrester and others argue that the concept of feedback is a powerful theoretical, as well as heuristic, concept which can be used to explore the behavior of many disparate systems.

15

A conceptual model is defined by Innis, Schlesinger, and Sylvester (1977:695) as "the verbal description, equations, governing relationships, or physical laws that purport to describe the behavior of some or all of the aspects of an entity, situation, or system." The conceptual model is the basis for the simulation model, and its form, content, and structure determine the logic of the simulation model. Other equivalent terms are *general model* and *theoretical model*.

Many terms have been developed to describe the contents and some facets of the operation of simulation models. Although most of these terms were developed in very different scientific fields, they are roughly equivalent. Table 2.1a presents a list of some common terminological systems, and Table 2.1b demonstrates the equivalence of some of them. In this chapter, the terms defined by Zeigler (1976b) are used to describe model contents. *Components* are the discrete entities of the system. Depending on the subject matter of the model, the contents of a component can vary considerably. *Descriptive variables* are tools which describe the condition of the component at any point in time. A component may have any number of descriptive variables. *Component interactions* are the rules by which components can influence one another through the course of model operation. Depending on the representation of the system, component interactions can be mathematical functions, logical decisions, or sets of rules or algorithms. Finally, *parameters* specify constant model characteristics. These terms are relatively general in meaning. Compared to many of the terminological systems, they carry very little theoretical or methodological content from a parent discipline.

THE SPECTRUM OF SIMULATION MODELLING

The use of computer simulation in scientific research has generated a vast literature which spans many different scientific disciplines, subdisciplines, and interdisciplinary areas. Simulation has been applied to thousands of different problems ranging from the analysis of the voting behavior of delegates to the Southern Baptist Convention to the study of how ion sputtering methods can be used in the production of semiconductor devices. The contents of simulation models also vary considerably, from completely logical structures with little mathematical sophistication to the laws of behavior of subatomic particles, gases, or

TABLE 2.1a
TERMINOLOGICAL SYSTEMS: EXAMPLES

Naylor et al. (1966)[a]	Zeigler (1976b)[c]
exogenous variables	components
endogenous variables	descriptive variables
parameters	component interactions
operating characteristics	parameters
Mihram (1972a)[b]	Hall and Day (1977)[d]
entities	compartments
attributes	forcing functions
relationships	state variables
Reitman (1971)[b]	relationships
entity	parameters
attribute	Fishman (1973)[b]
set	entity
event	attributes
state	functions
rules	

a. Derived from econometrics.
b. Derived from operations research and engineering.
c. Derived from computer science.
d. Derived from ecology.

TABLE 2.1b
TERM EQUIVALENCES (APPROXIMATE)

Exogenous variables	Terms used to describe forces
Input variables	outside the operation of the
Forcing functions	model that affect model values
Driving variables	
Components	Terms used to describe discrete,
Compartments	definable contents of models
Blocks	
Entities	
Events	
Descriptive variables	Terms used to describe the condition
State variables	of the discrete contents of the model.
Attributes	Mostly descriptive, but can be dynamic.
State	
Parameter	
Operating characteristics	Terms used to describe linkages
Component interactions	between model contents
Rules	
Relationships	
Functions	

electrical systems. The avowed uses of simulation models range from the practical, such as the prediction of how a business will do in the next fiscal year, to the theoretical, such as determining the optimal foraging behavior of an organism in a patchy environment. Simulation models can be simple, containing few variables and components, or extremely complex with literally thousands of variables, components, and equations. Different types of computers are used in simulation modelling. Although digital computers have become popular for use in a simulation context due primarily to their abundance, analog computers have had a very long history of use in computer simulation, and they are profitably used in fields in which time is viewed in a truly continuous fashion, such as ecology, dynamics, and electrical engineering. Hybrid computers are now beginning to appear which combine the best features of digital and analog computering into a single machine.

Despite this bewildering array of topics, applications, and machines, there is nevertheless an underlying continuum which serves to organize the concept of simulation modelling into a coherent framework. This continuum is based upon the traditional (if sometimes overwrought) distinction between the "hard" and "soft" sciences. Although in many cases this distinction is meaningless, it has a clear heuristic value in a simulation context because the location of a particular simulation project on this continuum helps to determine the content, form, validation process, and, most important, the proper use of the simulation model in scientific research.

To many authors, the distinction between the hard and soft sciences lies primarily in the level of understanding of the basic processes and principles included in the domain of that scientific discipline. Hard sciences tend to produce laws of processes, and in general these laws take on a highly mathematical form which makes them suitable for use in deductive experiments in highly structured contexts. Although there may be much to learn in a hard science, what is known is clearly conceptualized, and agreement on the form, content, and operation of the basic principles and processes is common among most scientists in the discipline (Karplus 1977:6–7).

The soft sciences in general demonstrate little of this high level of understanding of the basic processes which structure the domains of the science. There is usually considerable controversy as to what these

18

basic principles are and how they operate. If important systems can be identified, the mappings between system elements is often unknown, and there may be debate as to what the system contains. The fundamental laws that do exist are usually very general, and the level of rigorous mathematical definition of these laws is usually very low. In contrast to the hard sciences, what is known in a soft science is not known particularly well, and the "big picture," or the interrelationship of the elements within the scientific domain, is usually inductive at best.

The degree of hardness or softness of a discipline strongly affects the type and content of a simulation model which can be built to represent a system or process within its domain. At the hard end of the modelling spectrum, systems and processes are described as "white-box problems" (Karplus 1977:7). These systems are represented by conceptual models based upon well-structured sets of mathematical equations. The linkages between the contents of the model are clearly defined, and the resulting simulation model is clear and unambiguous. Innis (1973:34) describes these well-understood equation sets as *sharp* laws. There is no need for these laws (or equation sets) to be global; they must merely be clearly defined.

As one moves toward the soft end of the spectrum, the white box slowly turns from gray to black, indicating that the level of understanding of the basic principles of a discipline is becoming increasingly low. Although mathematical relationships may still be used as the basis of a conceptual model in the gray or black areas of the spectrum, the model is now described as *fuzzy*. A fuzzy law (Innis 1973:34) is one which is not well structured or defined, and is usually highly tentative. Unlike a simulation model based upon a sharp conceptual model, a fuzzy conceptual model of a system or process may have many conjectural elements included in its structure, or the exact form of linkage between model components and descriptive variables may only be a crude approximation. Moreover, the values of many parameters and variables may be nothing more than guesses. That a law (or model) is fuzzy reflects not the state of nature but instead our understanding of the phenomena under its domain. At the extreme end of the spectrum, where most problems are best described as black boxes, the simulation model may be no more than a set of rules or heuristic procedures implemented on a computer.

THE UTILITY OF A SIMULATION MODEL

As House and McLeod (1977:26) note, a problem which has repeatedly plagued the use of simulation modelling in virtually every scientific discipline is misapplication. This is probably one of the major reasons why the acceptance of simulation into archaeology has been so slow, and it is based upon a mistaken notion of what simulation is and how it should be used. There is a close correspondence between the form of a simulation model and the uses to which it can be applied, and there is a continuum of possible model uses which parallels the continuum of simulation model sharpness defined above.

There are many reasons for the use of a simulation model, but most of them can be subsumed under one of three types of *utility* of a simulation model: conceptual, developmental, and output (Innis 1973). Conceptual utility is the benefit gained from simply attempting to create a model of a system or process. Although this type of benefit can be gained from any type of modelling, the benefit obtained through simulation modelling is often more comprehensive because of the strong demands for explicit structure and clarity which simulation models require. Even if the conceptual model is never implemented into a simulation model, the effort expended in conceptualization often forces a rethinking of stale concepts and assumptions and can provide new insights into old problems. This type of research points the way to new goals which are used to direct further research. Developmental utility is the benefit gained from creating an explicit, better structured conceptual model and attempting to translate that model into a simulation model. It is in this effort that explicit linkages between model components must be defined and acted upon. This process generally forces the researcher to obtain new data or to build new and possibly significant concepts of model operation and structure. If conceptual utility is gained by rethinking, developmental utility is gained by placing these thoughts into action and building a simulation model. Output utility, according to Innis (1973:34), "is restricted to the benefits derived by persons outside the modeling effort as a direct result of the printed computer output and its documentation." Output utility does not refer to any benefits which the simulationist may gain from the operation of the simulation model. These are more properly classified as developmental benefits. If the output of a simulation model is used to explore or explain some other event or process, then output validity has been achieved.

Output utility can only be gained from a simulation model at the hard or sharp end of the modelling spectrum (Innis 1973; McLeod 1973b; Karplus 1977). Only this type of model can provide specific answers to questions asked of it because the model is well-defined, and the structure of the model permits realistic experimentation. Simulation models based on sharp laws are *expected* to produce reliable output which can then be used in other areas of research. Although sharp models can also provide conceptual or developmental benefits, these are clearly secondary to the goal of the modelling exercise, which is to produce useful information.

Simulation models based on fuzzy laws cannot (and should not) be used to gain output utility. Does this mean that simulation is therefore inappropriate in fuzzy situations? Clearly not, because it is often in these poorly understood situations that simulation can be of great use. Under the right circumstances both conceptual and developmental benefits can be derived from the simulation of fuzzy systems. Simulation with fuzzy models is often the only possible way in which the workings of a system can be revealed. Even if the simulation model is inaccurate (that is, it is incompletely validated) the attempt at modelling may produce tremendous insight into hitherto unobservable and poorly understood systems. The simulation model may point out flaws or weak points in the fuzzy model which forms its basis and may direct the simulationist to new sources of data which can help to sharpen the fuzzy model or law. This type of insight is rarely gained from more traditional methodologies because most are not dynamic and do not permit the investigation of the interaction of simulation model components with variables.

In the gray areas of the modelling spectrum, simulation may produce even more important conceptual and developmental benefits. Here the operation of the model may point out model components which should be simplified because they are insensitive to input changes and therefore have a negligible effect on the operation of the modelled system. In many cases of gray models, the temptation to regard the output as useful in itself is strong, but it must be resisted.

The greatest danger inherent in simulation modelling is to assume that *all* simulation models have output utility no matter how fuzzy the conceptual model used to build the simulation model. Fuzzy simulation models cannot be used for prediction (the most obvious expression of output utility), but the increasing use of fuzzy models for prediction can lead (and has led) to serious misapplications of simulation methodology. This problem is clearly illustrated by recent experiences in the use of simulation in a resource management framework in ecology. Ecology resides somewhere in the dark gray of the modelling spectrum because of the tremendous complexity of ecosystems.[2] Models of ecosystems which are to be used in a management framework must be accurate because the prediction of real-world problems is of paramount importance in a management context. Unfortunately, most of the modelling efforts in this area have been unsuccessful (Orlob 1975; Russell 1975) because most of the conceptual models used to develop simulation models have been very fuzzy. These failures have led to recriminations, and simulation has been discredited in ecosystem applications. However, the failure does not lie with the model but instead with the demands placed on the model. Prediction is clearly incompatible with fuzzy models. It is most important to define carefully the range of applicability of a simulation model and to adhere to it throughout the entire modelling process. Models must not be used outside their capabilities. Although some may bemoan the lack of predictive capacity of fuzzy simulation models, it is better to restrict the use of the model to its clearly defined limits so as to avoid many theoretical, methodological, and practical problems (Dyke 1977).

THE PROCESS OF BUILDING AND USING A SIMULATION MODEL

To build a simulation model, a researcher must move through a long series of increasingly abstract stages of inquiry. A simulation model, unlike many other quantitative models of dynamic processes, is at least twice removed from the real-world system it seeks to represent. The first major abstraction is the conceptual model of the system; the second is the implementation of that model into a computer program. The process is complex, making simulation modelling one of the most exacting and rigorous techniques currently in use today. All of the research, of course, is directed toward the increased understanding (at some level) of a real-world system or process.

22

Figure 2.1 presents an idealized flow diagram (a reconstructed logic) of the stages of the simulation modelling enterprise. Seven major stages, each subdivided into more specific tasks, are identified. In the best of all possible research worlds, the success of each stage of inquiry is dependent upon the successful completion of the preceding stage. Although this prescription is doubly important for simulation modelling because of its considerable technical difficulty, a number of conditions conspire to interrupt and redirect the flow of events. This redirection is commonly known as a *logic-in-use*. The scheme presented in Figure 2.1 is my synthesis of the work of a number of authors, most notably Martin (1968:246–49), Mize and Cox (1968: 139), Dutton and Briggs (1971), and Mihram (1972a:209–60). The discussion below elaborates on this figure, and points out some of the more important problems and questions with which anyone interested in simulation should become acquainted.

Model Goals

The first step of the modelling process is the definition of the problem to be studied. The recognition of a suitable problem can come from any source, but most often it is derived from the observation of an existing system or process. In some disciplines, such as computer science, operations research, economics, electrical engineering, and many others, the choice of the problem to be studied is a practical matter. Economists and policy makers may need models of the firm or the national economy which can help them predict changes in organizational requirements or policy under new market conditions. Computer scientists often simulate to solve a wide variety of problems ranging from the study of inventory systems to the analysis of optimal search procedures. In these cases, a clearly defined need is identified, and this need becomes the focus of the modelling effort.

But in many sciences, most notably the so-called soft disciplines of the social sciences, practical reasons for problem choice are often difficult to obtain. Very often, many of the systems of interest in these disciplines are partially or completely unobservable. In such cases, theory usually serves as a guide to the choice of a suitable problem. The sharpness of problem definition will vary depending on the quality of the theory. Sharply stated theories with clear propositions and arguments will inevitably produce clearer problems for study, and, con-

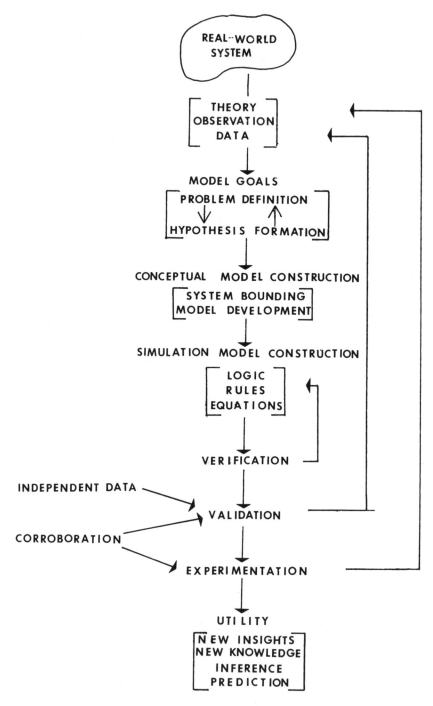

FIGURE 2.1. A flow model of the simulation modelling process.

versely, poorly articulated theories will produce less sharply defined (and consequently, possibly less useful) problems. The use of theory as a guide to problem selection is especially common in archaeology because many of the systems studied by archaeologists are long dead, are represented only by the material remains of more complex social and cultural entities, or are poorly described by analogies drawn from the ethnographic and ethnoarchaeological record. Thus, the use of theory as a guide to problem selection can be a double-edged sword, especially when simulation is used. The dangers are not significant when theory can specify clear problems for study, but the dangers increase as the theory becomes fuzzier. Although in many instances theory (however defined) is the only possible avenue to the study of some processes, the benefits of its use must be weighed against the well-known expense, frustration, and discouragement which often accompany poorly defined problems in a simulation context.

As the problem is defined, attention should also be directed toward the development of hypotheses. These two activities should be performed simultaneously, for each can sharpen the focus of the other. Since innumerable hypotheses can be drawn about or created from a single system or process, care must be taken to insure that the hypotheses selected for study are compatible with the problem which has been chosen for analysis. Only those hypotheses that are truly relevant should be formalized. Hypothesis formation also must be sensitive to the state of knowledge in the process of interest. Elaborate hypotheses based on poor empirical foundations are not of much use in a simulation context. Again, every effort must be made to determine whether or not the hypotheses posed are relevant to the problem, and that data are available or can be obtained to answer the problem using a simulation technique.

Many authors consider the formulation of a clear problem and the development of workable hypotheses to be of utmost importance to any simulation effort. Although both of these tasks are implicit in any modelling venture, the special technical complexities of simulation modelling demand that extra care be taken to complete these tasks *before* any development of a simulation model begins. Innis (1978) describes the importance of these tasks in the context of building a grassland simulation model for the US/IBP Grassland Biome Project. He stresses that this step is crucial because it serves as a focal point for the modelling effort. Explicit decisions as to what is intended of a

25

model affect both the strategy and tactics of further model development, such as the choice of simulation languages, details of model
content and structure, and programs of experimentation with the completed model. Moreover, the hypotheses developed at this stage of the
modelling process will ultimately serve as partial evaluations of the
success of the modelling effort because expectations can be easily
matched with results (Woodmansee 1978). One major practical benefit derived from early problem formation and hypothesis development
is that it often helps the researcher to stop tinkering with the completed
simulation model. Often a model is extended into distant applications
without a firm idea of where the model is going. Although such
modelling may be fun, it is expensive, and the usual result of unguided
and indefinite tinkering is a model which has no easily defined application nor a solid basis for use in other problems. Well-defined hypotheses
help to curb this tendency to tinker inappropriately.[3]

It is usually in the first stage of the modelling process that the
decision is made to use a simulation technique. By this point, it
usually becomes clear whether or not simulation is appropriate. This
decision is based upon a consideration of exactly for what purpose the
model is to be used and the quality of the data or the theory which has
been used to guide hypothesis development. Such consideration will
eventually guide model construction and the availability of other,
possibly more appropriate techniques which can be applied to the
problem. This is certainly the ideal situation, but it is more likely that,
given the present state of knowledge about simulation in archaeology,
the technique is chosen first, and then a suitable problem is created—
which may explain in part why so few successful simulation models
have yet been developed by archaeologists. This type of "experimentation" with simulation will undoubtedly decrease as archaeologists become more aware of the appropriate conditions for its use.

Conceptual Model Construction

The conceptual model provides the basis for the development of the
simulation model (or the computer program). Although conceptual
model construction as a stage appears before the simulation model
construction stage (Figure 2.1), there is a strong feedback process between these two stages of the modelling process. Although the concep-

tual model is almost always completed before the simulation model is programmed, the prior knowledge that a computer simulation model is planned exerts a direct influence on the course of model development. Depending upon the nature of this influence, this knowledge can bode either ill or well for the development of a conceptual model. It is likely that the conceptual model will suffer, for instance, if a simulation language with a particular structure is chosen before model development begins. Although the language provides structure, it is possible that the language can severely limit the generality of the resulting conceptual model. The outcome of this type of influence is a conceptual model that is probably a poor representation of systemic interactions even though the model may seem at the time to be adequate. However, knowledge that a simulation model is to be built helps the simulator to face some of the demands of computer simulation models before too much time has been invested in the development of a good but unsuitable conceptual model. The rest of this section deals with some of the more important aspects of conceptual model building in a simulation context.

Definition of System Boundaries

Early in the modelling process, the simulator must decide on what is to be included in the model. As most researchers are aware, this is not as easy as it sounds, for the process of erecting the boundaries of a system is strongly affected by epistemological and methodological issues. System bounding is especially difficult in the case of disciplines characterized by fuzzy laws. In the harder sciences, system bounding is much easier because the structure of the sharp laws and existing models has already identified the components, variables, and parameters of interest. Both the problem definition and hypotheses defined prior to the outset of conceptual model development should be used to select the appropriate variables for inclusion into the model.

Beyond these guides, there is very little methodological assistance available to the simulator for the bounding of a system. In some disciplines, especially those characterized by sharp (or at least gray) models and laws, the techniques of systems analysis are useful in the identification of the appropriate elements of a conceptual model. Systems analysis, related to systems theory, is a set of mathematical and statistical methods which can be used to tease apart complex combinations of components and variables so as to place them in a more coherent, compact structure (Bennett and Chorley 1978). Another technique is graph theory, which can be used to specify the direction and quality of connections between possible model components (Levins 1977).

One feature of this discussion on system bounding is that causality is implied when the components and variables of a model are chosen. Some decision has been made as to which of these components and variables exerts influence on others and which is of little importance for the problem at hand. The recognition of causality is more explicit in sharp models and laws, but causal relationships become blurred as one moves toward the soft end of the modelling spectrum (Karplus 1977).

The Importance of Data

Most conceptual models need copious amounts of data for their successful development. Data are used to identify crucial components and variables, and help to define the values of variables and parameters. Although fewer empirical data are required when dealing with sharp laws and models, which usually only require the experimental estimation of a few parameters, models based upon fuzzy laws need data to help sharpen weak relationships between model components and variables or to provide some estimate of the direction and magnitude of the interaction of model components. Data are obtained from observation of the real-world system or from the study of similar systems.

Despite the need for data, having too many data is almost as bad as having too few. If too few data are available to build a conceptual model, the resulting simulation model provides less conceptual and developmental utility. The result of having too many data, however, is often a conceptual (and simulation) model which has become bogged down in too much detail to be of much use in any possible definition of utility (House and McLeod 1977).

Aggregation and Simplification

Conceptual models are necessarily simplifications of real-world systems, and as simplifications, they indicate that choices in both model content and organization have been made. Two basic processes oper-

28

ate to define how and what is included in a model: *aggregation* and *simplification*. In practice, these two processes are complementary.

Most of the components in fuzzy models that are at the soft end of the modelling spectrum are highly aggregated. Aggregation is the process of lumping small-scale components of larger entities into a more inclusive component. For instance, econometric models of the national economy are necessarily based in part on the buying behavior of individual households. No model could include all of these households; therefore they are lumped into a single component. Aggregation inevitably leads to bias in both measurement and the subsequent interaction of systems components in the simulation model and will therefore produce inaccurate (at some level) results. But this is one price of building a model.

The problem with aggregation is that there is very often no legitimate way to combine the entities which make up the components of any system. As Berlinski (1976:86–92) notes, most aggregation is done on an ad hoc basis with little consideration for how the aggregated entities interact. The most common form of aggregation is to lump entities together in an additive manner (that is, the sum is the whole of the parts). But as Berlinski (1976) observes, additive lumping often leads to linear assumptions, and, in an obviously nonlinear world, models based on these linear assumptions will not be accurate or useful. Although this may be true, it is often the case that some form of aggregation must be performed simply to make any observations on the behavior of the modelled system at all.

Simplification is the process of dropping, combining, or modifying different components of a model to achieve a less complex model structure. The method of simplification depends on the level of understanding the interaction of the components that are to be combined or dropped. In sharply defined models, it is often possible to subsume one variable under another through an explicit mathematical function. Jacquard and Leridon (1974) have devised a simple model of human reproduction based on fertility functions. In fuzzy models, this type of combination is more difficult because the nature of the relationship is often not known. The dropping of components and variables is also acceptable, especially when it is felt that their inclusion would lead to problems of model validation and use. Zeigler (1976a, 1976b) and Cale and Odell (1979) provide discussions of a wide range of possible simplification procedures.

29

Continuous vs. Discrete

How time is handled in a conceptual mode is an important feature of the simulation modelling process. Two possible representations are *continuous* and *discrete* time models. In a continuous representation of time, the value of any variable in the system can change instantaneously and smoothly. Continuous time models are usually represented by *differential equations* (Gordon 1969; Shah 1974; Howe 1977). Discrete time models, however, move through time in intervals. Although each interval may be very small, the flow of time is not continuous and smooth, and the model "jumps" through time according to the interval of time advanced. Discrete models are excellent for the representation of easily definable events of a process or a system. The most sophisticated mathematical representation of the discrete event model is the *difference equation* (Innis 1974). Determining whether or not a conceptual model should be either continuous or discrete depends on the problem to be studied and state of knowledge on the components and the variables of the system. Also, some of this choice is guided by the orientation of the modeller and the purpose behind the model. For instance, Innis (1974:103–7) notes that differential equations, implying a continuous model, have long been used in biology and ecology. Despite this long tradition of use, he argues that this type of equation may not be the most suitable for use in ecological modelling, and that difference equations are a very acceptable substitute. He further remarks that difference equations are much more easily translated to nonmathematically inclined biologists, thus helping to enhance communication and the design credibility of the simulation model based on the conceptual model.

Stochastic vs. Deterministic

In general, the values of the descriptive variables in a conceptual model, and thus ultimately in a simulation model, can be either *deterministic* or *stochastic*. In deterministic models, none of the variables can be considered random variables, and the linkages between conceptual model components are such that in the simulation model, for any given set of input values, the output values produced by the simulation model with identical inputs will also be identical run after run.

In stochastic models, at least one variable is random, and its value may vary according to the type of probability density function which defines it. Random variables are created in the simulation model by random number generators, and through a repeated series of runs, the values of the output variables produced by a stochastic simulation model are not uniquely determined. The values of these variables are determined by the joint probability density function of the random variables in the model and by the interaction of these variables with other components and variables in the model.

The decision to build a stochastic or deterministic model is often difficult to make. What are some of the reasons for the inclusion of random variables in a model? Mihram (1972a:11–17) presents some answers. One obvious reason is that the system defined for study has random variables within it. In such cases, it is often difficult to determine any reasonable way to represent this variable deterministically, and thus the variable remains random in the model. Another reason is that a poor understanding of the system to be modelled often leads to the inclusion of random variables simply because the values of many variables and parameters are not well known, or the linkages between model components are not well defined. Finally, Mihram (1972a:15) suggests that models *should* include stochastic variables because of the essentially uncertain nature of any biological, economic, social, or physical system. He further suggests that as knowledge about a system increases, stochastic elements will necessarily be included in conceptual and simulation models.

This position contrasts strongly with opinion in other fields of modelling. Ecologists and system dynamicists, for instance, tend to shy away from stochastic models. Both disciplines acknowledge that stochastic features are more realistic and possibly even more appropriate in most modelling applications, but they further note that stochastic variability in many of these models can be ignored or damped down by the operation of feedback loops of processes in other parts of the system (Innis 1974). One further problem with the use of stochastic variables in conceptual models, especially those based on relatively sharp laws, is that it is difficult, if not impossible, to solve a set of deterministic equations with stochastic elements. Thus, it is the case that even if stochastic elements were desired, it would be difficult to implement this desire because of the traditional form of conceptual models in many scientific fields.

The choice between deterministic and stochastic variables is also influenced by the purpose behind the model. If a model is to be used only to obtain conceptual or developmental utility, simple models with few or no random variables may be preferred. However, if output utility is desired, then it may become necessary to include stochastic variables in the model.

Simulation Model Construction

This stage of the modelling enterprise is concerned with the transformation of the conceptual model into a computer program which then becomes the full-fledged simulation model. As Reitman (1971: 14–17) notes, much of the programming process, no matter what programming language or technique is used, is primarily a question of logic, rules, and equations. Logic is the overall structure and organization of the computer program which serves as the implementation of the conceptual model; rules help to implement the operation of the program by providing criteria to be met or rejected at decision nodes specified by the logical structure of the program; and, finally, equations are the operators of the model which manipulate, store, record, and transform the values of the descriptive variables and components throughout the operation of the program. Since a discussion of programming technique is beyond the scope of this paper, I will concentrate on a series of problems which usually arise as the computer program is developed.

The ultimate determinants of the logical structure of the computer program which becomes the simulation model are the form, content, and structure of the conceptual model. However, as will be demonstrated below, the programming language used often exerts a subtle but powerful influence on the structure of the computer program also. The biggest difficulty remains the problem of transforming a multiple-pathed, complex conceptual model into a linearly ordered computer program. The accurate representation of these events demands a high degree of ingenuity and skill on the part of the programmer, but the success of the transformation is not known until the verification and validation stages of the modelling process.

Different types of conceptual models present different problems in the process of building a computer simulation model. Models for continuous, deterministic systems of differential equations generally cannot be solved analytically; therefore, numerical solutions must be sought if the program is written for the digital computer. Much of the concern with this type of model centers on the accuracy of the algorithm which produces the approximate solution to the equation set

(Kleijnen 1977; Dewit and Goudriaan 1978:6–7). In discrete-event models, especially those with stochastic components, the problems associated with the generation of stochastic or probabilistic variables are of paramount importance. Virtually every paper or book which discusses stochastic, discrete-event simulation at length spends considerable time presenting alternatives and strategies for the generation of random variables. The point of this effort, of course, is to be as sure as possible that the values generated are truly random or truly distributed according to the appropriate probability density function. Errors or flaws in the subroutines which create these values can have serious effects on the validity of the output variables of the simulation model (Tocher 1963:50–93; Mize and Cox 1968:76–93; Emshoff and Sisson 1970:159–88; Maisel and Gnugnoli 1977:133–58; Mihram 1972a: 18–146; Stiteler 1974; Fishman 1978:345–479).

The choice of time scheduling in discrete-event models also presents problems. Two basic options are the fixed-time (or unit) advance and the event advance (Mize and Cox 1968:158–59; Emshoff and Sisson 1970:159–61).

The fixed-time advance moves the components and descriptive variables of the model ahead by a uniform increment. If an event is to occur during that increment, all actions are evaluated, new values for variables are calculated, and the master clock of the model is advanced to the next unit. In contrast, the event advance, instead of moving through time in uniform increments, "jumps" ahead to the next event which is to occur. It is always possible to simulate any process by the fixed-time advance method, but many processes cannot be represented by event advances. But it is also clear that the expense of computation and run time is higher for unit advance models than it is for event advance models. A further complication appears in that the unit time model is more advantageous if there is a high probability of an event occurring in a time unit. Each of these pros and cons must be weighed to determine exactly what type of structure is best for both the problem as defined and the conceptual model used to explore it. A brief study of the simulation literature reveals many more problems of this type which must be faced in the implementation of a conceptual model as a simulation model.

One of the most important decisions made in the modelling process is the choice of a programming language. There are probably dozens of programming languages which can be used in the development of a simulation model (Buxton 1968; Kay 1972). However, two basic types of languages are usually used in simulation: (a) general-purpose languages such as FORTRAN, PL/I, ALGOL, BASIC, and APL, and (b) special-purpose simulation languages such as DYNAMO, SIMSCRIPT, GPSS, GASP, SIMULA, CMSP, CSSL, DYSTAL, and SIMPL/1. General-purpose languages, as their name implies, can be used in simulation models, but as many authors have noted, these languages are usually not as sensitive to the special problems that simulation models present. In fact, some authors have claimed it is a "tragedy" that more simulators do not use languages such as GPSS and SIM-SCRIPT in their work (Kay, Kisio, and Van Houweling 1975). Special-purpose simulation languages are built solely for the simulation of systems and processes, and these languages usually are highly responsive to the special needs of the simulator. Indeed, as Kleine (1971) and Shannon and Wyett (1973) show, most simulators strongly prefer special-purpose languages over more commonly used general-purpose languages such as FORTRAN and PL/I.

Special-purpose simulation languages offer a number of attractive advantages:

(1) Many authors have claimed that these languages are very helpful in forcing the simulator to develop a structure for the system or process to be modelled (Moore 1978). In many instances, this conceptual benefit outweighs the actual use of the simulation. Moreover, the structure of the language is often easily adapted to a wide range of problems from many scientific disciplines.

(2) Most special-purpose simulation languages have relatively natural syntaxes which help to make them somewhat simpler to use than more abstract general-purpose languages.

(3) Conceptual models are often more easily programmed by special-purpose languages, and the total amount of programming work is often less. In some languages, such as SIMSCRIPT, a single line in the program can replace an entire FORTRAN subroutine (Kay, Kisio, and Van Houweling 1975). Special-purpose languages offer more flexible list-processing facilities, which are often required in a simulation model, and most have options for the generation of random numbers.

(4) Special-purpose languages generally offer special debugging aids useful in a simulation context which are often difficult to replicate when using general-purpose languages.

34

(5) Special-purpose languages usually have a large number of diagnostic aids and graphics which help to interpret the simulation output. These languages routinely monitor the operation of the simulation model and can quickly and easily produce large amounts of interpretative information which is often difficult to implement by general-purpose languages even when the appropriate graphics or output subroutines are available.

Despite these obvious attractions, there are a number of cautions to be considered before any language is chosen:

(1) As Moore (1978) points out, special-purpose simulation languages are often based on a particular "world view." For instance, DYNAMO is a language that implements the feedback-structured model of the system dynamicists, whereas SIMULA is known as a "process-oriented" language. The simulator must decide carefully whether or not the language is appropriate for the structure of the conceptual model. Moreover, the implicit structures of these simulation languages can *impose* a structure on a conceptual model which is not appropriate or is not the best approach to model implementation. These languages often exert a subtle pressure to consider this structure as *the* structure of the model, but this of course happens with the use of any modelling language.

(2) Special-purpose languages are still limited in portability. Unlike a general-purpose language like FORTRAN, not all simulation languages are easily transferable to other computing systems or even other similar machines located at other installations. A lack of portability makes it difficult to use or modify a simulation model if a computer is unable to understand the language in which the model is written. This is probably the reason why FORTRAN, despite all of its problems, is probably the language most often used for simulation modelling. As other simulation languages such as GPSS and SIMSCRIPT become better known, it is likely that portability will not be as difficult, and in that case, the use of FORTRAN as a simulation language should decrease.

(3) Special-purpose languages often have special jargons which have been created to describe them. These jargons are often adopted by the simulator when the results of the simulation are presented or when the simulation model itself is described. Unless special care is taken to define these terms accurately, it is possible that

35

the use of this jargon can inhibit the communication of the simulation model to others not initiated in the language. Since the credibility of a simulation model is such an important issue, the jargon problem cannot be stressed too strongly.

(4) Although some simulation languages are easy to learn, others are much more difficult. In fact, many of these languages are complex in that they offer the user a bewildering array of options. Generally, as flexibility increases, usability decreases. The general-purpose language PL/I, despite its excellent flexibility, really has not lived up to its potential, and it is likely that many special-purpose simulation languages also suffer from this problem. It often takes considerable time to learn these languages, and in already crowded schedules, time is not easily found (McLeod 1977:230). Moore (1978:12), attempting to provide a solution to this problem, claims that it is possible to get experts to help with the programming, thus freeing the archaeologist for other work. If only it were so easy! From past experience, I would suggest that obtaining long-term professional assistance in simulation programming is likely to occur only under special circumstances. Also, as the complexity of archaeological simulation increases, professionals will only be enticed to provide assistance by offers of financial support.

Verification

Verification is the process of determining whether or not the simulation model has been programmed correctly and produces accurate output values. Verification is concerned only with debugging the computer program which turns the conceptual model into a computer simulation. The logic of the computer program is checked only insofar as it is necessary to determine that the program produces accurate output. In the verification stage, no attempt is made to insure that the output from the simulation matches data from the real-world system or process. Instead, the emphasis at this stage of the modelling effort is to insure that the program is logically and mechanically capable of producing correct output.

Verification is a tedious but important step. Depending on the complexity of the program and the representation of system components and variables, a number of tests and techniques can be performed to insure program accuracy. As in many other areas of simulation modelling, there is an important difference between the verification of deterministic and stochastic simulation models. In many ways, it is reasonably simple to verify a deterministic simulation model because under the right conditions, a particular known input into the model should produce a single, unique output value. This is especially the case if the model is not complex or well defined in terms of explicit mathematical relationships and functions. If the output values do not match expectations, then it is likely that an error in coding, program logic, or even conceptualization of the model has been made. This simple process, however, becomes more difficult as deterministic models become more complex, and verification becomes especially difficult with these models when they have explicit feedback loops or time lags, as is the case in many modelling situations in economics, ecology, and management.

The verification of stochastic simulation models is more difficult because random variables are specifically built into the structure of the simulation model. As noted above, random numbers can be used in two general ways: (a) as "seeds" to initiate certain operations or processes in the simulation model, and (b) as members of specific probability density functions which are used to mimic the variability found in real-world systems or processes. It is usually simple to verify that subroutines or functions are producing random variables in accordance with a specific probability density function. In such cases, the values of the function derived from multiple runs of the simulation are compared to ideal values by nonparametric statistical tests, such as the Kolmogorov-Smirnov test or Chi-squared test. Acceptable goodness-of-fit is taken as successful verification of these subroutines and functions.

In the case of the random "seeds," however, verification proves to be much more troublesome. A brief example illustrates the problem nicely. Some time ago, I wrote a short computer program that simulated the dealing of cards of a bridge deck into four hands. Such a program naturally included a random number generator which would randomly select a card to go into one of the four hands. The program was soon finished, and it successfully created four hands of cards with no duplicates or omissions. Success? Alas, no. If the program worked correctly, then a change in the random number seed should *necessarily* produce four completely different hands of cards. Unfortunately, changing the random number seed did not change the content of the hands, and further experimentation demonstrated that regardless of the seed, the same hand was produced. Although in one sense the program "worked" (it created hands of cards), in its most crucial meaning it did not work at all.

Such is the case in more elaborate simulation models. It must be determined beyond any doubt that the output variables produced by the model are random variables which have been created by changing the "seed" of the simulation model and are *not* artifacts of the logic, operation, and structure of the simulation model itself. Although it is true that the simulation model will manipulate and change the value of the input variables, or any variable created by the operation of the simulation, it is also true that the random nature of the output variables created by the simulation must only be due to the random "seed." Mihram (1972a:245–50, 1972b) discusses this problem at length and presents a number of procedures which can be used to verify stochastic simulation models. For example, it is often possible to suppress stochasticity in the model, that is, use a constant value in place of a random variable and then compare the output variables with an expected response. In some cases, the distribution form of the output variables are known, and the goodness-of-fit between the calculated and expected values can be determined by use of the appropriate statistics.

Validation

Validation, aside from conceptual model development and implementation, is the single most important stage of the simulation modelling process. Surprisingly, it is also one of the most controversial areas of simulation methodology (also see the comments by Bell, Chapter 3, and Cooke, Chapter 8). At the most basic level, the validation of a simulation model is the measurement of the goodness-of-fit between data generated by a simulation model and the data generated by the real-world system itself. Validation also involves other issues, however, which are at the same time both practical and philosophical in nature. The practical issue is concerned with *design credibility*, which is simply the level of acceptance of a model by a set of users or consumers. A model may be validated by traditional methodologies, but for a variety of reasons may not be accepted by potential users. The problem of credibility is closely related to the issue of the corroboration of the simulation model with known theories and hypotheses which purport to explain the phenomena which have just been modelled. Simply put, why is this model better than any other model of the same system which seeks to represent and ultimately explain the operation of the real-world system? This question is concerned with hypothesis testing, inference, and theory construction, and it quickly moves into the realm of the philosophy of science for analysis and solution.

The traditional meaning of validation stresses the measurement of the accuracy of output from a simulation model when compared to data obtained from the real-world system. Certain types of methods are more appropriate for models with different structural and operational features. Empirical validation for deterministic, continuous models often found in ecology is achieved through the use of various curve-fitting procedures (Overton 1977:56–58). Sensitivity analysis—more commonly used in the analysis of experimental changes in parameter values—has been used in a validation context in ecology (Patten 1969; Miller 1974; Steinhorst et al. 1978). It has also been used to validate the essentially continuous, deterministic models commonly developed by systems dynamicists for a number of scientific fields (Britting and Trump 1973). Other methods are used when the simulation model has stochastic features. Mihram (1972a:263) notes that if a simulation model that uses random numbers is properly constructed and verified, its output variables are considered to be random variables. Hence a wide variety of statistical tests can be used to assess the validity of the simulation model which uses them. Which test is used depends upon the type of variables encountered and the specific aspect of the simulation output which is being tested. For instance, Student's t-test can be used to compare the means of two simulated populations. Similar measures can be used to determine how well the simulated data matches that from the real world. Student's t, the Chi-squared, Kolmogorov-Smirov, Mann-Whitney U, and many other tests have been used for this type of comparison. More elaborate techniques such as ANOVA, linear regression, time series analysis, spectral analysis, and factor analysis have been proposed for use in certain situations (Naylor and Finger 1967; Maisel and Gnugnoli 1977:67–88; Naylor, Wertz, and Wonnacott 1969; Gilmour 1973; Mihram 1972a:265–77; Kleijnen 1974:74–76; Fishman 1978:219–73). As with the use of any statistical test, every effort must be made to insure that the assumptions of the

39

technique are not violated when they are used to validate simulation models. Since the distribution form of the output variables of a simulation model is not often known, those techniques which violate the fewest parametric assumptions should be used when doubt about the distribution form exists (Gilmour 1973:129–30; Kleijnen 1974:74–76). Parametric tests should only be used in situations in which there is little doubt of their applicability (Van Horn 1971).

A number of problems plague the application of statistical methods to simulation model validation. One of the most common is the problem of sample size (Kleijnen 1974:82–87). For their proper use, statistical tests require that random samples be drawn from multiple observations of a population. Most statistical methods also require a minimum number of observations to insure that their results are accurate. The total number of observations depends on the confidence intervals of the test and its power. To obtain a sufficient sample size for the use of these tests, a simulator has two options: a large number of independent runs with independent random "seeds" or a single long, continuous run begun by a single "seed." Research has shown that a large number of relatively short, independent runs is preferable to the continuous run, because the continuous run produces serially correlated observations (Kleijnen 1974:87) and provides biased estimates of population movements (Mihram 1972a:448–50). Both of these problems seriously complicate validation. But the practical issue of cost also enters into the picture. Depending on the structure of the model, it may actually cost more to obtain the required sample size by a large number of independent runs than it would to get it by a single, long, continuous run. This is especially true if it takes the simulation a long time to reach "steady-state" conditions.[4] Since cost is always a crucial feature in simulation modelling, some sort of compromise between cost, number of runs, and sample size must be worked out.

One difficult issue in traditional validation is the problem of inadequate or insufficient data to be used for model validation. Very often, a lack of suitable data leads to an incompletely validated model. This problem is simply one facet of a much broader problem which is concerned with the definition of the appropriate conditions for the development of a simulation model.

In most applications of simulation, it is possible to obtain data for both model construction and validation. It may also be possible to obtain good data for validation during the modelling process (Nolan

1972; Naylor 1973). But what if these data are poor in quality, or what if only a theory has been used as a basis for simulation model development? This situation almost inevitably leads to the incomplete (and, to some, insufficient) validation of the model. The key to the solution of this problem is to distinguish between model validity and model utility. As House and McLeod (1977:160) and Mankin et al. (1975) have pointed out, a simulation model may still be useful even though it has not been completely validated. In fact, it is usually the case that it is impossible to validate a simulation model completely except under very stringent conditions of model homomorphism with the real-world system (Zeigler 1976a:343– 52; House and McLeod 1977:66– 75). Mankin et al. (1975) define a *valid* model as one that has no behavior which does not correspond to the behavior of the system, and a *useful* model as one that predicts some systemic behavior correctly. Even partially validated models are of importance in the overall development and use of simulation models. In general, there is no absolute set of criteria that can determine whether or not an incompletely validated model is useful because the decision of model utility ultimately rests upon the purposes for which the simulation model was constructed (see below).

Other approaches to the use of poor quality data in a validation context are available. Richards (1973) and Ward (1977) suggest a type of evolutionary model building in which the process of validation is directed at insuring the "reasonableness" of the output variables. The model (lacking a real-world data base) nevertheless has theoretical maxima and minima which the simulation output should not exceed. Intuition and experience may also suggest the values of reasonable validation criteria. In developing this type of simulation model, the model is "fine-tuned" when it is discovered that the output values are not in accordance with expectations. The structure of the model "evolves," eventually converging on the appropriate values.

The distinction between model validity and utility leads to the second major concern of validation: the problem of design credibility. In many fields that use simulation, the development of simulation models often seems to take place in a vacuum. Many of the models are simply not used by other researchers, and there is considerable concern by many simulators that simulation is not being taken seriously in many applications. House and McLeod (1977:160) note that the better a model fulfills its goals, the more likely it will be that the model will be accepted and, more important, *used*. Although this does not insure that the model is valid (in the traditional meaning of the term), it helps to establish the simulation model as an acceptable element of the body of current scientific thought. Such acceptance is crucial for the continued use, development, and ultimate improvement of both the model and the insights it provides into the real-world system it represents.

What factors lead to the rejection of a model by consumers? Innis, Schlesinger, and Sylvester (1977) and House and McLeod (1977) show that the most important reason for rejection is that the model does not have a clearly defined set of objectives, and that often those which are defined have not been met by the simulation model. As Innis, Schlesinger, and Sylvester (1977:698) note, "validation is impossible except in the context of objectives." Even if the model is valid in the traditional sense, it may be rejected because the gap between what consumers want and what the model does is simply too wide to bridge. Thus it is obvious that the strong concern for clear problem definition as noted in the model goals stage of the simulation enterprise will not be wasted in later stages of modelling. Practical issues, such as the level of documentation of the simulation model, type of experimental program, and a failure to specify the range of applicability of the model, among others, may also affect acceptance (McLeod 1973a). Thus care must be taken to assure potential users of a simulation model that the assumptions behind the model are reasonable, that the objectives of the modelling enterprise are clearly defined, and that the model meets the objectives and does not stray into distant applications.

If the traditional validity and the design credibility of the simulation model have been established, the final aspect of validation moves to a consideration of the simulation model as a *general* model about a process or an entity. Simply put, how do the knowledge and insight obtained from this model fit in with other theories and models of the same or similar processes? As noted above, this becomes an issue in the philosophy of science, and it is concerned with the corroboration of the simulation model vis-à-vis existing information. Caswell (1976) discusses this issue, using an example from the biological literature on population growth. Van Foerster (1966), using a variant of the traditional logistic growth equation, shows that if present trends are continued, the total human population of earth will reach infinity by the year A.D. 2026.87 ± 5.5. This model has been shown to be highly accurate in its prediction of population figures in the past, and thus the model is traditionally validated. But despite its accuracy, the model is nonsense, because nothing can reach a value of infinity, especially human population. As in other populations, other factors would limit this growth potential. Although the model is accurate, it simply does not provide a *reasonable* description or explanation of population growth. The model is valid, but it is not corroborated.

The process of corroboration of the conceptual model behind the simulation model is a complex problem, widely debated. In many disciplines in which the reasons for simulation modelling are very practical, models are validated by consensus, or acceptance by the consumer. This is similar to the concept of credibility as noted above, and it stresses utility of results over some concept of global acceptability (Van Horn 1971; Gilmour 1973). In these fields, accuracy (traditional validation) is sufficient for further use.

But other disciplines demand a more systematic approach to validation, and they usually look to the philosophy of science for guidance. Schrank and Holt (1967), Caswell (1976), and Lehman (1977), among others, advocate the use of "strong inference" (Platt 1964) as a device for model corroboration. In this view, models are never proven correct, but only falsified. Emphasis is placed upon the testing of alternative models of the same process by means of critical experiments designed to eliminate one or more of the hypotheses successively until only one is left. The remaining hypothesis is thus corroborated. However, there are other approaches to corroboration and validation of conceptual models that attempt to avoid some of the worst restrictions of the positivist model (Bell, Chapter 3).

Experimentation

In many ways, experimentation lies at the heart of a simulation enterprise, because experimentation with a model of a system is one of the avowed major benefits of simulation models (also see Zubrow, Chapter 6). In fact, simulation models act as "laboratories" in which the representations of real-world systems can be manipulated at reduced cost and difficulty. Yet surprisingly, as many authors have noted, the methodology of experimentation with simulation models is primitive compared to the much greater concern lavished on methodological and conceptual problems of model development. Nothing is more fatal to the credibility of a simulation exercise than a poorly designed, ad hoc experimental program imposed on a sound simulation model.

Experimentation with a simulation model involves much more than simply watching the behavior of a modelled system change through simulated time. Useful and meaningful experimentation rests upon the successful answering of the following interrelated questions: (a) what type of change in model behavior is to be monitored, (b) how change in model behavior is to be accomplished, and (c) how the effects of changing the behavior of the model are to be analyzed. Together, these three questions form the basis of the experimental design of the simulation exercise.

What types of changes occur in model behavior depend upon what the simulation model has been designed to do. Problem definition and the hypotheses to be investigated clearly have an important influence on what changes in model behavior are to be measured. The hypotheses should be defined sharply enough to identify the focus of model changes. In many applied fields the choice of what is to be measured is directed at determining the "optimal response" of the model in a specific policy situation (Emshoff and Sisson 1970:209–11).

Changes in model behavior are produced in two ways: (a) by changes in the input variables, and (b) by changes in the descriptive variables and parameters of the modelled system. It is important to note that what may be external to one modelled system may be internal to a slightly different definition of model boundaries so that the concept of making input (exogenous) changes or value (endogenous) changes is relative to the system being modelled. Changing input values is similar to validating a simulation model by using known historical data as input. If the model produces the correct (historically known) response, the model is probably valid. The focus of changing input variables, however, is to determine how the behavior of the model responds to exogenous factors. No changes are made in the internal structure of the model or in any of the values of descriptive variables and parameters. This method of producing changes in model behavior assumes that the model tends to operate in equilibrium, and that *only* external forces operate to produce changes in model behavior.

The second method is to produce changes in model behavior by changing the values of descriptive variables and parameters. The input variables of this type of experimentation remain the same, but the values of selected variables and parameters are modified. Which values are changed again depends upon what the model is supposed to investigate. The hypotheses that guide experimentation should be clear enough to identify the key variables and parameters of the modelled

44

system, although in many cases it is often difficult to identify these variables *prior* to the analysis of the simulation output. Sometimes theory may serve as a guide to identify which variables and parameters should be changed. In simple systems, with relatively few variables and parameters, it may be possible to manipulate many of these values, but as the size and complexity of the modelled system increases (especially as measured by the total number of variables and parameters), the total number of possible experimental situations increases exponentially (Steinhorst et al. 1978:243–44). Limitations on computer time and funds severely restrict the total number of possible experiments; therefore changes in the values of variables and parameters must be made carefully. The simulation literature offers very little guidance on this problem, and most of the decisions as to what to vary in the simulation model are left to the ingenuity of the simulator.

Measuring the degree and direction of changes in model behavior is a very complex problem. Many of the methods used in the validation of simulation models are also useful in the analysis of output obtained by experimentation with the model, and the particular method used depends upon the nature of the output variables produced by the simulation and the basic design of the experimental program. Mihram (1972a: 261–77), Kleijnen (1974, 1977:34–36), and Fishman (1978:92–137), among others, present discussions of how to analyze the output variables in stochastic simulation models. Much of the effort in the analysis of stochastic models concerns methods to determine the distribution form of the output variables, techniques used to reduce the variance in output variables (thus making the output variables more accurate in their predictions), and statistical methods, including time series, autocorrelation, spectral analysis, and others which can be used to compare and contrast the values of different output variables.

Among the most powerful techniques used in the analysis of simulation output is the analysis of variance (ANOVA) as used in formal statistical inference applications of experimental design. A detailed discussion of this methodology is not possible in this paper, but Naylor et al. (1966:321–44), Mihram (1972a:314–401), and Fishman (1978: 274–303) all provide good introductions to the basic concepts and issues in experimental design using ANOVA. Briefly, ANOVA attempts to identify, among the variables and parameters of the simulation model which have been changed for experimental purposes, which of the changes produce statistically significant changes in model behavior. The model takes into account interaction effects between parameters and components, and it specifies which are the most sensitive to changes in the values of the variables and parameters in other subsystems of the modelled system. Sensitivity analysis (Steinhorst et al. 1978), combined with a well-designed ANOVA experimental design, is very useful for the exploration of model behavior. Importantly, ANOVA also permits the exploration of changes in model behavior produced by both quantitative and qualitative factors, or any combination of the two. However, ANOVA is not easy, and the selection of a particular ANOVA model (there are many) is a complex task. Unless the simulator is an expert statistician, the services of a statistician will be required. Other statistical methods such as multiple regression and other extensions of the general linear model can also be used to analyze changes in model behavior.

A failure to use sophisticated statistical methodologies does not necessarily indicate that an experimental program is not useful or meaningful. In many cases, the intent of the simulation is not to produce very neat and clean inferences as to the details of component interactions, but instead simply to try to gain some insight into complex systems. Experimentation may then consist of informally manipulating parameters of interest without ever attempting to get at global measures of model behavior or performance. Like so many other facets of simulation modelling, the level of sophistication attained in any stage of the modelling process depends greatly on the purpose of the model.

THE FUTURE OF COMPUTER SIMULATION IN ARCHAEOLOGY

Despite many practical and methodological problems, it should now be clear that computer simulation has a role to play in archaeological research. This role is best defined by a consideration of the benefits of simulation modelling in the light of present-day knowledge of things archaeological. Such consideration provides a framework that can be used to evaluate the contribution of any simulation model to the better and more complete understanding of complex systems and processes. Despite all attempts at "quantification" and the modification of the quality and conduct of research, archaeology remains a "soft" science, and as noted above, soft sciences are characterized by "fuzzy" laws and models that are poorly understood and incompletely specified. Many would argue that simulation is inappropriate and even a great waste of time in situations in which fuzzy laws and concepts form the basis of models. The simulation models created from these poorly defined concepts will inevitably lead, it is claimed, to serious problems in model validation and model use. Although these caveats are accurate, they ignore the fact that simulation models are created for different reasons. For instance, although a simulation model of cultural evolution presents enormous difficulties in conceptualization and implementation, to define the utility of this model on the basis of, say, its ability to predict, or retrodict, known evolutionary sequences, is to ignore the tremendous benefits that would probably be gained by *attempting* to build a simulation model of the evolutionary process. The conceptual and developmental benefits of model development would be substantial. The output validity of such a model would be almost nil, but that is not the point of the modelling effort. Understanding, not prediction, is the goal. Similar examples of conceptual and developmental utility are found scattered throughout the archaeological literature. The participants in a previous School of American Research Advanced Seminar (Hill 1977) found that merely the attempt to describe a model of warfare and redistribution in terms compatible with a simulation methodology demonstrated glaring problems and conceptual difficulties. This was true even when the subject of the modelling effort was the Hawaiian Islands, the scene of one of the better-known transformations from a chiefdom to a state in the ethnographic literature (Hill 1977; F. Plog 1977a). Similarly, Zubrow (Chapter 6) shows the benefits to be gained by applying the urban dynamics model of the system dynamics school to Imperial Rome. The modelling attempt has pointed out potentially weak areas in data, conceptualization, and methodology.

Does this mean that the only possible benefits in simulation modelling in archaeology are conceptual or developmental? The answer must be no. Already there are signs that some aspects of archaeological theory are becoming better understood, and it is possible that simulation models of these processes can be built and that some of these models will provide output utility. With the addition of more data and a more general orientation, Binford and Bertram's (1977) model of bone attrition could form the heart of a simulation model which could be used to explain varying frequencies of bone in archaeological deposits. Simulation experiments have proven to be useful in the study of sampling methodologies and other archaeological sampling problems (Kendall 1974; Matson 1975; Davidson, Richter, and Rogers 1976; Ammerman, Gifford, and Voorrips 1979). In fact, these simulations, especially the one devised by Kendall (1974), take on aspects of distribution sampling as applied to mathematical statistics. Finally, my own simulation, ABSIM (Chapter 4; Aldenderfer 1977), has a real chance of providing output utility in the use of multivariate methods in archaeological research.

But the likelihood of gaining true output utility in the near future for most archaeological processes remains remote. Most of the conceptual models used to represent such archaeological processes as settlement distribution are still far too fuzzy to permit valid output utility of simulation models. Progress in these areas is likely to be extremely slow.

Does this mean that simulation methodology will become extensively used in archaeological research? Although predictions generally return to haunt their foolish masters, I believe the answer must be no. Simulation, despite all its potential benefits, remains an expensive, time-consuming method that has often been shown to be non-cost-effective even in ideal circumstances (Innis 1973; Crosbie 1977). The cost of simulation must never be ignored, and a wise strategy is to determine if any other modelling process could be used before the decision to begin a simulation enterprise is made. Present funding levels in archaeology, the fuzzy nature of any archaeological processes, and the structure of the discipline itself, which tends to make long-term multidisciplinary research difficult, all combine to present a relatively limited future for simulation in archaeological research. But simulation does have a place in the future of archaeology, and as archaeologists become more aware of the potentials, problems, uses, and benefits of simulation, it will become a solid element in the repertoire of archaeological science.

NOTES

1. This paper is concerned only with computer simulation. It therefore excludes a discussion of simulation as a gaming technique which has seen considerable development in the social sciences (Raser 1969).

2. Some ecologists would disagree with this statement, because in some areas of ecological modelling, very sophisticated models are being developed (Patten 1976; Patten et al. 1976). Whether or not these models will begin to sharpen biological modelling for output utility remains to be seen.

3. Tinkering is a long-honored activity in simulation modelling, and it is best performed when the simulator is attempting to adjust the output of the model so as to make it conform to expectations.

4. Transient data are generated by a simulation model before it "warms up" and reaches a "steady state." According to Emshoff and Sisson (1970:190), a steady state in a simulation model is reached when "it is possible to define an observation such that it provides no new information about the future behavior of the system." Or, put another way, the values of the descriptive variables of the simulation model are *independent* of the starting conditions (the values of the input variables) used to begin the simulation run (Kleijnen 1974:69). Transient data, although they may be analyzed separately, tend to bias the values of the output variables, thus producing an inaccurate description of model behavior through time. But because it is not possible to tell exactly how long the transient state of a particular run is, there is no simple rule that can be used to determine how many data are to be thrown out. Many procedures have been developed to deal with transient data (Conway, Johnson, and Maxwell 1959; Conway 1963; Tocher 1963:174–76; Kleijnen 1974:69–72).

Scientific Method and the Formulation of Testable Computer Simulation Models

JAMES A. BELL

University of South Florida

"It is better to be clearly wrong than vaguely right."
—Origin unknown

In order to have value, artifacts of past civilizations must not only be precisely recorded and painstakingly preserved, but must also be interpreted and explained. This paper concentrates on one facet of archaeological interpretation and explanation: the formulation of testable computer simulation models. As explanations should be testable, so should the computer simulation models associated with them. Testable explanations and models are refutable—vulnerable to possible empirical error. When error is found, they can be adjusted so that they account for the error and yet are still testable at other points. Highly testable explanations and models become empirically sound when they have been adjusted properly and tested successfully.

Computer simulation models are a recent phenomenon in the physical and social sciences, but the qualities that make them testable are not newly discovered. The heart of this paper, Part II, will show how a refutationist view of scientific method is used to guide the development and adjustment of testable computer simulation models. It will also be argued that refutationist method is the preferred one for this purpose. Part I is background that provides a perspective for the discussion and arguments in Part II. The conclusion will summarize important guidelines for a practicing social scientist who wishes to create highly testable computer simulation models.

PART I: BACKGROUND

This section will consist of three parts. The first focuses on the search for explanation in modern archaeology. Since there are numerous controversies over standards of scientific explanation, a paper that endorses an explicit standard by which to formulate and improve computer simulation models must provide comment. The second part explores the role of systems thinking in the search for explanations. Some differences in the types of explanation encouraged by systems thinking will be reviewed. It will be shown, however, that the qualities of testability are the same as for all scientific explanation. The third part will outline the function of simulation models in explanation. The purpose is to pinpoint some particular advantages and disadvantages for testability stemming from different types of computer simulation models.

Search for Explanation

For most of this century, archaeologists have been devoted to accumulating a well-ordered data base. Search for artifacts, accurate recording of discovery, and placement of discoveries in chronological and geographical frameworks have dominated their attention and effort. Interpretation and explanation have not been entirely ignored, of course, but they have seemed less pressing. This tradition of careful field work for the generation of an accurate data base was crystallized by Boas, who maintained that interpretation and explanation could be left for future generations. [1]

Boas's mandate for archaeological research was beneficial to a field in which civilization was encroaching dangerously; if the artifacts were disturbed, they might be lost forever. Furthermore, his view fit nicely with the all-dominating inductive prescription for the growth of science: that science should be advanced by gathering the facts first and then inducing explanations (hypotheses, theories, laws, models, and so forth) from the facts. We need to take a closer look at this inductive view and some of its consequences.

The inductive view was systematically formulated by Francis Bacon in the seventeenth century (Bacon 1960). Inductive elements have dominated views of scientific method in the English-speaking world ever since.[2] The digging and fact gathering by which a professional archaeologist gains basic credentials is a ritual that pays tribute to Francis Bacon as well as to Franz Boas.

Despite the emphasis on factual description in the inductive tradition, interest in explanation has not been totally rejected. Inductive theory even provides a standard for scientific explanation: it should be generalized from, and hence reducible to, the facts. The trouble is that this inductive standard for explanation faces an insuperable difficulty. As any logician knows, an infinite number of different explanations can be generalized from a finite set of statements (factual statements, for our purposes here). But if an infinite number of explanations is possible, what criterion can be used to judge among them? Unfortunately, inductive theory provides no adequate criterion.

Even the probabilistic modification of the inductive view—according to which the more probable explanation is the preferred explanation—provides little help because calculating such probabilities for important explanations is impossible. Furthermore, the refutationists contend that, even if it were possible, such calculation would not help to advance science because it would not contribute to finding error in explanations. For a summary of probabilistic induction and a history of its establishment, see Bell and Bell (1980). For detailed arguments against induction and probabilistic induction, see Popper (1965, 1968).

As a result, archaeologists operating in the Baconian tradition are forced into a dilemma. Either they must return to digging, recording, and categorizing, or they must use nonlogical criteria for judging the merits of an explanation, criteria such as the reputation of archaeologists holding it or the school of archaeology from which it emanates. Appeal to authorities or schools is not good science, however.

In recent years, as archaeologists have become much more interested in explanation of their data bases, attention has been given to other standards of scientific explanation. In particular, some archaeologists turned to the standard proposed by Carl Hempel. Perhaps partly because of Hempel's reknown and partly because of the popularity of his ideas among historians, his view of science swept into archaeology. Despite questions about its usefulness, about its soundness as a view of science, and even about its interpretation, one cannot help but commend Hempel for recognizing and reacting to a very important problem in the historical sciences: the need to establish a standard for scientific explanation that would supercede appeals to authorities and schools.[3] Comments on Hempel's ideas will be made in Part II.

Systems Thinking

Formulating and testing systems models is not significantly different from formulating and testing other types of explanation in science, but, to avoid confusion, two special qualities of systems models need discussion.

First, systems thinking encourages the introduction of a great number and variety of explanatory mechanisms. A reasonably simple model may have three or four different interacting causal mechanisms, and a complex model may have hundreds. While the complexity of phenomena explainable by such models may be greater because of the number of causal mechanisms, testing the mechanisms themselves can be more exacting. In addition, models of systems often introduce an extensive variety of causal mechanisms. For example, mechanisms involving physical parameters, such as food supply, can be associated with mechanisms involving value parameters, such as "honor," "merit," or "prestige." A major advantage of systems thinking for the social sciences is that physical and value mechanisms can be interrelated. Approaches to the social sciences that attempt to exclude "values" from explanation—as is often the case when the approaches attempt to emulate those in the physical sciences—may discard a crucial aspect of social investigation.

Second, systems thinking encourages endogenous rather than exogenous explanation. In endogenous explanation, in theory, the principal causal mechanisms should all be included in an explanation; external factors should not be crucial. In practice, endogenous explanation requires that an investigator alter the boundaries of a system so that important factors affecting the system become mechanisms within it. For example, if earthquakes were frequent and influenced behavior patterns of a society, then a mechanism(s) accounting for them should be endogenated. On the other hand, if those earthquakes seemed to have no significant influence on behavior, they can remain exogenous.

Systems boundaries—literally, those which mark off the causal mechanisms of a system—are not fixed. They will depend upon the goal of an investigation and will almost always change as a simulation model is being structured, tested, and restructured. For example, a tribal system might contain a community neighboring it or might not, depending upon the problem under study and whether or not testing of a preliminary simulation model reveals anomalies that require inclusion of mechanisms from a neighboring community.

Actually, the notion of a system can be regarded as derivative, being dependent upon the goal of an inquiry. The word *system* is not crucial for building simulation models if the heuristic functions it serves—such as requiring endogenous explanation—are not forgotten. I do prefer to use the term because of its heuristic value and its place in some of the most significant literature on simulation modelling.

One reason endogenous explanation is advantageous for testability is that it discourages ad hoc adjustment of models that have failed tests. An appeal to external factors can only be made if an external factor itself becomes a testable element, in which case it is endogenated.

A corollary benefit of endogenous explanation is that it encourages the explanation of major discontinuities in system behavior by internal, incremental changes in its mechanisms. Appeal to a powerful external factor, an untestable *deus ex machina*, is discouraged. It is not surprising that systems thinking and the application of "catastrophe theory" are related (see Renfrew 1978 for an analysis of Thom's catastrophe theory).

Although systems thinking encourages introduction of a great number and variety of endogenated causal mechanisms, the fact is that these causal mechanisms, and hence the "system," are testable just as are causal explanations in other areas of science. With this in mind, it is appropriate to comment on the views of two well-known critics of systems thinking, Salmon and Berlinski.

Salmon (1978) bifurcates systems theory into either some explicit "Systems Theory" or some type of mathematical systems theory. A review of the literature could certainly suggest such a bifurcation. Some of the most enthusiastic proponents of systems theory, especially for use in the social sciences, recommend systems theories that are very difficult to understand, much less apply to empirical problems. Others concentrate on mathematical systems theory, but its use for the social sciences is very questionable. Given the bifurcation, Salmon's pessimistic conclusion that systems theory may be of little or no help to archaeologists is warranted. Systems as interrelated causal mechanisms

55

fall completely through her bifurcation, however. An underlying thesis of this paper is that such systems can be very fruitful for archaeologists.

Salmon's appeal, in a footnote, to the book by Berlinski (1976) conveys the hope that Berlinski's analysis might convince readers if her own analysis has not. Berlinski is certainly correct in pointing out that the real world cannot be generated by mathematics, and his criticism of systems theorists guilty of such a hoax seems appropriate. Unfortunately, his analysis ignores the fact that the usual function of mathematics in systems work, as in all science, is to quantify explanations which themselves transcend math. These are tested against an empirical world which also transcends math. He thus wastes the reader's time by criticizing much systems work under the inappropriate assumption that it is just a mathematical creation. Berlinski also ignores the fact that the testing of explanations against the real world via mathematical symbolism is often successful despite puzzling, even disturbing, formal qualities of the mathematics itself. A famous example was the successful use of calculus in testing Newtonian physics even though the foundations of calculus (until more recent times) seemed strange and even inconsistent. Despite this, Berlinski devotes countless pages to analyzing formal difficulties in the math of even good systems work, failing to realize that the formal anomalies are unimportant for the function served by the math. This oversight seems particularly ironic since Berlinski's book is supposedly devoted to the battle *against* those who try to make math do more than it can.

Simulation Models

All simulation models attempt to replicate aspects of reality. At one extreme are models for which every iteration should correspond to reality. Models developed by system dynamicists are of this type; every iteration is over time, and the model at any time should correspond to reality at that time. At the other extreme are simulation models that attempt only to simulate an outcome and do not attempt to emulate processes at different stages (see Renfrew, Chapter 10, for further discussion of types of simulation models). While models can be at either of the above extremes or in-between, the more points at which elements of a model are testable, the better. Models that attempt to emulate reality of every iteration, then, are often more testable. Models that attempt only to emulate an outcome tend to be much less testable.

Increasing the number of testable points is desirable, but so is increasing the risk at those points. The more precisely the elements of a model are stipulated, the more precise will be the computer outputs and hence the more severe will be the tests against reality. Even if a model concentrates on simulating outcome, if it has a precisely predicted outcome it can be highly testable. Cordell's model for predicting site abandonment at Wetherill Mesa is an example of such a model (Cordell 1975).

It is appropriate here to point out a difficulty with the precision of mechanisms invoking value parameters as opposed to mechanisms invoking physical parameters. Obviously one cannot quantify "increasing honor" of a social group; if it were quantified precisely, the quantification would be open to much doubt. If a modeller in the social sciences needs to incorporate value mechanisms into a model, and yet cannot quantify them precisely, what is to be done? The answer is to make a quantification that at least shows feedback direction (+ or −, increase or decrease) and to try to test the feedback directions in as many social contexts as possible, including tests in other societies.[4] For example, a modeller could stipulate that "whenever food supply falls to a critically low level, all other factors unchanged, the honor of the religious leaders falls" and "whenever predictions made by religious leaders come true, all other factors unchanged, their honor increases." The feedback directions of value mechanisms are then formulated in such a way that they can be tested even though any specific quantification would have to be somewhat arbitrary. Feedback direction of this value mechanism need not be tested only for a model of the social group under investigation, but might also be tested for any other group in which the honor of religious leaders is significant.

In short, while value mechanisms cannot be precisely stipulated, they are partially testable: the direction of feedback loops can be submitted to tests. While less rigorous than is often possible for mechanisms involving physical parameters, that type of testing is nonetheless extremely effective. As those familiar with computer simulation models will readily attest, the direction rather than the magnitude of feedback loops is usually the most significant determinant of model behavior.

In sum, the more points at which mechanisms can be tested and the more vulnerable the mechanisms to possible error, the better. The groundwork has been set for a discussion of the refutationist view of scientific method, which is well designed to uncover explanatory mechanisms and to make them as testable as possible.

PART II: REFUTATIONIST METHOD AND TESTABLE EXPLANATIONS[5]

Refutationist method was systematically formulated by Sir Karl Popper and has been expounded upon and improved by him and his followers over the past five decades. According to the refutationist view, the primary route of scientific advance is the exposure of explanations (that is, hypotheses, theories, laws, and models) to possible error. Corroboration of an explanation requires that it pass tests that could have shown it wrong. Refutationist techniques focus on increasing the variety and risk of tests to which an explanation is exposed.[6] The greater the refutability, the higher the corroboration when tests are passed.

Why is corroboration desirable? An explanation makes "contact with reality" at points of corroboration. The more highly it is corroborated at crucial points, the more likely it will account for the crucial mechanisms. The mechanisms have run risky tests but have survived.

Below are the principal guidelines for applying refutationist method both to formulate and to adjust explanations (including models, of course). The most noticeable difference between this method and that of Hempel, it will be seen, is the refutationist insistence upon avoiding purely correlative or statistical relations which reduce, rather than enhance, refutability.

Before beginning, it should be pointed out that the prescriptions of refutationist method can seldom if ever be fully employed in practice. The more closely modellers attempt to follow the prescriptions, however, the more likely that their models, and hence the explanations associated with them, can be tested against empirical data and improved when the models fail.

Causality

Causality provides a key tool for employing refutationist method. The overriding importance of causal explanations is evident throughout Popper's work. In his seminal book, *The Logic of Scientific Discovery*, he proposes a methodological rule which corresponds . . . closely to the "principle of causality." . . . It is the simple rule that we are not to abandon the search for universal laws and for a coherent theoretical system, nor ever give up our attempts to explain causally any kind of event we can describe. This rule guides the scientific investigator in his work. (Popper 1968:61)

Refutationists insist upon causal explanations for two reasons. First, causal explanations can always be interpreted as including universal statements and hence can offer multiple points for testing. The generality of causal explanations is obvious in such theories as Newton's laws of motion ("Wherever . . ." or "Whenever . . ."). However, even causal explanations of individual events can be understood to embody universal statements. For example, consider the simple causal explanation, "Demand for the society's earthenware fell because it was losing religious significance." This explanation can be analyzed into three component statements: (a) "demand for the society's earthenware fell," (b) "earthenware of the society was losing religious significance," and (c) "whenever the religious significance of objects becomes less, the demand for those objects declines." The third statement is universal; it claims that in *all* cases when the religious significance of objects declines, the demand for those objects becomes less (other factors remaining unchanged, of course).

Universal statements are refutable by a wide range of empirical facts. In the above case, any instance of a rise in demand for objects that are losing religious significance, all other things being unchanged, can be interpreted as a counterexample to the causal explanation. Even a counterexample from another society, in another epoch, would refute the original notion. On the other hand, a causal explanation can become highly corroborated precisely because a wide variety of evidence can be called upon to test the universal statement. In sum, the number of tests and hence the risk of an explanation are increased by searching for causal mechanisms.

Causal mechanisms are also important in adjusting explanations which fail tests. Refutationists can guard against ad hoc adjustments—adjustments that decrease risk—by requiring a causal statement which suggests *why* an explanation is in error before adjusting it. That is, all failures of tests must be understood in terms of causal mechanisms and be overcome by improved causal mechanisms. Such practice can actually lead to adjusted explanations that are *more* refutable than their predecessors. Refutability can be increased because the revised explanation can be corroborated at a point of prior refutation and because it can contain additional universal statements (causal mechanisms) subject to further testing. The above discussion oversimplifies the practical difficulties in distinguishing ad hoc from proper adjustments. Hempel (1966) has shown how proposed adjustments may be less refutable than they initially appear. Lakatos (1970:116–38) has provided a penetrating analysis of the pitfalls of adjusting explanations so that they become more rather than less risky.

Correlative and Statistical Relations

By contrast, correlative relations can compromise refutability because they embody only singular statements about reality. For example, consider the correlative relation "demand for a society's earthenware fell and the earthenware of that society was losing religious significance." The correlation consists of two component statements: "demand for a society's earthenware fell," and "earthenware of that society was losing religious significance." Each statement is singular in the sense that it applies only to one empirical event. The two events are correlated, but this implies nothing about future cases when demand fails or religious significance decreases. Such relations are normally not even assumed to hold for the original events outside the historical range of variation for which the correlation was observed. In addition, correlative relations are often statistically expressed, which enables improbable, but possible, refuting evidence to be acceptable rather than regarded as counterevidence. In short, purely correlative relations do not provide a solid basis for highly corroborated explanations: They set boundary conditions that can exclude, rather than increase, the number of risky points. Statistical correlations have the further disadvantage of allowing possible, even if improbable, evidence rather than seizing upon it for refutation.

Finally, even if there is an accepted statistical criterion for failure of a theory, no causal explanation of error is required. If a model is revised on the basis of statistical tests, the adjusted model makes no more universal claims than the original. In this way, statistical criteria can encourage ad hoc adjustments of explanations (see Mass and Senge 1978).

The primary difficulty with Hempel's views on method, in my opinion, is his encouragement of purely correlative and statistical relations even though he also strongly endorses causal explanations. He does not disallow purely correlative and statistical relations that reduce risk even though he does maintain that risk is important for scientific explanations. Hempel (1966) displays numerous instances of these inconsistencies.

It should not be concluded that correlative or statistical relations are unfruitful. For those using refutationist method, they can be helpful in suggesting areas to search for causal mechanisms and possible flaws in explanations. However, they should not serve as substitutes for causal relations.

Popper himself has analyzed extensively the dangers of "probability logic" and purely statistical criteria for refutability (see, for example, Popper 1968:251–81 and 1965:280–92).

Unobservable Relations

Insistence on causal explanations has one additional advantage which is especially relevant for the present discussion: it allows admission of "unobservable relations" in formulating causal explanations of complex phenomena. For example, Newton's causal explanation of planetary motion requires two universal statements: (a) a body in motion will stay in motion unless acted upon by an external force (inertial principle), and (b) all masses attract each other (gravitational law). Neither universal statement is observable directly in everyday terrestrial phenomena. Bodies do not stay in motion because they are acted upon by external forces such as friction. And masses do not seem to attract one another because the overwhelming influence of the earth's gravitational attraction holds them in place. Moreover, each statement taken individually contradicts observed planetary motion: the inertial principle alone implies that planets would move in a straight line, while the gravitational law alone implies that all planets would fall into the sun. Clearly, if Newton had restricted himself to purely observable relations, he could not have formulated his highly successful dynamic theories.

There is another important advantage of multiple universal statements; they increase the *variety* of points at which an explanation can be tested. The universal statements by which Newton explained planetary motion also explain the motion of bodies on an incline plane, pendulum motion, bodies falling free, and the reaction of bodies upon collision. Such a variety of testable points greatly enhances the refutability of theories. But it also makes the testing process more subtle than is required to test the explanations with single universal statements. Tests may need to be devised that are aimed at refutable points distant from the events initially explained. (Who would have imagined before Newton, for example, that a causal explanation of planetary motion would have universal statements that could be tested by pendulum motion or the motion of bodies on an incline plane?)

Function of Data

For refutationists, as must now be evident, data function to test risky points of explanations. Data that confirm explanations without risk are not significant. Furthermore, since data function to test risky points, it is unimportant whether the data are known or unknown prior to explanation formation. In practice, the use of unobservable relations in explanation formation and testing usually necessitates that refutationists use data unknown to them at the time. These points are made because they contrast quite sharply with analogs in the inductive tradition, a tradition from which Hempel has partially, but not completely, broken. Inductivist techniques normally constrain a scientist to generate explanations from a data base already accumulated. This tends to render explanations which are confirmed with little or no risk (because confirming data were used in explanation formation) and which are statistical (because some data will not fit). As can be seen, inductivist use of data leads to acceptance of correlative and statistical relations and the inevitable weakening of testability associated with those relations.

CONCLUSION: GUIDELINES FOR DEVELOPING AND ADJUSTING TESTABLE COMPUTER SIMULATION MODELS

The more highly tested an explanation, the better. Therefore, scholars should remember

(1) That models associated with explanations should be formulated in such a way that they are as refutable as possible.
(2) That models which fail tests should be adjusted in such a way that they pass tests at the failure points, but are still refutable at other points.

62

To formulate refutable models, remember

(1) To search for causal mechanisms; do not be satisfied with purely correlative or statistical relations.

(2) To attempt simulation of mechanisms that are testable at as many stages of model iteration as possible; simulate an outcome as a minimum.

(3) To make causal mechanisms as precise as possible.

(4) To test mechanisms in as many contexts—for as many social groups—as possible.

(5) To test the direction of feedback loops of value mechanisms, remembering that their magnitude is not likely to be of paramount importance in model behavior.

To adjust models that fail tests, remember

(1) To insist upon a causal explanation of model failure.

(2) To endogenate additional causal mechanisms if they are important in explaining error.

(3) To continue testing an adjusted model for other weaknesses.

When should the testing and adjusting stop? When one is satisfied that the crucial points of a model have been highly corroborated through successful tests. The model has faced reality at those points and has been shown correct. A simulation model will never emulate all points of reality, but the more its crucial points have been subjected to serve tests against reality, and the better it has been adjusted when tests are failed, the more likely it is that the explanation associated with the model is empirically sound.

NOTES

1. It is interesting that Boas's emphasis on description and proper field training is evident even in his personal letters. See, for example, Stocking (1974, especially pp. 286–92).

2. For a reconstructed history of the scientific, intellectual, and sociological roots of inductive method, see Bell and Bell (1980). The (mistaken) belief that Newton's dynamis and celestial mechanics were formulated and legitimated by inductive method, along with the use (by Anglicans) of inductive method as a weapon against the Aristotelian foundations of Catholicism, were two important reasons for the widespread acceptance of inductive method.

3. For concise review of the literature relevant to archaeologists concerning Hempel's view of science, see Sabloff, Beale, and Kurland (1973). This article also raises some questions about the viability of Hempel's ideas and reviews difficulties seen by others. A penetrating analysis of Hempel's method applied to the historical sciences is provided by Goode (1977).

4. While there is controversy concerning the necessity of feedback loops in systems, I believe it is clear that there must be feedback loops. After all, they interrelate causal mechanisms; if there

63

were no interrelationships, then there would be no models. Renfrew (Chapter 10) has further comments on the controversy.

5. Portions of this part are taken from Bell and Senge (1980). While that paper focuses on system dynamics modelling, the arguments apply to all modelling.

6. For the record, it should be noted that Popper himself and some of his followers are principally interested in the progress of theoretical science and that refutationist method was originally developed for that purpose. Theoretical science, in their view, should not become fixated on particular goals. Instead, goals can and do change with theoretical development. Empirical work that has applied goals as well as theoretical motivation, as is often the case with simulation modelling, may focus on a given problem (such as explaining the collapse of civilization) and hence require a corroborated explanation aimed at that particular problem. Refutationist guidelines for formulating and adjusting testable explanations are very similar, however, regardless of whether one has theoretical or applied goals or both.

PART 2

Case Studies

4
Creating Assemblages by Computer Simulation: The Development and Uses of ABSIM

MARK S. ALDENDERFER

State University of New York at Buffalo

One of the most difficult things a researcher can do is to illustrate the process of model building as it really happens. Kaplan (1964) describes this as a presentation of *logic-in-use,* a discussion of the actual sequence of events in the research process. A description of logic-in-use can be embarrassing to the author because it may point out flaws and weak areas in research design and conduct. But an understanding of logic-in-use often helps other scholars avoid problems in their work by indicating common traps and pitfalls in the modelling process. Understanding how modelling is done is often preferable to a reconstructed logic of the same process. A reconstructed logic is a detailed presentation of an ideal series of steps in the modelling process. Reconstructed logics closely follow flow charts which describe the proper conduct of science, and they often portray what *should* have been done in the research process rather than what was actually done.

Reconstructed logics have their place in scientific discourse, but the early consolidation of information on computer simulation in archaeology is better served by a frank, if painful, illustration of why a simulation is built, how it is built, and how it can be used. Plog's viewpoint on simulation is as apt as it is succinct. He says simply, "It's not an easy thing to do" (F. Plog in Hill 1977a:315). Simulation modelling probably has more traps and pitfalls than any other methodology currently in use in archaeology, and because it is new to the discipline, both developers and users are unaware of the many perplexing problems that accompany the technique. A logic-in-use description of how simulation modelling works is a start toward an increase of knowledge about simulation in the discipline. The following paper describes the hows and whys of a simulation of assemblage formation processes—ABSIM (Aboriginal Simulation). I have attempted to describe as many of the critical decision points in the model as possible. Although the style of model description is literary, it follows many of the recommendations offered by McLeod (1973) for the comprehensive presentation of a simulation model to potential users. As archaeologists become more familiar with simulation, the need for this type of expository paper will diminish. But until that day, "true confessions" of simulation model building will have their place in the archaeological literature.

WHY WAS ABSIM CREATED?

Behind every simulation model there is (or should be) a clearly defined problem which guides the research effort. In most fields in which simulation is used, the problem to be investigated is straightforward. Urban planners may need to determine how traffic flows will be disturbed by the erection of a 14-story building in a busy part of downtown. A building contractor must determine what is the optimal waiting time for an elevator at each floor of a building, or an ecologist may need to know why high concentrations of phosphates are seeping into a previously uncontaminated water supply. An unambiguous definition of the problem to be studied helps to establish a set of working hypotheses which will ultimately become the focus of research and experimentation with a simulation model.

Poor problem definition inevitably leads to poor hypothesis construction, and this in turn leads to a poorly designed simulation exercise. The set of hypotheses derived from the problem informs the users of a simulation model of what the model was *intended* to accomplish. Strongly defined hypotheses act as goals for research and measures of the success of a simulation effort.

Once the problem has been defined, the simulation modelling enterprise moves through three levels of increasing abstraction: (a) system identification and bounding, (b) development of a conceptual model of the system, and (c) implementation of the conceptual model into a computer simulation. The first of these levels is discussed in this section of the paper, and the others are discussed below (General Assemblage Formation Model and ABSIM: A Simulation Model).

The definition of the real-world system or process of interest is the first step in the modelling process. The problem to be studied inevitably leads to a consideration of what aspects of the real world are relevant to its study and ultimate solution. In the traffic flow problem, the real-world system is composed of the streets that surround the proposed facility and the vehicles which travel them. The system is also described by data that include the direction in which traffic flows on the streets, the location of stop lights, the direction of red and green lights, peak periods of traffic flow, and much more. Other aspects of the urban environment, such as the population density of the area surrounding the facility, the ethnic composition of the population, or the types of businesses along the streets, are not relevant to the study of this particular problem, and thus they are excluded from the definition of the system. Although researchers are figuratively dealing with real-world phenomena (that is, the flow of cars on the streets), there is nevertheless a low level of abstraction at work in the process of creating boundaries of the system.

In the traffic flow problem, for instance, it might be difficult to determine exactly which streets are a part of the system. In most applications of simulation, there are no rules which make the process of system bounding simple. Success depends upon the state of knowledge about the system, previous definitions of similar systems, and the intuition of the researcher.

The relationship between the problem and the definition of the system is intimate, and a successful modelling effort defines both as clearly as possible. Without these definitions, it becomes difficult to judge whether or not a simulation model has accomplished its goals successfully, or, of equal importance, whether or not a simulation model is required at all to explore both the problem and the system.

Problem Definition

ABSIM was developed to discover just how well multivariate statistical methods work to discover functional patterning in archaeological assemblages. The use of multivariate methods has increased dramatically since the publication of Binford and Binford's (1966) application of factor analysis to Mousterian assemblages from southwestern France and the Near East. Since then, other multivariate methods, such as cluster analysis, multidimensional scaling, and other pattern search techniques, have been applied to many types of archaeological problems. Much of the use of these methods has centered around the so-called functional argument (Binford 1973), which is an attempt to explain interassemblage variability in a settlement system in terms of differential organization of human activity performance in space and time. Simply put, the variability observed in stone tool assemblages is due primarily to people doing different things at different places at different times. Combinations of tool types in different relative frequencies are said to represent "tool kits," and sites can be placed into site typologies on the basis of these kits.

Because most assemblages are characterized by many tool types and because the interaction between these tool types in their relative frequencies can be subtle, multivariate statistical methods are required to discover the inherent structure of assemblage data. In most instances, the multivariate methods are used to generate hypotheses which can then be tested for goodness-of-fit to independent archaeological data. If significant patterning in the data set is discovered, the archaeologist then attempts to explain the origin of that pattern on the basis of his or her understanding of the form of the results provided by the multivariate technique. The success of this research orientation depends upon both the phenomenon under study and the reliability of the multivariate method in its application to this particular data set.

Although archaeologists have long debated the merits of the functional argument, they have neglected the study of the methods used to create the patterns of interest in archaeological assemblages. It is now well known that multivariate methods will provide some sort of solution to any data set. Pattern search techniques, despite their name, generally *impose* some type of structure on the data. The trick is to determine whether the method has reproduced a reasonable approximation to the "true" or inherent structure of the data set, or has imposed a pattern which is neither accurate nor correct.[1] In many applications, this problem is ignored; the results are interpreted without question. When the results are confusing (how many times has a researcher stated, "Factor X or cluster X is uninterpretable"?), considerable head-scratching takes place, but interpretation (and other use of the results) nevertheless continues! When the problem is recognized, the standard technique is to see if the results are "reasonable." This usually involves a prior classification of the data, which the archaeologist compares to the newly generated result. If they agree, the machine version is reasonable; if not, the machine version is usually rejected. Elsewhere (Aldenderfer and Blashfield 1978), I have argued that this position is untenable, and that the use of multivariate (or any other) methods in this context is essentially honorific.

Other methods for evaluating the results obtained from multivariate methods are available, and these derive from two general sources: theoretical models and empirical studies. Theoretical models are usually a set of expectations derived from theory. Whether or not a theoretical model exists depends upon the level of quantitative sophistication of the particular technique. Factor analysis has a series of different models, many of them statistical in nature (for example, maximum likelihood methods). The success of a method is demonstrated by a good fit between a statistic as generated by the application of the method to data and the theoretically determined value of the statistic for that type of situation. Theoretical models can be misleading, however. Many statistical models assume particular distribution forms of data which are not often met in practice. In such cases, it is quite possible for the model to be inappropriate, and thus provide misleading statistics. The model may also be inappropriate on other grounds. Factor analysis, despite its application to many fields, has a particular psychometric interpretation which is a result of its long association with psychology. The application of this method (and by implication its theoretical model) to problems in other disciplines is more rightly an empirical question, unless it can be demonstrated that the model is appropriate in the new context.

Other multivariate methods, especially clustering methods, have few theories that can be used as reliable guides to the validity of their results. Most cluster analysis methods are heuristic, or "rules of thumb" systematically applied to data to create groups. Many validation methods have been proposed to test the adequacy of clustering solutions, but most of these methods are biased toward particular techniques or produce conflicting results (Blashfield, Aldenderfer, and Morey in press; Dubes and Jain 1977; Milligan 1978). Researchers have discovered that certain methods work well under certain conditions, but the reasons for this are not yet clear.

When theory proves to be a poor guide, or when applied research is unable to produce consistent results, the *empirical* evaluation of multivariate methods becomes important. "Typical" data sets with *known* structure are either created or discovered. Multivariate methods are applied to them and the results are compared with the true typology for goodness-of-fit. This type of research is important in disciplines that often use the same type of data in a variety of applied problems. This methodology assumes that certain data sets have a particular structure, and that even though this structure is presently unknown, certain methods will be more successful for the discovery of patterns of interest than will others. As particular clustering methods are found to work well on certain distribution forms of data, much of the guesswork of validation will be eliminated.[2] Schiffer (1975c) has applied this methodology to the use of factor analysis and its ability to reconstruct tool kits under simple conditions.

The empirical methodology for validation is ideally suited to archaeological assemblage data. Theory suggests that these assemblages are created by the same general processes worldwide. There is thus considerable uniformity to assemblage data. But theory does not go beyond this general statement, and it does not predict assemblage content or the relative contribution of various forces to the creation of assemblages. Nor does it offer the archaeologist a completely ascertained set of assemblages. An empirical methodology offers the opportunity of a more complete understanding of the processes of assemblage formation, and it provides a concrete set of results which, if accepted, can be put to immediate practical use. The results can then be applied in theory building.

System Definition

To obtain data on archaeological assemblages with known functional structure, it is necessary to define that set of social, cultural, biological, and natural forces which combine to create and modify the content of archaeological assemblages. For convenience, these forces are labelled *assemblage formation processes*. The definition of these forces should be general so that any resulting conceptual model of the system can be applied to any level of sociocultural integration.

A step in the definition of these processes involves the assessment of the state of knowledge on how assemblages are formed. In many applications of simulation, it is almost always possible directly to observe the system under investigation to obtain information on its structure and on the value of some of its components and variables. Although the costs of obtaining data from the system can be high, the system nevertheless acts as a repository of data for model construction, tuning, and validation.

In most archaeological problems, the system which produced the archaeological remains cannot be observed, and in most cases it is the focus of the modelling effort. To build models of these past systems, archaeologists rely on a diverse body of knowledge often of questionable reliability and quality. Ethnography, ethnoarchaeology, experimentation, and history all serve as substitutes for information which cannot be directly obtained from observation of the existing system.

The system of assemblage formation processes should include at least the following:

(1) That set of activities capable of producing durable outputs into the archaeological record must be delimited. These outputs must be further specified to be stone or other nonperishable materials, and for this problem, other types of outputs, such as features and middens, are not included in this definition of the system. Information on the frequency of activity performance should also be included. An activity structure or sequence should be defined, and the set of conditions which initiate a bout of activity performance should be included in the system.

(2) There must be an unambiguous definition of tool types in the system, and this definition should be based primarily on functional attributes. The relationship between each tool type and an activity in which it may be employed must be specified. The concept of the "tool kit" as understood by the users of the tools is irrelevant, as Binford (1976) has shown. Some estimate of the use-life (the expected length of time a tool can be used before exhaustion or breakage) of each tool type must also be made. Non-use-related pathways into the archaeological record must be

identified, such as loss, scavenging, and recycling. Data on stone tool manufacture may or may not be useful, especially the information on reduction strategies for different tool types.

(3) The location of activity performance is obviously important, and some attempt must be made to include all locations which may be the scene of activity performance which includes durable outputs into the archaeological record. However, the problem of "the threshold of archaeological visibility" must be considered. As Hayden (1978) notes for some Australian hunter-gatherers, certain types of procurement sites have a high threshold of visibility, meaning that these sites would be extremely difficult to find under most circumstances. Logically, such sites should be included in the system because activities are performed at them, but the problems of obtaining data on their distribution and location may be great. If the system has many sites, some mechanism must be defined which moves tool users from place to place.

(4) Natural and cultural forces which affect the content of assemblages should be included. The former are known as *n-transforms* (Schiffer 1976). These can add or subtract elements from assemblages, and thus affect the relative frequencies of tools in them. The type of archaeological deposit may also have an effect on assemblage content and its interpretation (Schiffer 1976).

Although relatively few concepts have been discussed, it is obvious that, taken together, this definition of the system involves a large amount of information. One important point must be stressed. System definition and bounding often lead to the inclusion of more processes than will be ultimately included in the conceptual model or the computer simulation. Although a process may be relevant to a system, and it may be important in the solution of the problem, it may not be included in further steps of the modelling process. The most common reason for exclusion is that too little information on the process is available to relate it to the better-known elements of the system. This has happened repeatedly in the development of ABSIM. System definition corresponds to the development of a base model of a system (Zeigler 1976a) in which all relevant information is included. Base models often have "too much" information in them to handle easily and are streamlined and modified in later steps in the simulation modelling process.

Is Simulation Necessary?

To evaluate the performance of multivariate methods, archaeological assemblages with known functional structure are required. These assemblages must be created and modified by a combination of forces in the system of assemblage formation processes. The ideal source of information on these processes is a group of stone tool users practicing a "traditional" subsistence-settlement adaptation. Multivariate methods could be directly applied to the data derived from the observation of this group, and a sophisticated methodology using simulation would not be necessary if enough of these groups of tool users were available. But even the briefest look through the modern ethnographic literature shows that no such group is available for study. Although some groups still use stone tools, and others still have traditional adaptations, no single existing group combines the extensive use of stone with a reasonably unmodified subsistence-settlement regime.[3] Without these groups, data on the system of processes which leads to the creation of assemblages cannot be directly obtained. The only alternative for the study of how multivariate methods work is to *create* assemblage data.

How can assemblages be created? One way is to contrive a simple example of tool use and deposition. Schiffer (1975c) has done this in his study of factor analysis. Although this study is useful, its simplicity limits its applicability to other archaeological situations which are considerably more complex. Another approach is to create them with a mathematical model. Ammerman and Feldman (1974) have built a matrix model which represents some of the important features of assemblage creation. Using the model, a number of tools can be deposited at a site, and this deposition can be compared to an expected number of tools. Differences between the expected and actual number of tools can be related to variability in dropping rates, activity bouts, and other variables. This model is important, but again, its utility to create a number of assemblages is limited. One of the major assumptions of the model is that it represents activity at only *one* site. In its present form, the model cannot be extended to create assemblages at a series of sites, because there is no mechanism to move the tool users to new locations, and there is no "memory" in the system which keeps track of modified tool use-lives after activity performance. The model cannot create a settlement system of sites which is reasonably realistic. A similar model by Schiffer (1976) suffers from the same weakness.

What is needed, then, is a model with a memory and a capacity to create assemblages at more than one site. By definition, such a model is dynamic because it moves through time as well as space to create new assemblages. Although there may be a static mathematical model at its core, the ideal model of assemblage formation processes must have this dynamic structure. Computer simulation fulfills the requirements for both memory and dynamic operation; it is thus the methodology of choice for the solution of the problem.

A GENERAL ASSEMBLAGE FORMATION MODEL

After problem definition and the selection of simulation as the appropriate methodology, the next step of the modelling enterprise is to create, borrow, or find a conceptual model of the process or system under study. Depending on the state of knowledge of the system, this step can be relatively simple or enormously complex. Problems in other disciplines often have similar structure despite differences in content. Simulation programming languages exploit this similarity and thus are widely used in many fields. Other problems, however, require substantial modification of existing models or the development of new models to include everything desired. The necessity to build new models which can be implemented as computer simulations is especially important in fields such as archaeology, in which many of the basic processes which structure the archaeological record are still unknown or poorly understood.

Despite a universal concern for a better understanding of how assemblages are created and what the data from them mean, little progress has been made toward the development of a formal, general model of assemblage formation processes. Only three models have yet appeared: those of Ammerman and Feldman (1974), Binford (1972b, 1973, 1976, 1978), and Schiffer (1976). Although each of these models has merit, none of them is sufficiently general or well structured for the successful construction of a computer simulation model.[4]

The general model described below has been built specifically for use in a simulation context. It is based on a set of *components, variables, parameters,* and *component interactions* which describe its structure and operation. The definition of these terms follows Zeigler (1976a). Components are simply the entities of the model. Each component

76

has a set of variables and parameters that describes its content and the condition of the component at any point in time. Finally, component interactions are rules which determine how one component influences another. The operation of these rules changes the value of the variables of the components, and thus the state, or condition, of the component is changed. Changes in the state of the components describe the behavior of the model through time.

Although other sets of similar terms could have been used to describe the general model (Aldenderfer, Chapter 2), these terms were chosen because they provide a common language or jargon which is important in the communication of the simulation model to other users (Zeigler 1976a:3–26). Moreover, their use enhances the design credibility of the entire modelling enterprise because it places the general (or conceptual) model in a rigorous, unambiguous framework which can be more easily compared to the structure and content of the resulting simulation model (Innis, Schlesinger, and Sylvester 1977; McLeod 1973).

The general assemblage formation model is behavioral in content, and it focuses upon the consequences of different types of human activity as they structure the archaeological record. Conceptually, the model acts as an interface between models of resource utilization (Joachim 1976; Limp 1978) and models of refuse deposition, disposal pathways, and site disturbance factors (Schiffer 1976). It can be used to describe many different types of settlement systems and activity sets. But the model is hardly exhaustive, and in fact, it cannot be. Many of the components of the model, such as "social factors," are no more than convenient terms which simply label much more complex human behaviors. This treatment of many components is necessary because the number of social factors, for instance, which can affect the composition of stone tool assemblages is very large. The model acts only as a heuristic device which demonstrates linkage between components. The content of each component (and thus the set of variables and parameters needed to describe it) varies from problem to problem.

Components and Variables of the Model

A heuristic device useful in the interpretation and presentation of a conceptual model to be used in a simulation context is the block diagram. Similar to flow charts, block diagrams demonstrate the influ-

77

ence of each component or variable on every other entity contained in the model. Often, block diagrams assume that the links between components or variables are causal, but this is not necessarily the case in all block diagrams, such as those which describe energy flow. Figure 4.1 presents a simple block diagram of the general assemblage formation model, and Figure 4.2 presents the same model in an expanded form. Table 4.1 lists these components and variables.

Artifact set. This component is composed of variables related to the set of artifacts included in living assemblages of tools. The *types* of variables are obvious. The variables contain all of the tools a tool owner is likely to use. There is no implication that the tool owner has all of these objects at any single moment in time.

The *use-life* of a tool is the expected length of time a tool can be used before exhaustion or breakage. Binford's (1973) concepts of curate and expedient behavior in the use of tools can be subsumed under the definition of use-life as a function of time. Time as a basis for the definition of use-life has been developed in engineering and the biomedical sciences under the concept of reliability theory (Bazovsky 1961; Gross and Clark 1975), which includes a number of statistical models of use-life based on different distribution types. Alternative definitions of use-life, such as the number of strokes a stone tool possesses, may prove useful in specific applications. The number of

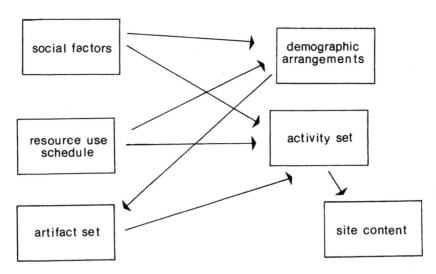

FIGURE 4.1 Simple block diagram of the assemblage formation model.

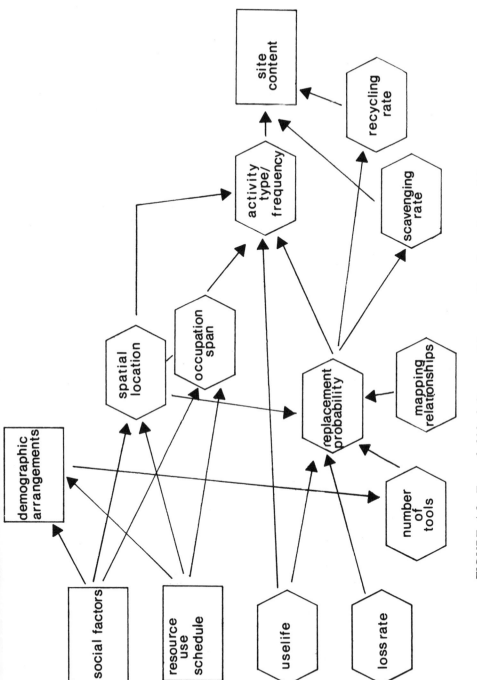

FIGURE 4.2. Expanded block diagram of the assemblage formation model.

TABLE 4.1
COMPONENTS AND VARIABLES OF THE GENERAL
ASSEMBLAGE FORMATION MODEL

1)	Artifact set	component
	a) types	variable
	b) mapping relationships	variable
	c) loss rate	variable
	d) recycling	variable
	e) scavenging rate	variable
	f) use-life	variable
	g) number of tools	variable
2)	Activity set	component
	a) activity set	variable
	b) activity frequency	variable
	c) replacement probability	variable
3)	Resource-use schedule	component
	a) spatial location	variable
	b) occupation span	variable
4)	Social factors	component
5)	Demographic arrangements	component
	a) number of individuals who perform a task	variable
6)	Site content	component
	a) number of tools deposited	variable
	b) types of tools deposited	variable

tools is the total number of tools which exist in the system at any point in time. Some of these tools may be in storage, or may only see sporadic use, but as long as they have not become a part of the archaeological record, they are included in this variable.

Mapping relationships, a concept introduced by Ammerman and Feldman (1974), refers to the set of relationships between the tool types and the tasks in which they are used. Some tools have only one function, but other tool types may be used in a variety of applications. A mapping relationship is the probability that tool type X will be used in activity Y. The *loss rate* is simply the frequency of loss of a particular tool type, and this rate should vary from type to type. Loss represents a non-use-related pathway to the archaeological record. The *recycling rate* is the frequency with which a tool, once it has ended its use-life for its originally intended function, is shifted to a new function (Schiffer 1976). Recycling may or may not involve modification of the original tool. The importance of recycling is that it can prevent a tool from entering into the archaeological record in its exhausted form, and depending on the use-life of the new function, the spatial location of its ultimate deposition may be different as well. Recycling thus obscures the relationship between the use of a tool and its appearance in the archaeological record. The *scavenging rate* refers to the use of already exhausted or ad hoc tools as substitutes for the appropriate tool type. This is slightly different from mapping relationships, for it refers to the use of tools or other objects which already have become a part of the archaeological record. Scavenging also obscures the relationship between a particular tool type and an activity.

Activity set. This concept includes all activities that may produce some type of output into the archaeological record. Many activities do not have archaeological consequences, and they are not included in this component. *Activity type* is the set of activities performed by individuals or groups over a specified period of time, and the *activity frequency* is the rate at which the activity is performed. As shown in the block diagram, activity frequency is determined by (or depends on) the action of a number of variables and components. The *replacement probability* is the likelihood of replacement of an object after loss, exhaustion, or breakage. Replacement depends on, among other things, the need for a tool, the availability of a substitute (mapping relationships), scavenged tools, and raw material needed to construct a new tool.

Resource use schedule. This component describes how the cultural system is adapted to its environment. The system can include groups at any level, from hunter-gatherers to sedentary agriculturalists. Although it is possible to define a large number of subsistence types, it would not be useful to include them in a general model simply because this model is not meant to be exhaustive. Some of the more pertinent factors in this component are food and raw material procurement systems, settlement locations and degree of seasonality. Accordingly, two variables are used to describe the state of the resource-use component. *Spatial location* refers to the locus of activity performance. There are two levels to this variable. The first is the general location of the group in its settlement system. This definition assumes that the group performing the activity is at a "site" or discrete location. The second level of the variable refers to the location of activity performance. Some activities are often performed near a camp or at its periphery. Others are located within its boundaries. Special-purpose sites or task sites act as "satellites" around a habitation location. Where any activity is performed is thus an empirical question. *Occupation span* is the length of stay at any site within the settlement or resource procurement system. Schiffer (1975b) is one of the first archaeologists to observe the effect this variable may have on the deposition of artifacts into the archaeological record.

Social factors. This component is a mixed bag of variables. Briefly, social factors are any set of beliefs, customs, or practices that can affect the performance of an activity or the locus at which the activity is performed. This simple definition includes a vast set of ideas too numerous to discuss here. The term "social" is used only for convenience; economic, political, military, trade, and ideological variables among others may affect assemblage composition. This component suffers from very fuzzy boundaries, and thus it is difficult to precisely define any single variable within it. The social forces which operate to deposit tools into the archaeological record in a chiefdom which operates a set of craft specialities will certainly be very different from those in a society of nomadic hunter-gatherers. Again, the content of this component depends entirely on the problem under investigation.

Demographic arrangements. This component refers to the number and types of individuals involved in activity performance. Depending on the problem, the number of individuals can range from one tool user to an entire guild. In some societies, task groups often perform many activities, and their composition can vary considerably. Like the artifact set and activity set components, this component refers only to that set of individuals or groups which performs activities that may lead to the deposition of artifacts into the archaeological record. In this version of the model, the *number of individuals* is the number of tool users involved in an activity. They may be involved as individuals, or in a cooperative venture.

Site content. This component is simply the accumulated *number* and *types* of tools deposited at a site in the settlement system. Additional variables can be included which describe the condition of these tools. The variable *types* also includes, if the problem demands, by-products of tool use or manufacture such as certain flake types. If stone tool manufacture is important in a cultural system, it may be necessary to include the results of this manufacture as a variable in the component.

ABSIM: THE SIMULATION MODEL

The heart of any simulation exercise is the computer program used to implement the general or conceptual model to be studied. This aspect of the modelling adventure must be well described because it is here that all of the implicit and explicit biases of the researcher are translated from ideas into practice. Any evaluation of the adequacy or utility of a simulation model must first grapple with the logical, theoretical, practical, and, at times, inexplicable choices made by the researcher during the construction of the simulation model. The following discussion describes most of the important structural and operational features of ABSIM as well as some of the choices as to model structure I was forced to make. To aid in the exposition of these choices, Figure 4.3 displays a simplified flow chart of the computer program, Table 4.2 briefly describes each of the subroutines it uses, and Table 4.3 demonstrates the linkages between the structure of ABSIM and the general assemblage formation model. Other tables and figures are included in the discussion to expand upon selected topics.

As will become obvious, ABSIM is based primarily upon a Western Desert of Australia ecosystem and an Aboriginal subsistence and settlement technology. These data have been used to transform the conceptual model of assemblage formation processes into a computer simulation model and in many cases have provided the value estimates for a number of parameters and variables used in the simulation model. Despite this heavy reliance on Australian data, ABSIM is *not* a simulation model of Aboriginal adaptations to the desert. The model is not intended to faithfully mimic or replicate the behavior of any *particular* population of hunter-gatherers anywhere in the world, nor is the model meant to be a detailed microsimulation of the arid Australian (or any other) ecosystem. The simulation model must have data for implementation and validation, but it does not necessarily follow that the use of these specific data changes the goal of the simulation exercise.

The goal of ABSIM is to produce data *similar* to that produced by human groups through the exploitation of the environment. ABSIM is thus quite different from BASIN I (Thomas 1972) because in that model, the goal of the modelling exercise was to determine the veracity of Steward's (1938) model of Shoshonean subsistence behavior. For that purpose, Thomas was compelled to produce an accurate replica of the Great Basin environment, a Shoshonean tool kit, and a set of food procurement systems. In contrast, ABSIM contains no detailed procurement systems, and it does not replicate the Australian tool kit or any other. Instead, ABSIM is general in scope, for it represents a set of processes which are common to many different human groups adapted

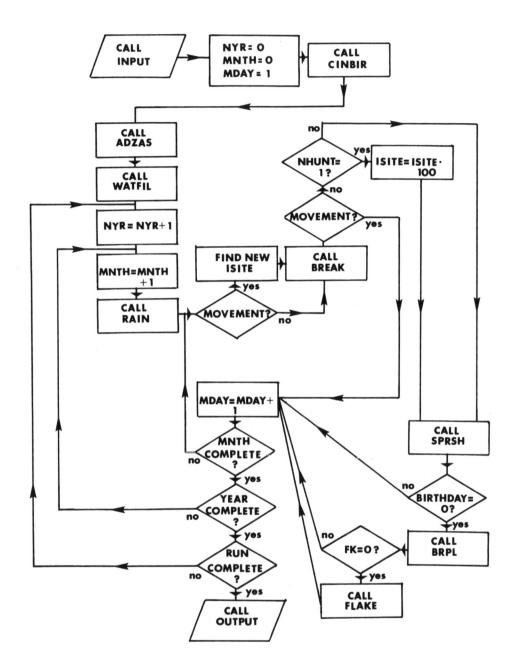

FIGURE 4.3. Flow chart of ABSIM.

TABLE 4.2
DESCRIPTION OF SUBROUTINES USED IN ABSIM

INPUT	Reads all input arrays and values
CINBIR	Creates an assemblage of tools for each individual according to empirical estimates. Assigns each object a "negative" birthday to start the stimulation with added realism.
ADZE (optional)	Creates two arrays of 1500 adzes each for use in the simulation.
ADZAS	Assigns adze to each male and subtracts random amount from each to signify stage of use on each.
WATFIL	Fills up water sources at start of simulation. Values are in gallon amounts.
RAIN	Selects total number of rainfall events for the month, total effective and noneffective rains, and distributes them over the span of 30 days in the month for each site in the settlement system.
BREAK	Assesses the age of all wooden tools against the reliability function to determine tool survival, and breaks tool if required.
BRPL	Replaces all tools broken in BREAK. Subtracts amount of use in strokes from each adze used and replaces it if exhausted.
SPRSH	Sharpens spears and subtracts number of strokes used from adze. Assigns new adze if exhausted.
FLAKE	Deposits number of waste flakes at site if chipping occurs. Distributional values of waste flakes known.
OUTPUT	Prints all relevant information desired.

to many environments. Under the appropriate conditions, ABSIM can generate data similar to those produced by hunter-gatherers with high movement frequencies or it can represent more sedentary peoples exploiting a series of seasonally available resources. Although the data generated by ABSIM will not be identical to those produced by any single group with a particular adaptation, the data should be similar to many different types of tool-use systems and adaptations to environment. The success or failure of ABSIM must be judged on how well the simulation model represents the general process of assemblage formation and not on how well the model represents any specific adaptation or tool-use system. Thus to criticize ABSIM because it does not represent "reality" very well or because certain aspects of it are unacceptable simplifications of more complex situations is to misunderstand the nature of ABSIM and the reasons for its development.

TABLE 4.3
LINKAGES OF ABSIM AND ASSEMBLAGE
FORMATION MODEL

Resource-use schedule	RAIN, decides number/type of rainfall events. Segments of MAIN which implement movement algorithm.
	Calculation of THRESH parameters. Assignment of water by WATFIL on basis of known distribution of water resources.
Social factors	None presently built into ABSIM.
Use-life	Use-life into exhaustion for stone tools built into BRPL, SPRSH.
Replacement frequency	Defined by variable OTTU. Variable replacement rates built into BRPL.
Activity set	Defined by BREAK for tool placement, SPRSH for spear sharpening. Decision in MAIN for hunting.
Activity frequency	Defined by occurrence of breakage in BREAK. Replacement rates built into BRPL, use-lives of some stone tools.
Demographic arrangements	Constant, NMALE = 5.
Spatial location	Monitored by simulation, defined by resource use. Decision in MAIN for hunting in blinds. All other activities at habitation site.
Occupation span	14 days at site maximum values determined by recency of occupation. Occupation also determined by THRESH parameter.
Mapping relationships	Defined by variables OTTU and SCAV.
Number/type of tools	Personal assemblages filled by CINBIR according to empirical estimates.

Operating Characteristics

ABSIM currently runs on an IBM 370/168 computer under OS/MVT. It is written in FORTRAN IV, and it is compatible with the WATFIV, G, and H compilers. IBM general-purpose subroutines and functions are used, but plans are under way to convert those to the similar, more generally available IMSL subroutines and functions.

ABSIM, because it uses random number generators, is a dynamic stochastic simulation model. Because it is stochastic, the output variables of the simulation, such as the number of tools deposited at a site, vary from run to run. Note that the use of random numbers does not mean that the process of tool use and deposition itself is random. Instead, these random numbers are usually transformed into elements of a *probability density function* (pdf), which describes the range of variability of a process or event. Any number of different pdfs can be used in a simulation model depending on the distribution forms of the components or variables of interest in the real-world system. Among the uses of random numbers and associated pdfs in ABSIM is the determination of how many flakes are to be deposited at a site after one instance of stone-tool flaking (empirical pdf), the probability that a wooden tool will break (Weibull, gamma, and exponential pdfs), and the distribution of rainfall frequencies and amounts at sites within the settlement system in any given month (empirical pdf).

The use of random numbers and random variables of known pdfs is essential to the realistic modelling of ill-defined systems in which there is too little information available to develop deterministic equations of systemic processes. In such cases, it is almost always safer to use stochastic model features rather than to falsely assume a particular deterministic solution of a process which will probably produce results of spurious accuracy and dubious reliability. Probabilistic elements are also useful when the system under study has a strong stochastic component. Finally, the results derived from stochastic simulation models can be compared and their reliability assessed using common statistical procedures. This is so because the use of random numbers in the model insures that the output variables will also be random variables (Mihram 1972a:15–16,265–313). Multiple runs of the simulation will thus produce a random sample of all possible responses of the model.

Two random number generators are used in ABSIM: RAND and PRAND. RAND returns a quasi-random number between 0.0 and the real-mode argument which can be set to any integer value. The generator can produce 2^{29} random numbers before recycling. PRAND generates a quasi-random number which is serially independent and distributed between the values of 0 and 1. This generator also produces 2^{29} values before recycling. Both algorithms are written in IBM assembly language.

The statistical properties of these two generators are well known. PRAND is the best known, and it has been subjected to intensive study (Lewis, Goodman, and Miller 1969). Significantly, it has been shown to produce independent values over long simulation runs. Since the total number of calls to PRAND during a typical run of ABSIM is relatively low (20,000 values per 50 years of simulated time compared to 2^{29} possible values), the probability of autocorrelation between these generated values is extremely low.

The Structure of ABSIM

There are two major structural features in ABSIM: subroutines and loops. The subroutines in ABSIM do the "work" of the simulation model. Each subroutine contains a logically discrete activity or set of activities which may be repeatedly called by the main program of the simulation. The subroutines are linked through statements in the main program, which in the case of ABSIM are primarily bookkeeping operations, logical checks, and transfer statements.

Subroutines, or subprograms, are necessary for success when using general-purpose programming languages such as FORTRAN or PL/I for the development of simulation models. Subroutines offer the following advantages:

(1) Logical sequences or operations can be isolated. Complex operations dealing with a single phenomenon can be placed outside the body of the main program and called when needed. This makes the program more efficient by reducing both compilation and run time.

(2) Subroutines permit much more rapid debugging and initial verification of the simulation. Since subroutines can be first tested as independent programs, costly and time-consuming debugging, a common result of linking program elements prematurely, may be considerably expedited.

(3) Subroutines permit the easy modification of program. Changing the type of subsistence system used in ABSIM from the deserts of Australia to the temperate woodlands of the United States would be difficult if subsistence activity had been implemented as a portion of the main program. Experimentation would then necessarily involve a possibly fatal tinkering with the "guts" of ABSIM. The program would then have to be recompiled, reverified, and revalidated before research could procede. Because subsistence activity is based within a subroutine, all that needs to be changed to grow oak, pine, and hickory trees in ABSIM are a few values on cards input into the simulation program.

The three major loops of the program provide the "path" or the "route" for the operation of ABSIM. In Figure 4.2, the outermost loop is to insure that the simulation runs through the required amount of simulated time. The next loop is the month loop, permanently set at twelve months to the year. A representation of time in months is required in this model because rainfall, and thus, ultimately, subsistence regime and movement frequency of the simulated population vary substantially on a monthly basis. The month counter insures that a new rainfall regime is initiated at the proper time. The innermost loop is that of days, and this is fixed at a constant 30-day month. Days are incremented one by one until a new month is reached. A new month begins and the daily cycle is repeated. Most of the activities built into ABSIM, such as movement, stone tool loss, breakage and replacement, and hunting, occur within the day. Thus in ABSIM, time is represented by discrete intervals, in this case the simulated day.

The three-loop system of years, months, and days was chosen over such competing systems of time bookkeeping as year/month/week/day, year/month/week, or even year/day, for a number of reasons. The most important is parsimony; the current structure of the model is both realistic and simple given the state of knowledge of both the Australian environment and the activity sequences of the Aboriginal groups used to estimate the variables and parameters of the model. A weekly representation of population movement and tool replacement is unrealistic because Aboriginal groups often move camp and replace certain tools daily. Condensation of seven days into a week would certainly impose improper constraints on these activities. Similarly, a finer structure to the model, such as hourly increments of time within the day, is also unrealistic. In this case, not enough information exists on Aboriginal activity structure to create a realistic sequence of events based on such small increments of time. Even if such information became available, it is likely that the addition of an hour loop would not be a benefit to the model, for it would increase run time without substantially enhancing the realism of the model. As I will describe below, an activity sequence has been developed that is both realistic and simple, given what we know about how Aborigines live.

What Flows Through ABSIM?

In various applications of simulation, many types of entities can be said to "flow" through the structure of the model. Energy, automobiles, money, people, innovations, information, and blood are just a few of these elements selected from many disciplines. These elements are important because a change in their value (however defined) through time provides an indication of the changing states of the entire system. Although these elements are not necessarily the primary focus of the

89

model, they are the entities which are transformed, combined, and manipulated by the dynamic operation of the system.

Stone and wooden tools flow through ABSIM. Each tool has both an owner and a "birthday," the day it was created. Tools are lost, used, and broken according to simple rules built into the simulation. In some cases, exhausted or broken tools are left at a site, and others are created to take their place. Sometimes tools are lost between sites, and they are replaced at the next opportunity. In ABSIM, tools are not transformed but combined at sites to produce inventories of varying frequencies of types. This inventory of tools at a site is a function of a complex series of actions defined in part by the fixed structure of the model, such as the arbitrary sequence of the activity structure, and in part by the operation of the probabilistic elements within the model such as rainfall frequency and amount at any site within the system, probabilities of tool loss or breakage, and the proximity of a tool owner to the resources required for tool replacement.

The tool owners, band members, or people of ABSIM exist only as repositories for the tools currently in use in the system. Tool owners are more of a bookkeeping device than a crucial element of the system. I could have omitted them entirely as did Moore (1978) in his simulation of projectile point disposal. I retained them, however, because I felt that identifying tools by individuals provided an aspect of versimilitude to the model with little additional programming effort or cost. For most of my experiments, I set the total number of tool owners at five. This figure represents, in anthropological terms, five adult male tool users. This figure is probably close to the average number of males in most hunter-gatherer bands except in times of aggregation (J. Martin 1973). Tool owners do not die, and they are not replaced regardless of the length of the simulation run. There is no random or probabilistic element that varies the number of tool owners present at any site at any instant of time. Tool owners are in a sense automata, losing, breaking, and making tools until the end of time (simulated time, that is).

Objections can be immediately raised over the choice of tools rather than people as the crucial elements flowing through the system. People (and their tools) move in and out of bands constantly, and the number of individuals at any location *must* vary considerably. Therefore, to people these simulated bands with constant numbers of undying automata is certainly not reasonable. Or is it? Given both the purpose of the model and the nature of simulation model building, I believe that my choice is reasonable. As observed repeatedly, simulation models are often complex despite all attempts at simplification, and they contain a multiplicity of variables which can act in counter-intuitive ways. To mimic adequately the movement of individuals between bands, a whole new series of internal monitors would have to be added to ABSIM. Since solid empirical data on interband movement is not readily available, movement would have to be treated as a stochastic process. To represent realistically the replacement of tool owners at death might require the addition of a microsimulation of birth and death processes such as that recently developed by Howell and Lehotay (1978).

Despite the elegance of these additions, they would not substantially improve the present operation of ABSIM for the purpose for which it was created. The addition of the stochastic element for movement between bands by individuals creates a new variable, individual movement frequency. Because it is stochastic, a large number of simulated runs would be required to factor out its contribution to assemblage variability *before* any other type of experimentation could take place. A much better strategy is to hold this frequency constant (in ABSIM at zero), and then, once a reasonable baseline of variability has been established by the interaction of the other systemic variables, to begin to vary the number of people. This type of movement, despite its potential importance to the study of assemblage variability, is likely to contribute noise to assemblage variability.[5]

The addition of program elements to "kill off" tool owners would add more complexity to an already complex model. Run and compile time would be substantially increased, but the movement of tools through the system, the reason why ABSIM was created, would not be much improved. Given the intent of the model, the handling of the tool owners in ABSIM is both reasonable and sufficient so that a baseline estimation of the basic causes of assemblage variability can be made.

Where Does ABSIM Work?

To effectively model assemblage variability, some sort of settlement system is required. The sites in this system are the locations at which activities take place and tools are discarded or broken. The sites become part of the archaeological record after the required amount of simulated time has elapsed.

ABSIM can accept any type of settlement system as long as it is compatible with the structure and operation of the program. One set of experiments planned for the future will feature a settlement system based on the famous "infinite plain" familiar to students of geography. Sites will be uniformly spaced on a hexagonal grid, and movement costs will be proportional to distance. The purpose behind the use of this type of system will be to minimize the effect that variable distances between sites have on the probability that a site will be occupied. This experimental program will factor out the effect of distance as one of the determinants of assemblage composition, thus providing a measure of its relative strength.

ABSIM is currently based on a Western Desert of Australia settlement system. This system (Figure 4.4) is hypothetical, but it is closely tied to examples of similar systems reconstructed by Berndt (1959, 1970) and Gould (n.d.). It consists of two routes which connect the Warburton Mission, located in the Brown and Warburton mountains of Western Australia, with the Giles Weather Station, located at the eastern end of the Rawlinson Ranges (see Gould 1969:257 or Aldenderfer 1977:69 for a detailed area map). Most of the sites in the system are still used by Aboriginal populations when moving between Warburton and Giles and beyond.

Although the system does not recreate a set of sites used by viable bands of Aboriginal peoples, it is nevertheless a reasonable approximation of a complete settlement system. Many of the sites in the system are associated with hunting blinds where game can be trapped. The presence of a blind is based on Gould's observations. Beyond blinds, no other special-purpose sites (task sites) are built into the system. The reason for their exclusion is simple; there is insufficient knowledge at present to build in reliable estimates of the number of these sites. Length of occupation or duration of activity performance at them is also unknown. As information on these problem areas is made available or is estimated, specialized activity sites will be added to the system. Plans are under way to add wood-procurement sites, initial tool-knapping locations, kill sites other than blinds, meat-processing stations, and other miscellaneous activity sites to the model. At present the basic composition of ABSIM is a set of habitation sites with attendant hunting blinds.

92

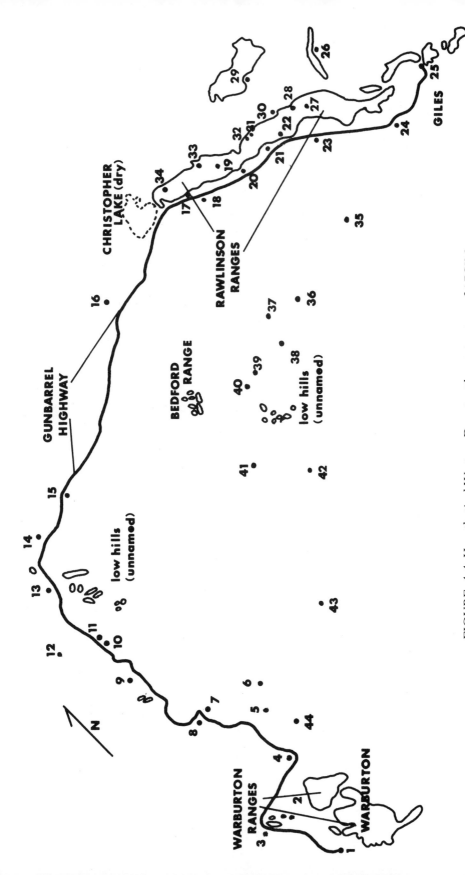

FIGURE 4.4 Hypothetical Western Desert settlement system of ABSIM.

Rainfall, Subsistence, and Movement in ABSIM

Getting tool owners from site to site is an important feature of ABSIM. Both rainfall and subsistence are subsumed under the resource-use schedule component as defined in the general assemblage formation model, and movement is determined by critical changes of state in these two components and in the variables which define them. Although the general model indicates that social forces have an effect on movement, and thus ultimately on assemblage composition, I have not built these forces into the simulation model.

ABSIM currently is based on a Western Desert of Australia ecosystem in which, as in most deserts, rainfall is the driving variable. Rainfall in this area of Australia is highly variable, both temporally and spatially. There is some predictable monthly variation in the occurrence and amount of rainfall, with rain more likely to occur in the early winter and summer months, but this trend is obscured in the short run. Long periods of drought are common, and these appear to be stochastic in frequency (Beard 1968). Rainfall occurs in rainfall events (Beard 1968; Noy-Meir 1973) in which sequences of rainy days are interspersed with periods of completely dry weather. These events tend to "persist," meaning that some rain continues to fall over a period of up to five days. The amount of rain that falls during these events has only a weak positive relationship with the duration of the event.

If rainfall is variable, what is the best method for its implementation into the simulation model? Three alternatives are possible: (a) a detailed microsimulation for storm-cell genesis and movement, (b) the actual sequence of rainfall events as they occur in the desert, and (c) the construction of a model that faithfully replicates the frequency of occurrence and duration of rainfall events. The most realistic of these alternatives is the creation of storm cells which are moved across the desert to drop rain. Unfortunately, there is no reliable information on the processes of storm-cell generation in the Western Desert (Ross 1969). Any attempt to create storm cells by analogy with other arid regions would be difficult, because the wind currents and air masses which cross the Australian continent have no close analogues (Gibbs 1969). In any case, I am not competent to construct such a complex model, which would necessarily include a number of climatological and meteorological variables.

The simplest alternative for the representation of rainfall is to use the empirical sequence of rainfall events which actually occurred at

Warburton and Giles over the past 25 years. This alternative is sensible when the data are of good quality or the expense or difficulty of building a model of the process is prohibitive (Mihram 1972a). Although the data are of good quality, there are not enough; the sequence at Giles lasted only 11 years. This is too short a time period to be useful for inclusion in the simulation model. Also, these data could introduce an unrealistic periodicity and regularity into rainfall frequency that would undoubtedly affect movement frequency and direction. These data would introduce a period of 11 years into rainfall, which is not supported by time series analysis of rainfall events (Maher 1967).

The third alternative, a model of Western Desert rainfall, has been developed out of necessity. A number of different modelling approaches are possible. The simplest of them is a random sequence of wet and dry periods. Limits on the length of each period could be established, but the occurrence of a dry sequence would in no way affect the probability of occurrence of another dry event immediately afterward. These events are independent under the random model. Despite the appeal of this approach, it has been demonstrated repeatedly that rainfall in the Western Desert, although highly variable, is not random. A better model which reduces the variance in the prediction of rainfall frequency is a first-order Markov chain (Fitzpatrick and Krishnan 1967). Runs of wet or dry pentads (five-day sequences) fit known rainfall event sequences for nearby Central Australia reasonably well. The model is flawed, however, because it assumes a wet pentad to have at least 0.1 inch (2.54 millimeters) of rain. For most desert plants, this threshold value is too low to stimulate growth (Beard 1968; Mott 1972), and thus pentads based on this value are not valid from an ecological perspective.

The rainfall model used in ABSIM combines empirical rainfall data (Beard, personal communication) with a Markov chain approach. It is similar to a model proposed by Goodall (1969) for a semiarid region west of Warburton and Giles. For each month, an empirical frequency distribution of rainfall events can be constructed. A random number generator is used to select a number of rainfall events to occur within that month according to these empirical values. The Markov chain model is used to insure that no sequence of rainfall events will overlap or follow one another too closely. The Markov model is also based on empirical information regarding the duration of rainfall events and the expected length of time between events of the month.

The spatial distribution of rainfall presents another problem because again there are no data which describe how and where rain falls in the Western Desert. Given the paucity of information, ABSIM assumes that the theoretical rainfall probabilities are identical for each site in the settlement system, and that the probability of occurrence of rainfall events between even close sites (approximately one kilometer apart) is independent. What data exist tend to support these assumptions (Ross 1969).

Two types of rainfall events have been built into ABSIM: effective and noneffective. Effective events are those which drop enough rain to stimulate plant growth. Beard (1968) has shown that at least 0.25 inch (6.35 millimeters) of rain is necessary to initiate growth of both perennials and annuals in the Gibson Desert, immediately northwest of Warburton Mission. Because the thermal efficiency of this desert is high, this value does not vary on a monthly basis. Noneffective events, by definition dropping less than 0.25 inch per event, are still monitored by ABSIM because even rains of minimal intensity help to fill natural water cachements such as soaks and rockholes. Since water availability is a prime factor in the decision to move from one site to another, ABSIM must create all important rain types at all locations in the settlement system.

The modelling of Aboriginal subsistence behavior has proved to be one of the major stumbling blocks in the development of ABSIM. Unlike BASIN I (Thomas 1972), ABSIM does not have a set of food procurement systems built into its structure. Although a number of ethnographic and ethnoarchaeological studies (Gould 1967, 1969; Tindale 1972), supported by ethnobotanical research (Cleland and Johnson 1933, 1938; Cleland and Tindale 1954, 1959; Johnson and Cleland 1943), have provided a general model of Aboriginal subsistence in this portion of the Western Desert, there is not enough detailed ecological information available on the distribution, variety, and variability of the indigenous flora and fauna used as food resources to build even the most rudimentary ecosystem model. Australian ecologists and biologists have concentrated their efforts toward an understanding of the potential of desert soils for the grazing of sheep and other ruminants. Consequently, their studies have focused on the introduction of non-native species into the desert ecosystem and on other facets of land management and modification. Those studies which have investigated the dynamics of adaptation of indigenous species have almost wholly ignored flora used as food resources by the Aborigines (Chippendale 1968; Fitzpatrick, Slayter, and Krishnan 1967; Mott 1972; Winkworth 1967).[6] The ethnobotanical studies are only descriptive at best and provide almost no clues as to seasonal abundance or variability in availability.

Because detailed data are unavailable, a more general model of re-source availability has been developed. In the original version of ABSIM, each site in the settlement system is assumed to have the same basic set of staples, and depending on rainfall at the site during the year, some staple food resource will always be available. The availability of a food resource depends on the recency of an effective rainfall event. Two weeks (14 simulated days) after an effective rainfall occurs, a food resource at that site is available for use. The amount of the staple available is assumed to be enough to feed the band of tool owners for 14 days.[7] This is the maximum occupation span at any site in the settlement system. A food resource may "rot" or "dry out," meaning that the band did not exploit that resource which became available after the last effective rainfall at that site. Untouched by the band, a resource is diminished one day at a time in its capacity to "feed" the band. For instance, if a band arrives at a site 17 days after an effective rain, the band may remain at the site for only one day.

Australian fauna, such as kangaroo, emu, euro, and wallaby, are not directly represented in ABSIM. Although hunting is an important activity for males, the band as a whole obtains the majority of its subsistence needs from flora, grubs, and small game collected by the women. Consequently, faunal availability is not a major component in the decision to remain at a site or move to a new one. Since males will hunt at almost any site, no special treatment of faunal availability is required. In any case, success in hunting is not important to ABSIM as a model; instead, the *act* of hunting (and its associated activities) is the more important consideration.

This model of resource availability is obviously unrealistic, but it is the best alternative given the paucity of data on the indigenous flora and fauna of the Western Desert. Although the model violates some of the common assumptions of arid ecosystems, such as patchiness in availability of certain resources, the *general* treatment of resource avail-ability is reasonably well supported by what we know of Australian desert ecosystems. In the expanded version of ABSIM (still under development), it is possible to create a more varied environment with

97

seasonal fluctuations in both rainfall and resource availability. It also allows the user to select certain sites as the only locations of certain resources. These additions make ABSIM much more realistic. However, for the purposes for which ABSIM was created, the basic model of resource availability is adequate for the initial exploration and quantification of the processes of assemblage formation.

Movement in the desert by Aboriginal peoples is strongly influenced by three interrelated information sources: (a) the direction in which rain is seen to be falling; (b) the direction of known staple food resources in the direction of the rains at that time of year; and (c) the trend of known "lines" of waterholes as they correlate with the above two points (Gould 1969:267–68). These factors mean that aboriginal peoples, whenever possible, "follow" the rains. However, Gould (1969) notes that although rains can be seen up to 50 miles away, the maximum distance a band will travel in a single day is 25 miles (40 kilometers), such trips being made only in extreme conditions.

A factor that directly determines movement is the availability of water. Some catchments are larger and more reliable than others. The more a catchment holds, the longer a band can remain at the site (all other factors remaining equal). Evaporation is a serious problem with these catchments, and even protected and shaded water sources quickly diminish unless they are very large. Because the Aboriginal peoples have no water storage technology, they depend completely on the availability of water in these catchments. Consequently, the band will move if it perceives that too little water is available.

These many decisions which affect movement have been implemented in ABSIM in the following fashion, in order of consideration in the program:

(1) The probability of a rainfall event is assessed for the current site. If it does rain (either effectively or noneffectively) at the current site, *and* if the food resource level (THRESB) has not been exceeded, the decision is to stay at the current site.

(2) If no rain occurs, *but* the water level threshold has not been exceeded (THRESA) *and* THRESB has not been exceeded, stay.

(3) At this point, ABSIM evaluates rainfall probabilities at all other sites in the settlement system.

(4) If the band must move (THRESA or THRESB limits have been reached), find all sites within a 25-mile (40-kilometer) radius

and determine the recency of an effective rainfall event at each of them. Also determine the value of food resources by reference to the recency of an effective rainfall event at each of them. Also determine the value of food resources by reference to the recency of the effective rainfall *and* date of last occupation. Rank the sites by these criteria.

(5) Go to the highest ranking site within the 25-mile (40-kilometer) radius.

(6) In the case of ties (that is, two or more sites within 25 miles [40 kilometers] with identical THRESA and THRESB values), go to the one closest to the current site.

(7) If no site within this radius satisfies these criteria, determine which sites within the radius have had recent noneffective rainfall events. Determine the recency of occurrence of rainfall (within the last 14 days), and the *closest* site of those which have had noneffective rains.

(8) If no site is suitable for occupation by any of the above criteria, go to the closest site regardless of food or water availability.

This movement algorithm works surprisingly well under the conditions used for the validation of ABSIM. The number of "default" moves—step 8 above—never, in all experimental runs, has exceeded ten, and in most years the value was five or below. Note that the model assumes that the band members have almost perfect knowledge of rainfall conditions in the desert. For most arid-land hunters and gatherers, this assumption is generally true. Although it is well known that bands will occasionally make mistakes, and thus die, the requirement of good decision making in hostile environments is supplemented by good information networks between bands and the individuals within them. Knowledge of the environment is constantly passed around as individuals move back and forth between bands and their segments. Although ABSIM does not directly implement this information system, the movement algorithm seems unintentionally to include its effects.

The evaporation of water from the catchments always takes place before it rains and before a decision is made to move. This method of implementation represents the early morning evaluation of the necessity of movement. The rate of evaporation from a catchment varies monthly, and these rates have been estimated from Australian meteorological publications (Aldenderfer 1977:267–69).

Variable and Parameter Estimation in ABSIM

Variables and parameters in simulation models are essentially descriptive quantities that measure the current or changing values of the different aspects of the components of the system. With any model, every effort must be made to obtain reasonable estimates of the expected values of these entities. This is especially important in simulation modelling because variables and parameters (with their expected values and ranges) are used in the validation phase of the modelling process to estimate the accuracy of the output data generated by the simulation.

In ABSIM, the initial values of the variables of the tool kits and activity structure of the simulated band have been estimated from ethnoarchaeological descriptions of the Ngatatjara, Pitjandjara, Nyatunyatjara, and Ngatjara Aborigines of the Western Desert of Australia. Most of the information on these peoples is found in Richard A. Gould's field notes of two expeditions to this area in 1966–67 and 1970 and in a series of publications based on these studies (Gould 1967, 1968, 1969, 1970, 1971, 1978). He was fortunate enough to study a group of relatively unacculturated desert peoples who still practiced their traditional subsistence/settlement regime and who still used stone tools in their daily activities. Although metal has gradually replaced stone, most of the men studied by Gould knew how to make and use a full assemblage of stone tools. Gould's field data on the artifact assemblages of these peoples have been supplemented by a number of other studies of Australian material culture, most notably Akerman (1974), Boness (1971), Bronstein (1977), I. Hill (1976), Love (1944), Mountford (1941), Thomson (1964, 1974), and Tindale (1965). These studies have proved invaluable for the verification of Gould's original estimates, and they have often provided new insights into Aboriginal tool usage, breakage, and disposal.

The environmental and subsistence-related variables have also been derived from Western Desert sources. The local information on the subsistence potential of each site has been gleaned from Gould's notes, and more general information on ecology, rainfall, and weather from a wealth of other publications. Table 4.4 presents information on the source of data used to estimate environmental variables and the general reliability and usability of that data.

100

TABLE 4.4
SOURCES AND RELIABILITY FOR ESTIMATES OF
ENVIRONMENTAL VARIABLES

Rainfall frequency and amount	Arnold (1963) Beard (1968, 1969) Fitzpatrick and Krishnan (1967) Gentilli (1971) Gibbs (1969) Maher (1967) Noy-Meir (1973, 1974) Slayter (1962)	High
Local rainfall distribution	Chapman (1970) Duckstein, Fogel, and Kissel (1972) Fogel and Duckstein (1969) Shanan, Evenari, and Tadmor (1967) Sharon (1970, 1972)	High
Local water sources, including capacity and reliability	Basedow (1904) Farbridge (1968) Gould (n.d.) Maclaren (1912) Talbot (1910, 1912) Talbot and Clarke (1917) Twidale and Corbin (1963)	Fair
Subsistence, including distribution and abundance of flora and fauna	Beard (1969) Cleland and Tindale (1959) Gould (1967, 1969, n.d.) Mott (1972) Ross (1969) Thomson (1974) Tindale (1972)	Poor

In most anthropological and archaeological simulations, behavioral data for variable and parameter estimation are obtained primarily from ethnographic, ethnoarchaeological, experimental, and historical sources. In many cases, ethnography is the only available source on processes of interest. Despite their superficial plausibility, ethnographic and even most ethnoarchaeological sources must be used with caution. This is so because most of these sources are *normative* in nature. They tend to describe the "typical" situation and, in so doing, often fail to include the range of variability in an activity or process. Information on variability is of great importance to simulation models, for it is well known that extreme conditions can have a significant effect on the operation of an activity or task. The variability in the value of a variable may help the simulation model express some of the counter-intuitive results that these models are famous for producing.

Some variable estimates were relatively easy to develop. The most comprehensive data Gould recovered were on the composition of the tool kits of his Aboriginal informants. He could easily count the number of tools in use at any time, and compare these empirical counts to estimates of assemblage size elicited from his informants. Since few special-purpose tools are used by these Aborigines, and because, to the best of his knowledge, no tools were used seasonally at specific locations, he could be reasonably sure that his estimates of the range of variability in numbers and types of tools in the Aboriginal assemblage were valid. Because these data are strongly confirmed, they have been used with confidence in ABSIM. Compared with data from other sources, notably Balfour (1951), these data are as comprehensive as possible.

Other variables, such as use-life, proved more difficult to estimate. All stone tools with long use-lives, such as adzes, have use-lives derived from experimentation. Using native wood and stone, Bronstein (1977) determined the use-life of the adze as the number of strokes of use before exhaustion. Gould was unable to obtain evidence of use-life because the length of his stay at a site was often short. Although this allowed him to estimate the number of strokes used from an adze during an episode of activity performance, it did not help him determine the *total* number of strokes possessed by any given adze. Attempts at questioning informants on this method of reckoning use-life were unsuccessful. Experimentation was the only available route to the required information.

Wooden tools in ABSIM have use-lives based on the statistical theory of reliability. Reliability is concerned with the "time to failure" of any object. Statisticians have developed a number of different statistical models which describe the times to failure of various classes of objects. These statistical models take the form of different probability density functions (pdfs), which can be used to determine the probability of failure of any object at any instant of time (Tsokos 1972:183–92). The first archaeological application of statistical reliability was by Hatch (1976), who constructed a reliability function of the use-life of Fulani pottery, using David's empirical information (David 1972; David and Henning 1972). Using David's census information on the ages of pots, a histogram was constructed. Curves were fit to the shape of the

102

histogram through standard statistical tests (Box 1960; Daniel and Wood 1971). Hatch discovered that the exponential distribution, a common reliability function, fit the Fulani data.

A similar procedure was employed for the estimation of the use-lives of wooden tools. Unfortunately, the data on these tools were not as extensive as the Fulani data, and no empirical histograms of tool age could be constructed. Thus, no estimate of the correct pdf for each tool type could be made. Gould did, however, collect information on the expected length of life and frequency of replacement of these objects. Gould noted that the correspondence between the expected length of life and the actual use-life of the object was quite high. But this is not satisfactory for my purposes. Given only three points on a curve, birth, some midlife determination of age, and death (breakage), innumerable curves (or pdfs) could be constructed. What to do?

The only recourse was to the general literature on the reliability of systems and components. A considerable number of reliability functions and their associated pdfs have been studied, including the normal, Weibull, exponential, gamma, and many others (Tsokos 1972: 183–92; Weibull 1951). The behavior of these functions is well understood, and some distributions have been demonstrated to be more useful than others under certain circumstances. The exponential distribution is useful when the failure rate of the system is constant through time.[8] The Weibull distribution is useful when it is assumed that the failure rate may vary through the life span of the system. No reliability function has a simple, linear pdf.

Wooden tools probably do not have constant failure rates. Wooden bowls are very sturdy until relatively late in their use-lives, when they become extremely dry. They tend to crack easily and are then discarded. Spearthrowers, although similar to bowls in shape, are subjected to greater stresses, and break more rapidly. Spears are usually replaced very rapidly because they become brittle and thus splinter and shatter more easily. The failure rate, then, at some point begins to increase. The concomitant value of the reliability function decreases, thus making it more probable that the tool will be broken or discarded.

A distribution which is skewed to the right with a variable failure rate is required. One likely candidate is the gamma distribution (Tsokos 1972:161–63, 187–88).[9] Figure 4.5 shows the graphed reliability function for selected values. This curve has intuitive appeal, because it seems to "fit" the reality of bowl, spearthrower, and spear breakage

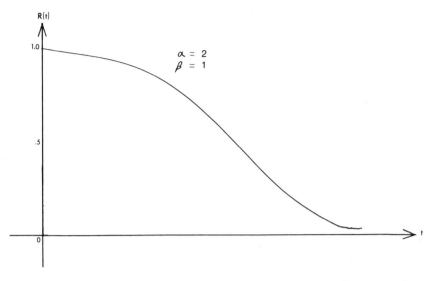

R(t)

1.0

α = 2
β = 1

.5

0

t

FIGURE 4.5 Graph of the reliability function of the gamma distribution for selected values.

very nicely. As implemented in the model, it performs *exactly* as required, with no fudging. Moreover, the values predicted by Gould for midlife age and final breakage for these objects were replicated almost exactly by substitution into the formula which defines the gamma distribution.

Is this procedure valid? In some ways, it probably is not. These data are scanty and thus weak. But no other data are available, and these values seem to be adequate. Could other distributions with other failure rates do a better job of representing the breakage of wooden tools? This possibility was tested using the exponential, Weibull, and normal distributions. None of these distributions were as accurate as the gamma for predicting the expected value of the reliability function for any of the tool types.

Activity Sequence Within ABSIM

Human activity performance is a complex, multilineal aggregate, often difficult to parcel into discrete units of behavior. This creates a problem for the archaeologist working with simulation models, for this unwieldy aggregate must be placed into the strictly linear sequence of commands demanded by the computer. Any attempt to structure activity performance on a probabilistic or random basis would lead to serious programming problems which would increase the complexity of the simulation model considerably. Although such a sequencing of activity would be more realistic, it would also require too much effort for implementation. To implement activity structure effectively, a balance must be struck between realism and efficiency. This balance is delicate, and its attainment requires that skillful use be made of existing data so as to insure that no decision point or activity alternative of importance has been omitted.

One useful way to analyze activity structure so as to place it into a linear framework is to adopt a method similar to the concept of behavior chain analysis as developed by Schiffer (1975a). Modified "decision trees" of all possible sequences of activity performance can be built. These trees are similar to flow charts but do not incorporate any of the symbols used in flow charting computer programs. Of course, not all discrete sequences of activity performance can be built, especially in cases where the number of activities is large. In most cases, there is an obvious hierarchy of importance of the different aspects of activity so that a preliminary ordering can be made. The creation of these trees becomes an analysis of logical alternatives, and running through a few cycles of competing trees usually indicates which tree is probably the most reasonable representation of activity structure. However, a final determination of its adequacy cannot be made until the entire simulation model has been validated.

Two basic activity types are implemented in ABSIM: the use of stone tools and the replacement of stone tools. All other activities built into the model are subsumed under these two types. The goal of activity performance, of course, is to produce materials which will become a part of the archaeological record. Since stone tool assemblages are the focus of the model, no other residues of activity performance, such as bone, wood, and vegetable remains, or features, such as hearths, post molds, or middens, are created by ABSIM. Only those activities which use stone tools are represented. Important tasks such as vegetable food procurement, resin procurement, and some types of hunting, because they do not use stone, are not built into the model. Table 4.5 summarizes the activities of ABSIM. Sources of data for activity performance are Gould (1967, 1969, n.d.).

The following sequence of steps is a verbal description of the activity structure of ABSIM. At each step, all the possible options for action are specified. Figure 4.6 is a decision tree of this process. Note that this description (and the tree) must be repeated for each tool owner in the

105

TABLE 4.5
ACTIVITIES BUILT INTO ABSIM

Wood carving	Includes all replacement and maintenance of all wooden tools, from digging sticks to bowls.
Spear sharpening	The process of keeping spears well sharpened and in balance, either at hunting blinds or habitation sites.
Wood procurement	Involves the removal and rough shaping of blanks for wooden bowls and spear-throwers, the act of locating suitable wooden shafts for clubs, spears, fighting sticks, and digging sticks.
Stone procurement at site	Nonquarried stone picked up from immediate vicinity of activity. Minor retouch possible, but not likely.
Stone flaking	Involves the reduction of specially prepared adze flakes into finished tools. Also spokeshaves and flakescrapers produced from suitable flakes.

band. After all tool owners have been processed and the appropriate activities performed, the simulation starts a new day.

(1) The necessity for movement to a new site is first assessed. If movement occurs, no activities of any kind are performed.

(2) If the band remains at the site, then

    (a) The probability of breakage of every wooden tool in the personal assemblage of the tool owner is evaluated. Spears are checked first, followed by spearthrowers, bowls, clubs, and throwing sticks.

    (b) If spears or spearthrowers have been broken, or if too few spears are available for hunting, these items are replaced first, *if* wood is available. If it is not, and no tool owner can hunt because he cannot replace his spears or spearthrowers, the program steps out of activity performance and starts a new day.

    (c) If spears and spearthrowers have been replaced, and if hunting is possible, the replacement of other tools is postponed for that day for that person. The hunter proceeds to the hunting blind and sharpens his spears there.

    (d) If spears and spearthrowers have been replaced and if hunting is *not* possible, other tools may now be replaced. Spears may be sharpened if such an activity is scheduled. Other artifacts may also be replaced, but within limits. Only *one* labor-

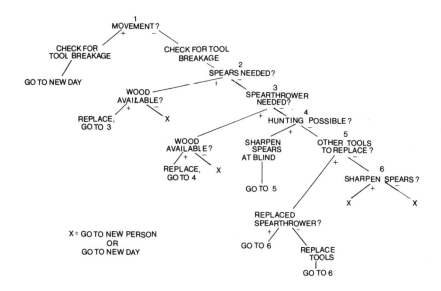

FIGURE 4.6. Modified decision tree of activity structure in ABSIM.

intensive wooden tool (spearthrowers and medium and large bowls) can be made by an individual in a single day. This is a realistic constraint, because these objects often take two to three days to finish. One amusing but painful incident with an early version of ABSIM was that one Aborigine replaced four spears, two bowls, and one club in a single day. It was a prodigious feat, but not very realistic. That such a feat occurred meant that although the general structure of activity performance was realistic, the exact method of implementation was not able to prevent unreasonable events. Thus logical checks on the daily *frequency* of different segments of the activity process were built into the model. These checks effectively make the probability of herculean efforts nil.

How does this implementation compare with what we know of aboriginal activity? It does surprisingly well because the totality of activities of these peoples is not highly complex. A discussion of the main points of the decision tree may help demonstrate this.

(1) Movement in general precludes activity. Males and females usually forage on the march and often spend most of the day in search of food. The only exception to this is when the distance travelled is short. In such cases, ABSIM must treat the day as if movement was the only activity.

107

(2) Spears and spearthrowers are replaced first since hunting cannot occur without these tools.

(3) After these tools have been replaced, the tool owners "go" to the hunting blinds near the site. In these blinds, they sharpen spears, a common activity performed while waiting for game.

(4) After hunting, the tool owners return to camp. If no labor-intensive object is to be replaced, the simulation moves to a new day. If only one of these objects must be made, replacement begins (if wood is available). Love (1944) and Gould (n.d.) note that the replacement of large wooden objects takes considerable time, often up to two days. It is often not possible for the tool owner to replace these items in a single day even if no hunting occurs. Therefore, replacement is postponed until the next day or some later date.

The actual use of stone tools occurs only when wooden objects are replaced or maintained. Figure 4.7 displays a modified decision tree for the use and replacement of stone tools in ABSIM. The use of the word "continue" as a step in activity performance means that the program must see if more wooden tools of the current owner must be replaced, or if a new owner must have his tools replaced, or if the program as a whole is finished with activity performance and must move on to another day. Other stone tools have similar decision trees which describe their mode of use. At each node in the decision tree of activity performance where a wooden tool is maintained or manufactured (Figure 4.7), the stone tool decision tree is called in to determine what type of tool is used and how much use-life should be subtracted from the tool. Combined, these trees provide a complete description of activity performance in ABSIM.

WHAT DOES ABSIM PRODUCE?

In the most general sense, ABSIM creates archaeological assemblages at the sites in a settlement system. The contents of the assemblages are whole, broken, and exhausted tools, and various types of stone waste associated with tool use and construction. These assemblages have special characteristics, and a set of assumptions about their structure has been developed. These assumptions distinguish the created assemblages from their real-world counterparts in many ways, and the as-

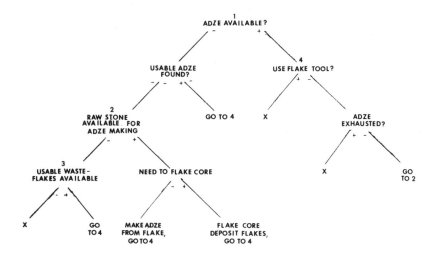

FIGURE 4.7. Decision tree for stone tool usage in ABSIM.

sumptions must be considered before the data generated by ABSIM can be put to practical or experimental use. In most cases, the assumptions act as limits on the realism of the created assemblages in that they represent conditions or situations not likely to occur in the archaeological record. These assumptions are necessary, because many of the details of assemblage formation processes are still poorly understood. Few models of these processes exist, especially for the natural forces which affect site content and the various cultural or social factors which govern trash disposal at sites. The use of these assumptions permits the modeller to avoid assuming too much knowledge, and thereby attempting to build such poorly known details into the simulation model. These assumptions represent a compromise between the demands for realism and the obvious dangers of using poorly defined models in the simulation context. Despite these limitations, the data from ABSIM have a wide range of potential applications. The assumptions are as follows:

(1) In the original, and most basic, version of ABSIM, no strata or levels of occupation are produced at any site. All materials that have been deposited are recovered by the archaeologist. This type of site is most closely related to the "blowout," common in arid and semiarid regions, in which the individual strata originally created at the site have been destroyed by aeolian forces. This process combines the contents of the strata into a single assemblage or component. To avoid the problem this mixing can

create, two strategies of data generation and manipulation have been developed. The first, and easiest, is to run ABSIM for relatively short periods of time. Most runs used in experimentation with ABSIM lasted 50 years of simulated time. This time span is often the shortest duration which can easily be recognized in the real-world archaeological record through the use of common dating methods. The second strategy permits the user to create strata of arbitrary duration.[10] This strategy in effect creates a series of distinct assemblages at each site.[11] The inventories of discarded tools and waste materials accumulated at each site during previous occupations are "hidden" (incorporated into buried strata) from the next set of tool users to occupy the site. This procedure often has an effect on the availability of raw stone used in tool replacement and other activities.

(2) No cultural forces which pattern waste at habitation (or other) sites have been built into ABSIM. Many cultures have specific trash disposal methods, and the application of these methods often leaves distinctive concentrations of artifacts in middens, spoil heaps, or other features. Although data on the location and form of refuse can be used to postulate "activity areas" or other discrete uses of space, there is no spatial information contained in the assemblages created by ABSIM.

(3) No n-transforms (Schiffer 1976) or postdepositional cultural forces affect the contents of the assemblages created by ABSIM. It is well known that certain forces affect the recovery probabilities of different materials at sites (such as the size effect), but these have not been systematically studied. Also, the sites created by ABSIM are not subjected to erosion, alluviation, cryoturbation, or any other force which would subtract artifacts from the assemblages. No collector has ever sullied the assemblage. The closest real-world approximation to this situation is a site in a recently plowed field, in which *all* the materials have been brought to the surface and scattered about, thus destroying any spatial patterns of refuse disposal.

Although these assumptions certainly stretch the limits of reality, the assemblages created by ABSIM are nevertheless useful, especially in the role of a baseline. Given complete information, it is instructive to determine just how well analytical methods do in the *best* of all possible research worlds. The results obtained in these experiments can go far to establish the limits of inference of the methods in the less-than-ideal real world of the archaeological record. For the problem as defined above, the data generated by ABSIM are sufficiently realistic and complete for use in a variety of experiments and research designs.

ABSIM creates a large number of data on a number of different processes. Of greatest interest are the data on activity performance at each site for each year of simulated time. These data have the following features:

(1) The type of activity performed is recorded. Each discrete bout of activity performance for each day of the year is monitored. A complete list of all of the activities at the site can be recovered, even if these activities did *not* result in the deposition of tools or other waste materials into the archaeological record.

(2) The type of tool(s) used in activity performance is noted.

(3) If a stone tool is used, the program records exactly how much use-life was subtracted from the tool even though the tool was not deposited into the archaeological record.

(4) The program maintains a complete inventory of all tools and waste materials deposited at the site. This list is cross-referenced to the list of activity performances by date and type so that the effects of each activity performance on the archaeological record of the site can be evaluated.

(5) In all of these lists, the person who discards or uses a tool is recorded. This is important, because not all tool users will perform an activity at a site. Keeping track of the number of participants in activity performance aids in the evaluation of the degree of variability in the frequencies of tools deposited due to the number of persons.

A second major category of data is the frequency and duration of movement of the tool users through the settlement system. The occurrences of rainfall at each site in the system for each day of the year and the total length of occupation at the site are monitored. Also, the number of reoccupations at each site within the year is recorded. These data represent the effects of the resource-use system on assemblage composition. From these data, maps of band movement can be generated which are useful for the evaluation of the reliability and reasonability of the movement features of the simulation model. Figure 4.8 displays the movement of tool users in a very poor year.

111

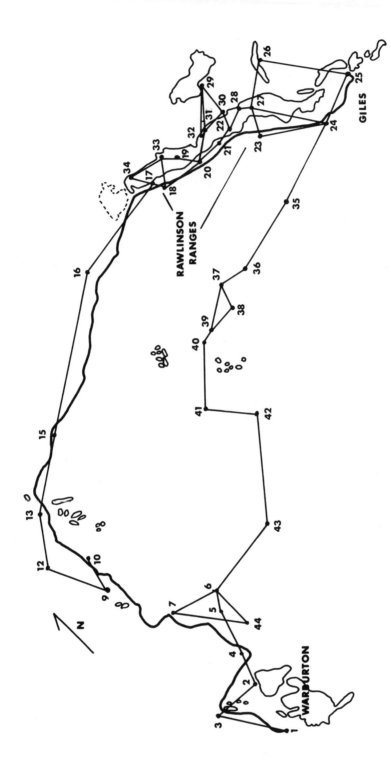

FIGURE 4.8. Diagram of movement of tool owners in a year with low rainfall.

These two major data types can be used in a number of experimental situations. For instance, a "true typology" of sites based on any set of attributes can be constructed, and the typologies created by different multivariate methods can be compared to them for goodness-of-fit. One of the important "true typologies" used for recent experimentation with ABSIM is based on the intensity of activity performance for each type of activity at each site in the settlement system. This typology combines the concept of function with the relative contribution of each type of activity to the creation of assemblages. This "functional" typology can then be combined with other data such as occupation span, reoccupation frequency within the year, and other measures to create other typologies. "Tool kits" can also be created and the ability of factor analysis to successfully reconstruct them from the relative frequency of different tool types can be assessed.

THE FUTURE OF ABSIM

I think ABSIM may be regarded as a success in that it has provided insights into how assemblages are created, and how data gathered from these assemblages can be used legitimately. It has also served to notify archaeologists that there are distinct and powerful limits on the use of certain statistical tools when applied to archaeological assemblages. Under the right conditions, most of these tools will work correctly. But under many circumstances which are likely to be common when dealing with archaeological resources, the techniques will not be of great help. ABSIM has helped to identify some of these circumstances, but much more work is needed in order to make full use of this new information. The experiments and the results are described in Aldenderfer (1977).

There are a number of legitimate extensions of ABSIM which can be pursued. ABSIM should be generalized and expanded so that different environmental and tool-use systems can be more easily accommodated. This expansion is well within the original scope of the project because it simply makes ABSIM a better program.

More research should be directed toward the construction of a quantitative model of assemblage formation processes beyond the simulation context. Such a model would be among the first of its kind, and could possibly serve as an example of quantitative model building in archaeology. I envision this model to be similar to the Binford and Bertram (1977) model of the attritional processes which affect the frequency of occurrence of certain types of bone in the archaeological record. It will be difficult to develop this model because it will have to be simple in order that it can be described in mathematical language. Archaeologists, however, will probably not be comfortable with the need for simplicity, for as the general assemblage formation model indicates, many variables affect the composition of assemblages. One possible form of the model, and one which I am presently working toward, is based on the familiar Leslie matrix model used in demography and ecology. Usher (1972) presents some of the recent advances in the use of this type of model.

Further studies should also be made to determine the relative contribution of different variables to assemblage composition. Such studies can take the form of a path model of the process of assemblage formation (Li 1975). These models are also known as causal models (Blalock 1971). The block diagrams of Figures 4.1 and 4.2 are similar in structure to a path model. Arrows depict causal linkages between variables and components, and the strength of relationship between them is derived by correlation analysis and multiple regression. These estimates of relative contribution could have a practical use when investigating any archaeological assemblage.

One extremely important addition to ABSIM will be subroutines which represent cultural and postdepositional disturbance factors. ABSIM at present assumes that all of the material deposited at a site will be recovered. This is unrealistic, of course, but it is a practical solution to the problem of deciding exactly what should be found in the absence of useful information. Most of the existing literature on these processes is descriptive at best (but see Wood and Johnson 1978). As more work is done to develop models of these processes, it can be added to ABSIM to portray more realistically the recovery of archaeological data.

Studies with ABSIM have indicated that "noise" seriously disrupts our ability to reconstruct many aspects of prehistoric behavior. Noise obstructs pattern, thus making explanations of assemblage variability or other processes difficult to generate. ABSIM is an excellent device for generating data to study the effects of noise on archaeological assemblages, because the data are completely understood and ascertained. Theoretical studies of noise may have excellent practical benefits because they may identify common causes of noise. In addition, such studies may possibly suggest robust methodologies for the analysis of archaeological data that minimize its effect.

There is always the temptation in a simulation exercise to look ahead to the widest possible set of applications. This desire for expansion often leads to extensive modification of the simulation model in hopes that the new structure will be capable of dealing with new problems. Despite the allure of new discoveries, this temptation must be strongly resisted. This type of extension often takes on the air of "playing games" with the simulation. Research often proceeds without first establishing explicit and solid hypotheses and goals. Without these goals, it is often difficult to evaluate the success of a simulation exercise, and it is even difficult to stop pushing the model into still more distant applications. The modelling exercise at that point operates under a "more is better" instead of a "more is less" philosophy. Too much of anything is unhealthy, but too much simulation can be disastrous. Simulation should be the methodology of last resort as Crosbie (1977) suggests, and it should in no case be extended beyond the original purpose of the model.

Nevertheless, the use of simulation models and their results in inappropriate contexts is becoming increasingly common. This usually involves the use of the model to act as a guide to practical, real-world problems. Although a model may be relevant to a specific real-world situation, it is seldom accurate or complete enough for use in a management context. Most simulation models, especially in the "soft" sciences, are not much more than a set of hypotheses transformed into a computer program. The results of the model may be useful, but they are *not* definitive answers or solutions to any problem. Managers of real-world projects demand solid data so that their decisions have a high probability of being correct. To use a simulation model in this context is unfair to both the model and the manager. The model (and by inference, its developer) gets a bad reputation, and the manager (and the project) are poorly served. This problem is becoming prevalent in ecosystem management situations (Innis, Schlesinger, and Sylvester 1977; Innis 1978), and, given recent trends in cultural resources management, it may begin to appear in archaeology. Already the first skirmishes of the methodological battle have occurred in the recent spate of articles which compare different areal sampling strategies (Mueller 1974; Matson and Lipe 1975; S. Plog 1976; S. Plog, F. Plog, and Wait 1978). Simulation has been pressed into service to generate distributions of archaeological sites according to different locational and statistical models in order to test the differences between sampling strategies more completely and efficiently (Matson 1975; Davidson, Richter, and Rogers 1976; Voorrips, Gifford, and Ammerman 1978; Ammerman, Gifford, and Voorrips 1979). Simulation will be used more extensively as this type of evaluation becomes more sophisticated.

Simulation is also a likely candidate for integration into "predictive modelling" research designs, which are also becoming fashionable. I have been asked repeatedly if ABSIM could be used in a management context, and although I have been tempted, the answer I have given is no. ABSIM, despite its potential, is nothing more than an experiment. It has not been designed to reproduce any existing (or prehistoric) settlement system, and it would not provide useful data for management decisions. Although the *results* may be applicable to archaeological problems, the model itself is not. Simulation may become important in management applications in archaeology, but this will not occur until the basic processes which structure the archaeological record are better understood.

NOTES

1. Note that I am not claiming the existence of Platonic ideal types. In this context, the inherent typology is based on the set of attributes used to describe the entities to be classified and the interpretative concepts used to judge the success of a proposed classification. These attributes define a multidimensional space in which the entities arise, and these swarms of entities may have a distinct structure. In one sense, a true typology is created by the method which least distorts the positions of these entities in this space.

2. The identification of these distribution forms is likely to be difficult. Progress in the analysis of nonnormal multivariate distribution forms has been slow (Andrews, Gnanadesikan and Warner 1973), and most models are based on multivariate normal mixtures which are not likely to be common in many fields.

3. Although the San are probably better known than many Australian groups, especially from an ethnoarchaeological perspective, they no longer use stone tools. The hunter-gatherers of the Philippines, such as the Tasaday, have few chipped-stone tools. Some agriculturalists, such as highland Ethiopian peasants (Gallagher 1972), still use stone, as do a number of New Guinea peoples (White and Thomas 1972). In these groups, the range of tools used and the functions to which they are applied are limited.

4. Elsewhere (Aldenderfer 1977), I have described the reasons why these models cannot be built into simulations. Binford's model suffers from a lack of detail about many of the important processes of assemblage formation, and it relies heavily on the invocation of "principles" as

116

illustrative and explanatory devices. Among these principles are "organization variability," "expedient and curate behavior," and others. Although the concepts are important, and in some cases should be used, the model is never fully developed and never completely loses a polemical force, which detracts from its usefulness. Schiffer's model has more promise, but it suffers from a series of questionable assumptions which affect the utility of the formulae developed to predict the composition of the archaeological record.

5. Noise normally refers to randomness or error in measurement of a system, but in this case, it refers to extreme *variability* in resource-use systems, tools, and activity structure. Tools characterized by high variability have relatively long use-lives, high standard deviations of use-life, and overlap in mapping relationships. Variable resource-use systems have high movement frequencies, high reoccupation rates at sites, and little redundancy of activity at sites in the settlement system. The opposite of the variable (or noisy) system is an *ordered* system. Ordered tools have relatively short use-lives, low standard deviations of use-life, and little overlap in mapping relationships. Ordered resource-use systems show low movement frequencies and redundancy of activity at the sites in the settlement systems. Such systems are low in noise. The types of systems define the extremes of variability and order. Most cultural systems will fall somewhere between them.

6. Research on the kangaroo and euro is in much better condition than is the research on the indigenous flora.

7. In the only other report available on ABSIM (Aldenderfer 1977), the maximum occupation span was set at 10 days. In further validation studies, a 14-day maximum slightly reduces the amount of variance in movement frequency, thus providing a closer fit with the data available for validation.

8. The failure rate is defined as the number of item failures per unit of time. A more mathematical definition is "the integral of the failure density taken from some time t to t+Δt divided by the integral of the failure density is the probability density function which characterizes the behavior of item failure."

9. The reliability function under the gamma distribution is

$$R(t) = 1 - \frac{1}{\Gamma(x)} \int_0^t x^{\alpha-1} e^{-x} dx.$$

10. Hatch (1976) has used this method of strata generation in his simulation of ceramic breakage.

11. Most studies of deposit development are restricted to a single site or a set of sites, and are not generalized to other regions. Those models which do exist tend to describe special cases (Rick 1976; Wildesen 1973).

5
The Wetherill Mesa Simulation: A Retrospective

LINDA S. CORDELL

University of New Mexico

INTRODUCTION

I became interested in computer simulation because the technique adds a useful dimension to the hypothesis-testing procedure in archaeology (Cordell 1972:2–5). Simulations permit the investigator to model sets of dynamically interactive relationships; therefore they provide a relatively efficient means of viewing the consequences of "what if" statements. This is not the only advantage simulation may provide, but it is the one that I was attracted to first.

On a typically dreary day in Eugene, Oregon, I had the pleasure of reading Brues's (1963) pioneering study of selection in the ABO blood group system, a system in which the mechanism of inheritance is known. In order to study genetic drift, Brues developed a computer model of 60 populations that varied in size but had the same frequency of A, B, and O alleles. Individuals within each population "mated" at random for 20 generations, and the computer kept track of the genotypes of "offspring." In the absence of selection, Brues found that

119

simulated populations diverged at a greater rate than would have been anticipated and in fact lost alleles with rather alarming frequency. In effect, the rules of a selection-free model pushed populations into genetic cul-de-sacs.

Although there has been considerable refinement in work of this kind (Cavalli-Sforza and Zei 1967; MacCluer 1973; Dyke and Mac-Cluer 1974), I found the structure of the experiment exciting. It seemed to me that archaeology could profit from the use of the same general kind of study. In both cases, the factors leading to long-term change may be highly complex and poorly understood. Nevertheless, the contrast between genetic and archaeological modelling is marked. In genetics, the basic mechanisms that create biological variation are precisely defined by the "theory of the gene" augmented by the equally precise "theory" of the molecular structure of DNA. By contrast, most statements concerning process in the archaeological literature of the late 1960s and early 1970s were based either on poorly formulated assumptions about human behavior or on vague notions about the relationship between human activities and the archaeological record. Precise modelling of arguments relating to processual change was considered largely impossible (for example, see Doran 1970; Flannery 1973). When the outcome of a particular simulation experiment in archaeology proved contrary to expectations, this result did not necessarily provide information pertinent to the evaluation of the processual model. Rather, the investigator might conclude that the cultural process had not been modelled correctly, critical variables had been ignored, or the number of runs had been insufficient to generate consistent results (see Zubrow 1973; Zimmerman 1977). Thus, it is the absence of precise theoretical statements about how a system should work that precludes gaining insight when simulations yield unanticipated results.

A very different approach uses simulation to direct research into rewarding areas by focusing on the generated data. In this case, the data have been produced by defined, though not necessarily "realistic," processes. In fact, the only "process" may be noise (random events). Thus, biological studies of macroevolution by Raup and his colleagues have used simple probability functions and a random number generator to determine the "behavior" of "clades" (artificial taxa) over time. The fossil record of real taxa shows definite patterns of growth. Some taxa diversify quickly and become extinct slowly, for example, the trilobite configuration. Other taxa ramify very slowly but

120

become extinct rapidly, such as the dinosaur pattern. Raup (1977) reports that identical patterns were generated in the simulated clades. Of additional interest is the fact that during these experiments, a number of clades became extinct simultaneously through random chance alone.

The same group of biologists, all proponents of Darwinian theory, experimented with generating morphology in a random fashion (Schopf et al., 1975). In this case, they found far more regularity in patterning than they had anticipated. Certainly among the most striking observations was that highly specialized forms appeared late in the computer simulation, mimicking the increasing specialization of biological taxa in evolutionary time. As Raup (1977:56) states, "We were able to see, from example, that a selection-free model will inevitably produce certain patterns that we have always assumed were possible only as a result of selection." The lesson is *not* that natural selection is unimportant or that biological evolution is the product of random factors. Rather, the results of the simulations indicate that biologists should devote more research time to explaining patterned variability that cannot be generated by chance.

Archaeologists would, I believe, learn a great deal if we pursued a course similar to that of our evolutionist colleagues in biology. We might well find that many of our assumptions about patterned regularity are ill-founded and that we are committing our energy to exploring the wrong patterns. For example, the report of the site survey of Wetherill Mesa, Colorado (Hayes 1964), emphasized the changes in the locations of prehistoric Puebloan habitation sites over time. Thus, there appeared to have been an important shift from mesa-top locations to talus-slope and canyon-bottom settings and finally to caves. A simulation that I prepared (Cordell 1972) assigned each of the Wetherill Mesa sites to one of the four topographic situations (mesa top, talus slope, canyon bottom, cave) on the basis of chance alone. The simulated random distributions of sites in some cases matched the documented site locations better than distributions obtained with more "realistic" models. This result does not suggest that the choice of a particular setting for the position of a residence is governed by chance. Rather, I believe, the simulation indicated that the particular topographic categories were not as important as key environmental attributes that crosscut these features.

As I have noted elsewhere (Cordell 1972, 1975), the major focus of

121

the Wetherill Mesa simulation was to test hypotheses about the location and duration of Anasazi habitation sites. The hypotheses provided rules that are conceptually similar to those involved in the simulations of genetic drift cited above. Yet, there are no anthropological laws of settlement behavior that approximate the very precise rules of Mendelian inheritance. The simulation assumed that the loci of habitation sites were determined by the location of productive arable land. In this context, it is important to note that the simulation was concerned with the time period between A.D. 700 and 1300, the Anasazi portion of the Puebloan sequence. The conditions critical for the location of residences during the earlier portions of the Southwestern archaeological sequence are likely to have been quite different (see, for example, Glassow 1972; F. Plog 1974; Reher 1975; Allan et al. 1975). For example, although I suspect that wild plant and animal foods constituted important resources throughout the Anasazi period, after about A.D. 700, these were probably obtained some distance away from village sites. The material correlates of wild-resource collecting activities would be reflected in limited-use or special-use sites that were not incorporated in the simulation.

The assumption that arable land alone determined the location of residential sites should be understood to reflect my research philosophy, which is essentially to view cultural behavior *initially* as state-determined systems (Cordell 1977a). State-determined systems are simple systems which are treated as though they were independent of time. The behavior of these systems can be predicted by specifying external stimuli alone (Ashby 1964; Nauta 1972). I do not, of course, believe that culture is simple or that an explanation of any aspect of behavior as complex as settlement placement is independent of time. Rather, I believe that productive research may be facilitated by starting with simple models, pushing them to their logical and empirical limits, and only then adding complexity. The "problem" with the Wetherill Mesa simulation was that despite its simplistic (and mechanistic) approach to human behavior, it was remarkably successful in predicting the abandonment of some sites and the continued occupation or reoccupation of others (Cordell 1975). In effect, because the simulation worked, I felt that I had learned very little. In order to clarify this admittedly overly pessimistic view, I will briefly describe the simulation and provide a reanalysis of the variables used and the results obtained. I will then discuss criteria that seem useful for evaluating archaeological research and will comment on analytical and simulation techniques with respect to these criteria.

THE SIMULATION

Wetherill Mesa is a relatively small landform within the boundaries of Mesa Verde National Park, Colorado (Figure 5.1). The simulation was based on published archaeological, environmental, and paleoenvironmental data acquired during the course of the Wetherill Mesa Project (Osborne 1965; Hayes 1964; Erdman, Douglass, and Marr 1969; Fritts, Smith, and Stokes 1965). The Anasazi occupation history of Wetherill Mesa is generally similar to that of other areas of the northern Southwest. Sites dating from about A.D. 700 to 900 generally consist of concentric rows of surface rooms with associated pit houses. These sites are numerous on mesas or near other areas of abundant arable soils. The Wetherill Mesa survey located 139 of these sites, most on the widest parts of the mesa tops. Habitation sites dating

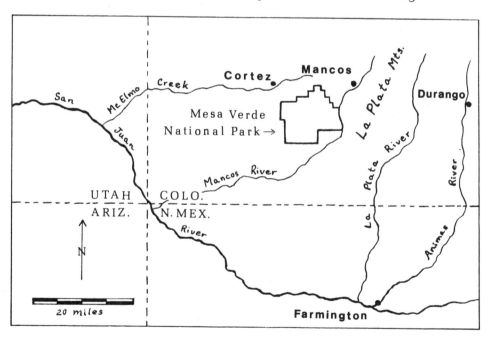

FIGURE 5.1 Location of Mesa Verde National Park.

between about A.D. 900 and 975 generally comprise fewer rooms, and the sites are more widely spaced. They are also more widely dispersed among various landforms. The Wetherill Mesa survey located 208 sites dating to this period. Between about A.D. 975 and 1050, sites are still fewer in number and more widely scattered. They may be associated with agricultural features such as terraces and check dams. At Wetherill Mesa, 166 sites dating to this time period were recorded, and most of these manifest debris from later occupations as well. Sites dating from about A.D. 1050 to 1150 consist of contiguous rooms arranged around well-defined plaza areas. Site size is larger than in the preceding period, but the number of sites may decline. The Wetherill Mesa survey recorded 60 sites dating to this period. The final phase of Anasazi occupation at Wetherill Mesa, and elsewhere in the Colorado Plateau country, dates between A.D. 1150 and 1300. Most sites consist of large, aggregated villages, but there are small one- or two-room storage structures or "limited activity" loci as well. At Wetherill Mesa, 150 sites dating to the final phase of prehistoric occupation were recorded by the survey. In general, the occupation history indicates a gradual aggregation of settlements. Site abandonment was a recurrent phenomenon, and the mesa was permanently deserted by Pueblo peoples by about A.D. 1300.

Despite the small area comprising Wetherill Mesa, there is considerable variation in elevation, exposure, slope of land, water sources, and soil composition (Figure 5.2). Although there were no drastic changes in climate during the prehistoric period, there were periods when it was cool and moist and periods when it was warm and dry. The events of the simulation were derived from the sequence of climatic episodes reflected in the local tree-ring chronology. The simulated consequences of these events were decisions predicting the abandonment or continued occupation of each habitation site found and assigned to one or more of the temporal categories used by the archaeological survey crews (Hayes 1964). The phase names, phase dates, and the number of sites evidencing occupation components during each are listed in Table 5.1. Summing the number of components, the simulation specified whether or not each of 726 components would be abandoned and during which phase abandonment would occur.

As discussed elsewhere (Cordell 1975), the simulation correctly predicted continued occupation for between 90 and 100 percent of all

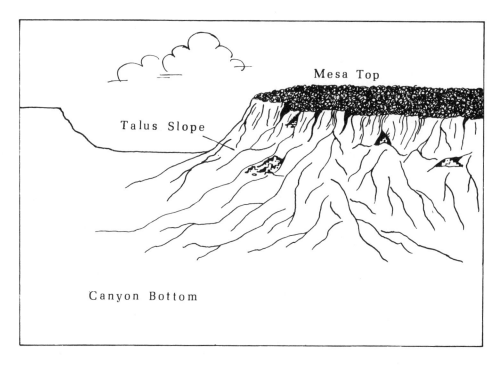

FIGURE 5.2. Schematic representation of major landforms at Mesa Verde.

cases. Abandonments were correctly predicted for 100 percent of the components abandoned during the Piedra and Mancos phases and for 87.68 and 66.66 percent of all components abandoned during the Mesa Verde and McElmo phases respectively. The fewest correct predictions were of components abandoned during the Ackmen Phase, only 31.76 percent.

Although certainly successful, the Wetherill Mesa simulation may be criticized for at least two reasons. First, it was overly complex. It involved the interaction of eight variables that had from 2 to 14 attri-

TABLE 5.1
PHASE NAMES, DATES, AND COMPONENTS IN THE
WETHERILL MESA SIMULATION

Phase	Years A.D.	Number of Components
Mesa Verde	1150–1300	166
McElmo	1050–1150	69
Mancos	975–1050	200
Ackmen	900–975	161
Piedra	700–900	130

butes. Second, it was situation-specific in the extreme. Ten square miles of Colorado do not tell one very much about the world in general. Furthermore, for a simulation to be useful to other archaeologists, it must minimally be comprehensible to the investigator. In some ways, mine was not. I suspected that my good results were based on spurious correlations built into the model and, probably, the inadvertent inclusion of a single noninformative causal variable, such as distance to water. The only aspect of the simulation in which I had confidence was that its success was not due to a single aberrant run. Unlike other simulations in archaeology, including some of my own, the simulation of climate change is completely deterministic. There are no random or probabilistic variables. Successive runs would have produced the same results.

In order to determine whether or not the results of the simulation depended on a single variable and in order to ascertain whether or not the variables could be redefined to make them applicable to other archaeological contexts, I have reexamined the results using two approaches. First, I used very simple analytical techniques in order to suggest reductions in the number of variables. Second, I compared statistically significant variables, as derived from the analyses, with variables that correlate with habitation site location in other areas of the Southwest.

EVALUATION OF VARIABLES

The simulation incorporated attributes of land that I believed would have had a direct effect on the reliability of agricultural yields. As much as possible, I considered the requirements of the variety of corn planted and the water and soil control features used by the Anasazi. The attributes of land are: local landform; proximity to canyonheads; exposure; degree of slope; elevation; type of nearest water source; distance to nearest water source; and an evaluation as to whether the location was sheltered with respect to prevailing wind direction. One relatively direct way of evaluating the importance of each of these variables is to compare units of land that lacked habitation sites with land that contained habitation sites with respect to each variable. Table 5.2, which presents the results of this comparison, indicates that in each case there is a statistically significant relationship.

126

TABLE 5.2
CROSSTAB RESULTS FOR LAND WITHOUT SITES AND
LAND WITH SITES

Variable	DF	Chi-Square	Probability
Landform	6	145.139	0.0001
Canyonhead	1	15.429	0.0001
Exposure	4	67.837	0.0001
Slope	3	37.499	0.0001
Elevation	11	122.800	0.0001
Type of Water Source	3	77.689	0.0529
Distance to Water	3	40.217	0.0001
Sheltered Location	1	8.838	0.0029

It should be noted that the Chi-square scores were not influenced by sample size. Of the 755 coded grids used in the simulation, 398 lacked sites and 357 contained sites. The data presented in Table 5.2 are not of much utility to one who is trying to reduce the number of variables important to understanding the *differential* abandonment of sites. However, Table 5.2 is important because it indicates that each of the relationships is statistically significant. Further, on an intuitive level, I doubt the independence of some of the variables. For example, canyonheads are also sheltered locations, although not all sheltered locations are canyonheads.

It is becoming increasingly obvious that estimates of site longevity for the Anasazi Southwest as a whole have been exaggerated. S. Plog (1977) suggests that most Anasazi sites were not inhabited longer than about 35 years. Estimates of 60 years for sites on the Colorado Plateau and 100 years for the Rio Grande Valley may be somewhat generous (for example, see Cordell 1979b; F. Plog 1979). An extensive land use strategy, coupled with frequent abandonments, seems to be characteristic of the Anasazi in general (Cordell 1977a, 1979a; Cordell and Plog 1979; F. Plog 1978). Although the data available do not permit estimating the length of time that multicomponent sites were actually inhabited, the survey records indicate that these sites either were occupied for two or more consecutive phases or were occupied during at least two of the local phases. The multicomponent sites, therefore, may be considered unusual in that they do not conform to the somewhat ephemeral character of Anasazi habitations. With respect to Wetherill Mesa specifically, the majority of sites recorded are single-component occupations. In view of the fact that multicomponent sites seem to be the exception rather than the rule, the environmental

127

TABLE 5.3
CROSSTAB RESULTS FOR MULTICOMPONENT AND
SINGLE-COMPONENT SITE LOCATIONS

Variable	DF	Chi-Square	Probability
Landform	6	17.519	0.0076
Proximity to Canyonhead	1	0.590	0.4426
Exposure	4	12.087	0.0167
Degree of Slope	3	15.294	0.0016
Elevation	10	29.357	0.0011
Type of Water Source	3	3.338	0.3424
Distance to Water	3	2.473	0.4802
Sheltered Location	1	0.028	0.8666

factors conditioning the location of these sites should depart significantly from those conditioning the locations of single-component sites. Further, if the assumptions underlying the simulation are correct, multicomponent sites should be in close proximity to land that would *reliably* be productive for agriculture despite minor climatic variations. Table 5.3 compares single- and multicomponent site locations with respect to the eight variables used in the simulation.

Table 5.3 indicates that canyonhead locations, sheltered locations, distance to water, and type of water source are not relevant to site longevity on Wetherill Mesa and could have been eliminated from the simulation. Although I suspect that canyonhead locations and sheltered locations were probably not important to the selection of field or house sites for the Anasazi in general, the same may not be said for distance to water and type of water source without some qualification. Wetherill Mesa is a small landform. There are at least 11 seeps and springs on the mesa as well as numerous washes (Hayes 1964). Slightly less than 5 percent (4.90 percent) of the total amount of land is more than one-half mile from any water source, and no land is more than three-quarters of a mile from a water source. It is the relative abundance of water, for both crops and domestic use, that determines its lack of significance for the location of sites. A similar situation was found to apply to Anasazi sites in the South Sandia–Tijeras Canyon area of New Mexico (Blevins and Joiner 1977), and apparently in the Grand Canyon area as well (Euler and Chandler 1978). In the Tijeras Canyon situation, no habitation sites were found in locations farther than one-half mile from permanent water, but there were no statistically significant associations of habitation sites and kinds of water sources or distance to water within that limit. Similarly, habitation sites reported for the Grand Canyon cluster within half a mile of water sources. Given a very broad, regional perspective, then, water sources are, of course, critical. It would be interesting to know if the half-mile distance represents a meaningful behavioral threshold or if it is an artifact of our recording procedures.

The variables that do seem to be important for site longevity (or site reuse) on Wetherill Mesa, and therefore presumably for sustained agricultural yields, are elevation, exposure, slope, and local landform. With respect to each of these variables, the pattern of differences between multicomponent and single-component sites is similar. Multi-component sites are found in more restricted situations than are single-component sites, and in each case, the difference can be related to long-term agricultural productivity.

Elevation in the study area ranges from 6,600 feet (1,980 m) to 7,900 feet (2,370 m), although no sites occur above 7,750 feet (2,325 m). The mean elevation of multicomponent sites is 7,241 feet (2,172 m), with a standard deviation of 226 feet (67.8 m) and a coefficient of relative variation of 3.43 percent. Single-component sites are not only more dispersed with respect to elevation, but the dispersion occurs primarily toward lower elevations. These lower elevations are not in the canyon bottoms. An examination of the distribution of sites with respect to local landform indicates that only seven (2.63 percent) single-component sites and one (1.11 percent) multicomponent site are located in a canyon-bottom setting. In fact, 177 (67 percent) of the single-component sites are on the mesa top. Low mesa-top situations at Mesa Verde are characterized by greater annual variation in precipitation than other locations. Soils are typically thin with high concentrations of calcium carbonate. The soils dry out fairly early in summer and, once dry, are subject to splash erosion and high runoff (Erdman, Douglass, and Marr 1969:27–30). These conditions are not favorable for sustained agricultural yields.

The situation with respect to slope is similar. Nearly all multicomponent sites (87.78 percent) are located on flat land. Single-component sites are on gentle, moderate, and steep slopes. The difference in distribution may be summarized by comparing indices of qualitative variation, expressed as percentages (Mueller and Schuessler 1969:178). For multicomponent sites, this index is 14.54 percent. It is 45.74 percent for single-component sites. The importance of slope for agriculture is reflected by the use of this dimension in the land class system developed by the U.S. Soil Conservation Service. The classes are not designed to monitor the fertility or productivity of the soil but rather those characteristics that influence its erodability, which is considered the major factor conditioning the length of time land can be success-fully cultivated. Slope is one of the permanent soil characteristics used in the classification. It determines the amount of soil build-up. Soil can accumulate only on level ground and on gentle slopes. The slope is therefore an indirect measure of erosion (Hudson 1971:152; Ramage 1977). There is now additional archaeological information that lends support to the notion that slope conditions both the establishment and the longevity of Anasazi habitation sites. Data from the Chevelon Drain-age, Arizona, discussed by F. Plog, Effland, and Green (1978) showed a high correlation between the location of habitation sites and arable land, with the latter defined only in terms of slope.

Interpreting the effects of exposure is rather more difficult with respect to analysis on the Wetherill Mesa simulation, although it is not hard to understand the importance of exposure for agricultural yields. In the latter case, exposure is considered an indirect measure of cli-mate and a guide to the moisture content of the soil. Thus, soil temperature, which is often of more importance to crops than air temperature, is directly affected by exposure. Generally, northern ex-posures have a greater moisture content than do western or southern exposures (Hudson 1971). For the simulation, exposure was recorded from topographic maps. These did not provide sufficient detail to determine exposure accurately on the relatively flat mesa top. For this reason, exposure was not recorded at all for these locations. Neverthe-less, comparison of locations of single-component and multicomponent sites with respect to exposure does indicate the same pattern noted above. Multicomponent sites are less dispersed than single-component sites. These distributions are shown in Table 5.4.

The absence of habitation sites on land with northern exposures is contrary to observed distributions elsewhere in the Southwest (Blevins and Joiner 1977; F. Plog 1978a, 1978b) but is understandable given the local situation at Wetherill Mesa. The "mesa" landform is in fact a cuesta with an abrupt northern scarp. The scarp prevents the accumu-lation of soils. The dip of the cuesta to the south also prevents the formation of seeps and springs in most north-facing situations. The observed relative importance of eastern slopes is therefore expected, in part because these situations approximate the moisture-retaining prop-erties of northern exposures.

130

TABLE 5.4
COMPARISON OF MULTICOMPONENT SITES AND
SINGLE-COMPONENT SITES WITH EXPOSURE

	Not Recorded	North	South	East	West
Multicomponent sites	38	0	10	23	19
	(42.22%)	(0)	(11.11%)	(25.56%)	(21.11%)
Single-Component sites	64	1	27	99	75
	(24.06%)	(0.38%)	(10.15%)	(37.22%)	(28.20%)

Local landform had been recorded as either mesa top (with subcategories such as mesa-top edge, mesa-top ridge, and so forth), talus slope, or canyon bottom. At Mesa Verde, these landforms are a general indicator of soil depth and texture, as well as growing season length. Canyon-bottom soils are light, fine, sandy loams with low storage capacity and are generally considered prohibitive to shallow-rooted plants (Erdman, Douglass, and Marr 1969:39). Growing season is also shortest in the canyon bottoms. Talus-slope soils are complex, having been derived partly from coarse colluvial-alluvial materials and partly from the underlying bedrock. These soils present the most variability with respect to water retention. The length of the growing season at talus-slope locations is determined primarily by exposure. Soils of the mesa top vary with elevation. At the higher, northern end of the mesa, soils are a stony loam, generally well drained and noncalcareous. These soils vary considerably in depth. At mid elevations of the central portion of the mesa, soils are typically deep loams with underlying clay loams. Moisture retention is good, and the growing season today is adequate for corn (Erdman, Douglass, and Marr 1969). Conditions of the lower mesa-top elevations have been described above. The distributions of multicomponent and single-component sites with respect to local landform shows essentially the same pattern as the distributions for other variables. Multicomponent sites are concentrated on the mesa top, as are single-component sites, but the latter are more dispersed among the local landform categories. The index of qualitative variation is 54 percent for multicomponent sites and 69 percent for single-component sites.

Of the four variables indicating significant differences between multicomponent and single-component sites, I now think that local landform has the least utility for future research. My initial emphasis on local landform (Cordell 1972) derived primarily from the attention that

131

the Park Service investigations gave to the observation that over time there was a shift from mesa top to talus slope and rock overhangs (Hayes 1964; Rohn 1977). Although local landforms may be important for agriculture, there are three good reasons for excluding them for future models. First, local landforms are not comparable from one area to another. This has emerged as a significant consideration in recent evaluations of regional Southwestern research. As succinctly stated by Dean (1978:111),

> a particular landform, however rigorously defined, is simply not the same thing in the high steppe of the Colorado Plateau as an identically defined landform in the low desert of the Gila-Salt drainage. These landforms, although typologically identical, are components of two totally different networks of climatic, topographic, geological, hydrological, and biological relationships that delimit two distinct environmental systems. Because of the interactions among all the variables within each system, no single feature, such as landform type, can be removed from its systemic context and equated with a similar feature extracted from a different system.

Second, the simulation used local landform as an index of two variables that I considered important for agriculture. These are growing-season length and soil texture, each of which can and should be measured separately. Third, as noted above, one of my simulation experiments (Cordell 1972) generated the distribution of sites at Wetherill Mesa at random and tabulated the resultant number of sites in each local landform category. Although this simulation was designed as a baseline control against which to evaluate the success of more realistic (or more reasonable) site-selection criteria, the random site-location model more accurately fit the known distribution of sites with respect to local landform features 50 percent of the time. The success of the simulation model's specific predictions concerning the effects of climate on arable land and the abandonment of particular sites is not duplicated by the random model. These observations strongly imply that observed patterning of site distribution in regard to landform, although certainly real, obscures far more significant configurations. These should be sought in direct measures of soil quality and growing season.

In summary, the Wetherill Mesa simulation was overly complex. Analysis of the eight variables used in the simulation indicates that four might be more appropriate for future models: exposure, elevation, slope, and perhaps general soil class (see, for example, Ramage 1977). These have the advantage of not being situation-specific and do seem to correlate with habitation site locations in other parts of the Anasazi Southwest.

The Ackmen Phase

Simulations, in general, seem to be most productive when unanticipated results are obtained. The Wetherill Mesa simulation was quite successful in predicting the continued occupation of sites as well as the abandonment of sites throughout a 600-year time period, with the noted exception of the Ackmen phase (Cordell 1975). At this point, I would like to abandon all caution, suggest that the simulation did realistically model behavior, and pursue the question of why it did not work for one specific segment of time.

Hayes (1964) applied the designation Ackmen phase to sites consisting of a few contiguous rooms of crude masonry with circular kivas placed to the south. The diagnostic ceramics of the phase are the painted Cortez Black-on-white and unpainted Mancos corrugated utility ware. Neither of these types is securely dated. Dates of roughly A.D. 875–950 for Mancos corrugated and about A.D. 900–1000 for Cortez Black-on-white are generally given (Abel 1955; Breternitz, Rohn, and Morris 1974; Rohn 1977). The dates that Hayes (1964) assigned to the Ackmen phase, the shortest phase in the Wetherill Mesa sequence, are A.D. 900–975, which seem to me to be "compromise" ceramic dates. Interestingly, Rohn (1977), in his discussion of Chapin Mesa, a neighboring landform at Mesa Verde, does not use the designation Ackmen phase; rather, he distinguishes Early Pueblo II and Late Pueblo II. He dates Early Pueblo II from "900 to 1000?" and Late Pueblo II from "1000? to 1100" (Rohn 1977:238). In his discussion of Early Pueblo II, which corresponds most closely to Hayes's Ackmen phase, Rohn (1977:237) notes that "no complete village or cluster of houses has been dug on Chapin Mesa or elsewhere in the Mesa Verde Region." He concludes his discussion by remarking that "this is the poorest known phase in the Chapin Mesa sequence, and much of our knowledge depends on what we know of its predecessors and successors" (Rohn 1977:238). My simulation of responses to climate changes used phase designations as the only temporal framework for archaeological sites. The events of the simulation (rules of site abandonment) were derived from the dendroclimatological chart and therefore rely on years and not phase labels. The simulation results departed from the archaeological observations in not predicting the number of sites which were apparently abandoned at the end of the Ackmen phase. The results were consistent in predicting sites which were not abandoned at the end of the phase.

Given the problems in both defining and dating the Ackmen phase, it is conceivable that the simulation is more accurate than the original survey, but I do not think this is the case. Rather, the difficulties in defining the Ackmen phase are symptomatic of much of the Anasazi Southwest during Early Pueblo II, and I do not think that response to climatic change reflects or can reflect what happened to settlements in the area at about A.D. 1000. The period between about A.D. 900 and 1000 in the Anasazi area witnessed both the maximum regional dispersion of settlement and the beginnings of regional population instability, marked by population aggregation in some areas and abandonments in others (Cordell 1979b; F. Plog 1979; Cordell and F. Plog 1979). For example, population seems to have increased greatly both in Chaco Canyon (Judge 1976) and at Mesa Verde (Hayes 1964). This is true of the Cebolleta Mesa area as well (Ruppe 1966; Dittert 1959). By A.D. 1000, or certainly by 1050, there were complete abandonments of the Navajo Reservoir District (Eddy 1966), and the Governador (Hall 1944). The dendroclimatological data from Mesa Verde indicate that between A.D. 900 and 1000 or 1050, conditions were slightly more mesic than they are today.[1] I would suggest that initially, quite small communities dispersed and farmed a diversity of local settings, and that most of these were unsuitable for continual cultivation. Most locations were probably doomed to failure because under less than optimal conditions they suffered from lack of sufficient moisture or were subject to erosion, nutrient depletion, or salinization (see, for example, Cordell and F. Plog 1979; Husler and Fosberg 1977; F. Plog 1979).

Of even greater importance are the social conditions prevailing in the northern Southwest between A.D. 900 and 1050. As argued in detail elsewhere (Cordell and F. Plog 1979), this period witnessed the breakdown of the first, ephemeral attempt to integrate most of the Colorado Plateau area into an alliance and exchange network. The alliance system is reflected in the ubiquitous White Mound, Kana'a, Kiatuthalanna ceramic "style" that crosscut technologically distinct trade types and in a noted general increase in evidence of long-distance

134

trade. The archaeological data suggest that, whatever its specific structure, the alliance system was relatively egalitarian and, as noted above, shortlived. By A.D. 1000 to 1050, events in the Anasazi Southwest were dominated by highly intensified agricultural production in some areas, increased productive specialization, and elaborate exchange systems that were maintained by groups of people who may have had differential access to positions of authority. The abandonment of some sites and areas at the end of Pueblo II as well as the subsequent aggregations during the Classic Pueblo period are probably better explained as the result of changes in the mechanisms of social integration than they are by reference to local climatic perturbations. In short, I think, the failure of the Wetherill Mesa simulation to predict adequately the number of sites that were abandoned at the end of the Ackmen phase indicates that these abandonments were largely the result of changes in the organizational strategies of the system and not directly related to variation in local rainfall and growing season. Thus, it might be suggested that the simple, mechanistic, time-independent model upon which the simulation was based failed to predict known site abandonments because the abandonments were the result of systemic, time-dependent factors.

SIMULATIONS, ANALYSIS, AND ARCHAEOLOGICAL RESEARCH

Scientific inquiry of any sort involves, in part, proposing hypotheses to explain phenomena, deriving test implications from the hypotheses, and testing these against further observations. Most hypothesis-testing procedures in archaeology are analytical, that is, testing the existence and strength of associations among variables. Analytical techniques have the advantage of being relatively simple and therefore fairly easy to interpret. But hypothesis testing through the demonstration of patterned covariation among variables is appropriate within a synchronic context. Correlations do not indicate causality without process statements. The search for and recognition of patterns of covariation in archaeological data generate questions and not answers. In addition, two important limitations are inherent in analyses designed to discover patterned covariation. First, as others have noted, pattern searches are frequently inefficient, and "wasteful in terms of the irrelevant data that have to be manipulated" (Dean 1978:113). Second, as I have indicated through the extended discussions of "clade" behavior in macroevolutionary simulations and of landform type in the Wetherill Mesa case, some pattern recognition studies will inevitably result in focusing on the wrong patterns.

Most of the time, of course, searches for patterns of covariation are not undertaken blindly but are guided by current theory. Nevertheless, as scientists, we must be able to demonstrate that the patterns which confirm our theoretical expectations cannot also be the result of chance and cannot be derived from another set of expectations as well (see, for example, Tringham 1978).

Archaeological inquiry generally concerns explaining past behavior. (Exceptions involve determining postdepositional effects on artifactual remains in order to refine archaeological method.) The problem that archaeology, and any other historic aspect of science, faces is being able to test past synchronic patterning without leaping entirely into metaphysics (Cordell 1977a). In a logical sense, metaphysical statements are those that are not falsifiable with contemporary data (Popper 1959; Lewontin 1968; Tringham 1978). Developing experientially falsifiable "tests" seems to rest with the ingenuity of the investigator. Either analytic or simulation methods may be appropriate. For example, *analysis* of trace elements in obsidian allows determination of specific source locations. The results of the Wetherill Mesa simulation suggested an experientially falsifiable test that I have discussed elsewhere (Cordell 1975). The simulation predicted an order of abandonment of sites within phases which could be tested through further excavation. The reexamination of the simulation results presented here suggests additional tests. New insight into Anasazi settlement systems might be gained by examining Pueblo II agricultural fields for evidence of soil depletion, erosion, and concentrations of salt. These tests need not be restricted to Mesa Verde. Having reduced the number of variables to be considered and broadened their potential applicability somewhat, these tests may be appropriate in other areas of the northern Southwest.

An important facet of archaeological research also relates to the temporal remoteness of its subject matter. Archaeologists must be concerned with long-term processes, with systems that *do* change over time; it is in this context that the potential contribution of archaeological research is greatest. The value of simulation is that it necessitates an explicit statement of processes, and there may be no other realistic way to model long-term systemic change. The results of the Wetherill Mesa simulation suggest that a simple, mechanistic process does accurately predict most site abandonments. I have noted that the lack of successful results obtained for the Ackmen phase indicates that an internal systemic change was taking place. I have also tried to show that the overall success of the simulation could not be reproduced by a random model. I have not, however, been able to demonstrate that a model of response to climatic variability is the *only* one that can generate accurate predictions. In fact, because of my conviction that neither life nor archaeology can possibly be that simple, I doubt that it should be the only successful predictive model. Certainly, directions that future research should take include deriving more experientially falsifiable tests, falsifying them, developing simulation models that address the same problem from a different perspective, and generating equally successful, if not better, results.

KINDS OF SIMULATIONS IN ARCHAEOLOGICAL RESEARCH

The comments made here are not meant to provide a catalog either of the current uses of simulation in archaeology or of the variety of problem areas that might fruitfully be examined by archaeologists using simulation techniques. The diversity of case studies in this volume and elsewhere (for example, Hodder 1978) suggests the potential versatility of simulation approaches. My comments are directed toward questions that appeared as themes during the Advanced Seminar and that relate to the kinds of simulations archaeologists have developed or would like to develop. The first question involves examining how complex simulation models should be. The second question relates to whether or not systemic change is best explained in terms of "internal" (endogenous) system structure or "external" (exogenous) events. As I argue below, these questions are aspects of a single problem. The answers to these questions are in part defined by explicitly stating the level of explanation we seek in order to account for particular system behavior.

In general, it can be argued that any realistic model of a system must include all variables that we believe are relevant to the behavior of the system. These variables are constrained by "the state of existing knowledge about the number and value of the parameters involved in the phenomenon modeled" (Jacquard and Leridon 1974:214). Archaeologists will probably have little difficulty identifying *many* variables that may be germane to any particular system. Those variables that can be measured with any degree of confidence will be very *few*. The structure of the Wetherill Mesa simulation incorporated components that I could measure; therefore, it is a very simple model. Low (Chapter 9) presents a system dynamics approach to Anasazi settlement pattern that incorporates a richer, and therefore probably more realistic, inventory of components.[2] Yet most of the components Low includes have no independently measurable correlates in the archaeological record. How does one determine a scale for vulnerability to changes in climate, for "organizational diversity," or even for "net birth rate"? In this case, Low's model is heuristic and not explanatory. It suggests that methods for obtaining indices for these components would be valuable. As Low notes, system dynamics models include internal model components that are "refutable by appeal to intuition, direct observation, experience, and expert advice" (Chapter 9, page 259). Archaeologists cannot directly observe past behavior, nor can they ask the advice of the dead. Appeal to our archaeological intuition or our own experience is anathema because as anthropologists we are, rightfully, concerned about our ethnocentric biases. We know that as twentieth-century scientists we cannot intuit the way an Anasazi farmer perceived "environmental and social stress." Finally, lest some Southwestern archaeologists *assume* that the values expressed by the descendants of the Anasazi are the equivalent of expert advice, I will reiterate that the Pueblo societies of today are not appropriate analogs for their ancestors (Cordell 1979b; Cordell and F. Plog 1979). In essence, I believe that although complex models may be attractive and desirable, they are also beyond the current methods of archaeology.

In view of the above comments, I would like to clarify my position with respect to the apparent contrast between Hill's (1977b:75) statement that "goals must originate in response to stress" and Low's (Chapter 9, page 253) remark that "it is the existence of goals, with or without any particular stress impinging on human actions, that keeps a system under control." It is my opinion that this particular dispute is at cross-purposes until a statement about the power or level of explanation is defined. I will use the Wetherill Mesa simulation and Low's Anasazi model as references. Like Hill (1977b), I believe that individuals and social systems have goals. Sometimes these goals must reflect external stress, and sometimes they may be internal and unrelated to stress or "perceived stress." When the latter is the case, I do not believe that archaeology is currently in a position to know what the particular goals of a system were. Low (Chapter 9) suggests that a system dynamics approach may enable the researcher to determine the nature of the system's goals by observing the trajectory of the system. This requires, however, that the system be defined and that system boundaries reflect "the role of one's *theory* about what's important and how things interrelate" (Low, Chapter 9, page 261, emphasis mine).

In his approach to Anasazi settlement patterns, Low prefers to use the "general" Anasazi phenomenon to explain the particular instance of abandonments at Wetherill Mesa. I agree that specific cases should always be explained as particular instances of general phenomena. In developing a general theory for the Anasazi, however, Low has focused on abandonment or "collapse" as the reference mode of behavior that the system *should* manifest. He therefore limits that portion of the system trajectory to the time that postdates A.D. 900. I might quip that Low's willingness to model the Anasazi "collapse" results from his having spent too much time reading about the Maya (Hosler, Sabloff, and Runge 1977). My simple Wetherill Mesa simulation very clearly shows that the abandonment of particular sites was a common, recurrent, and predictable theme of Anasazi life for six hundred years. My approach suggests that "abandonment" of a *site* (or sites) and of an *area* (the Colorado Plateau) are not the same problem and may well require two different theories.

In order to clarify the notion of how many theories might be required, I will resort to the expedient of using a familiar example. Newtonian physics does explain and allow accurate predictions at a certain level. It is adequate for apples falling from trees and for most of us on earth, but it is not appropriate for the entire universe, that is, for red shifts and black holes. Similarly, the concept of genetic inheritance is adequate for predicting phenotypic diversity in many characteristics and for estimating the risks of having children with certain kinds of disorders. However, the genetic theory will not help one to understand cell replication or certain kinds of mutation or protein synthesis.

Low's approach strikes me as akin to trying to model all the phenomena in the universe. That is, he seeks to place under one system a model of DNA as well as the distribution of wrinkled and smooth garden peas. The vision of system dynamics may be considered admirable, but I think it is no accident that Einstein lived long after Newton's death and that Mendel's work preceded that of Watson and Crick. Until we know the empirical limits of an explanatory framework, we do not know how broad the next theoretical level must be, how many discrepancies it should explain, or to what level of phenomena it should be applied.

In my discussion, I have tried to *simplify* the Wetherill Mesa simulation so that it can be applied more generally to the Anasazi area. If it is applied in its new form, we shall know its empirical limits very quickly. We will also determine whether or not the next theoretical step should be the development of a more complex model of "collapse" that incorporates site abandonment or whether we should develop a theory of *regional* abandonment that ignores individual sites because these may be explained by reference to purely local conditions.

In summary, while the examples from physics and biology are overdrawn, I think that all of us at the Advanced Seminar were concerned about the nature of change, the complexity of models, and the power of various kinds of explanation. In addition, we each expressed confidence in a refutationist approach to experimentation. As Bell and Low (Chapters 3 and 9 respectively) have indicated, system dynamics modelling conforms to refutationist principles because the "internal model components, derived independently of the behavior they produce, are refutable" (Low, Chapter 9, page 259). With respect to archaeology, however, the internal model components cannot be refuted in the usual ways, because the systems involved are no longer extant. In effect, we are in the process of developing the structure of the internal components when we deal with simple models that are empirically falsifiable. When we have confidence that the behavior of the internal components is modelled adequately, we should be able to model and explain system behavior primarily in terms of internal structure. Furthermore, because something like the Wetherill Mesa simulation must be seen as a small component of some larger system, I think that the simplest models are the most efficient. Simple models are comprehensible, and their empirical limits are relatively easy to find. It is probably no accident that response to local climatic changes failed to predict most site abandonments between A.D. 900 and 975.

This is the time period for which Low would begin his model of a "general" Anasazi collapse. The latter is, at this point, an interesting heuristic device that should inspire advances in method and theory.

NOTES

1. Rainfall in the Southwest is so spotty in distribution that the dendroclimatic reconstruction for Wetherill Mesa cannot be used to interpret past climate from the Navajo Reservoir District.

2. During the conference, Low was encouraged to develop a model of the Anasazi case in order to explicate the system dynamics approach. My comments on his model adequately reflect my response to the draft of his paper that appears in this volume. Low was to have had the opportunity to reply to my remarks in the final version of his paper, but his untimely death has made this impossible.

6
Simulation as a Heuristic Device in Archaeology

EZRA B. W. ZUBROW

State University of New York at Buffalo

INTRODUCTION

This chapter differs from traditional simulation studies; it uses simulation not to solve problems but to create new problems and view old ones in new and interesting ways.

The study is divided into two parts. The first is theoretical and provides the background information necessary to discern the contrasts between how simulation is most frequently used and how it is employed here. Part 1 focuses on a series of general questions about the nature of simulation and its role in research. Questions such as, What is simulation? What are its functions? and What is the methodology of development? are discussed.

While the first part is theoretical and couched in generalities, the second is applied and descriptively specific. It is the saga of my attempt to apply and modify a model of urban dynamics by Forrester to early cities. I include a description of his model, its assumptions and conclusions. I also present my modifications, strategy, exemplary data, and a variety of heuristic insights that have been derived throughout the simulation process.

PART I. THE GENERAL NATURE OF SIMULATION

What are simulations? Briefly, they are operational modes of reality. They encompass physical or analytical analogs. They may be static or dynamic, deterministic or stochastic. Simulations most frequently model systems. A system consists of inputs, outputs, components, and relationships as well as the environment in which they reside. If one simulates a dynamic system, the results will not only be dependent upon the values of the above factors, but also upon the structure and ordering of the various components and relationships in time and space. For example, consider a relatively simple system found in the archaeological record at the historical edge of prehistory, the famous Roman bakery excavated from Pompeii. The size and type of such components as the mixers, ovens, and cooking racks obviously have a significant effect on the baked goods. It is no less obvious because of our familiarity with the system that the temporal ordering of the same components may create important variants. The Roman baker could create different confections even by adding the same amount of yeast to the dough at different points in the baking process. The importance of temporal ordering is far less obvious in systems with which one is not familiar, as illustrated by the Roman monetary system. What is the importance of the temporal ordering of the large mandatory financial gifts to a given Emperor? Many archaeologists have noted how the size of the communication system may limit the size of early cities, but few have asked if there are significant differences in when the communication processes occur. In short, all simulations require that archaeologists carefully examine the components, environment, and relationships among the variables. Dynamic simulations require an especially sensitive examination.

What are the functions of simulations? Traditionally, simulations have been the methodology of last resort. One simulates because one cannot manipulate reality. Reality may be too valuable to experiment

144

upon, as is the case when the data are human lives or populations. Or, the data may be too unique to allow for multiple or replicable experimentation. In such cases, analytical solutions are possible but not feasible, owing to extraneous factors. Conversely, analytical solutions are sometimes feasible but not possible. There may be so many solutions to the systems of equations that the best choice among solutions cannot be determined efficiently. Or the problems of calculating an analytical solution may be so immense or expensive as to make it impossible. Finally, of course, some problems are impossible to solve analytically.

Simulations have important predictive and retrodictive functions. One may trace a component, a relationship, or a set of variables both forward and backward through time. There is also the manipulative or "let's try it and see" function to many simulations. One of the great advantages of simulations is that it enables the simulator to fiddle inexpensively with the variables and relationships. One may discover the feasibility and advantages of a particular strategy or a path of action without jeopardizing the system.

In addition, simulations have two heuristic functions. First is the oft-noted focusing of the researcher's attention upon the explicitness and completeness of the model. This takes place according to an informal evolutionary process. The model is transformed from intuitive insight through both verbal description and graphic approximation to mathematical precision. This process is demonstrated by a variety of recent papers on Maya development and collapse (Rathje 1973; Culbert 1974; Hosler, Sabloff, and Runge 1977; Freidel 1979). In many ways, it is analogous to a consciousness-raising experience. Step by step, new factors are recognized as important. Greater clarity and precision are demanded and must be provided. One of my favorite introductory class assignments is to ask the students to simulate a Maya ball game by actually playing it. One suddenly becomes aware how incomplete the most exact accounts are when faced with such problems as how the ball enters play, what one does if the ball is accidentally knocked out of the court, or any of numerous other mundane but operationally important problems.

The emphasis of this paper is to explore the second heuristic function. Simulations often will generate combinations of variables, components, and interrelationships that create unexpected results.

145

Sometimes, upon reflection, these will provide novel insights, new ways to perceive old problems. Often they will give rise to new explanations—particularly in complex systems where totally different interactions within the structure may take place when thresholds are passed or when new subsystems and variables are introduced. As complexity increases, so does the unforeseen. Furthermore, complex systems are often counterintuitive. Change a variable or a component and the results are the opposite of what one expects. This is not due to the ineptness of the simulator, who could predict the expected given sufficient time. Rather, it is due to the system's complexity. There are just too many intervening variables and too many logical relationships for the simulator always to be able to perceive the relationships between cause and result. In short, one does not really understand the operation of a sophisticated system or simulation until one is either in it or doing it.

What are some of the strategies for developing a simulation? Simulation has often been described as an art. The aesthetic aspect begins with the choice between the two, possibly three, strategies of development and is continued into numerous design decisions and stylistic preferences.

The first strategy can be described as *sui generis*. There have already been allusions to the evolutionary process by which scholars gradually change intuitive insights in the formal mathematical models. Reality need not follow theory exactly. Steps are sometimes passed over. In any case, once the model is in appropriate mathematical form, the traditional approach is to define the problem in terms of the model. One makes the appropriate simplifying assumptions and writes an original simulation from the model's equations. It is as simple and as problem-specific as possible. One tests this tightly conceived and narrowly defined simulation against reality. If it is found lacking, one systematically begins to relax the restrictive aspects of the simulation and to broaden its scope in order to find a better fit. In other words, this strategy is the tactic of originality and parsimony. The simulator is the creator and moves from the simple to the complex and from the narrow to the broad only under conditions of necessity.

The second strategy could be termed a strategy of borrowing and imitation. One often uses a large portion of another's simulation model. For example, if one wishes to use a mathematical model to simulate kinship systems, one may choose from a variety of extant samples (Hammel 1976; Skolnick and Cannings 1974). There are persuasive reasons for borrowing from an existing model or simulation rather than creating one from scratch. First, it is usually thought more cost- and time-efficient to make minor modifications of a working simulation than to begin anew. Second, one may wish to show the appropriateness and inappropriateness of extant models as well as the adequacy or inadequacy of existing simulations prior to the development of a totally new model or simulation. This is particularly useful when testing the operational limits of a model. Often an existing model will be adequate within a set of normal operating parameters. But one may wish to examine its behavior when it is functioning beyond normal constraints. For example, a simple gravity model of migration may characterize the migration of a standard region adequately but grossly distort the regional characteristics when it is found that no roads exist. The third reason for borrowing a simulation is that there may be no other alternative. For example, there may be only one effective way to solve a problem, and someone else may already have found it. In these cases, one might ask, Why bother? I would respond by pointing out that although the simulation has been constructed previously, new values of the variables may engender creative new research.

This paper is an example of the second strategy. It was originally conceived to show the inadequacy of existing models prior to the development of new ones. However, the heuristic implications of the old model were sufficiently interesting to warrant a report.

The third strategy is a synthesis of the first two. It is the development of a new model and simulation which includes the borrowing of some standard components. Consider, for example, a complex stochastic simulation of the economics of a prehistoric region in Peru. It may make perfectly good intellectual and financial sense to combine the population-growth algorithm originally developed by Keyfitz, an age-structure algorithm developed by the United Nations, and a settlement-locating component developed by the author. The existence of libraries of algorithms, components, and procedures as well as packages of the above in various simulation languages provide the standard tools for simulators. Most sophisticated simulations today are of this form. (One of the best references is Knuth's (1973) multivolume set entitled *The Art of Computer Programming.*)

PART II. APPLICATION OF A
SIMULATION MODEL

A Brief History of Forrester's Model in Urban and Archaeological Contexts

Forrester's model appeared in a book entitled *Urban Dynamics* (1969). It attempted to analyze the underlying causes of urban growth and decay. This work should be seen in the context of his other books; his subjects show a continuous growth in scope. Originally, Forrester studied problems of industrial location and dynamics. In the late 1960s, he turned the techniques he had developed to the urban situation; in the 1970s, to the world economy. Indeed, the now famous or infamous Club of Rome report by Meadows et al. (1972), entitled *Limits to Growth*, was·stimulated by Forrester's ideas. Over the last three decades, his work, using a consistent economic basis, has broadened in scope and repeatedly caused controversy.

Although Forrester's *Urban Dynamics* is the most widely known model and simulation of an urban area, it is not unique and should be viewed as part of a short tradition of modelling and simulating urban processes (Berger, Boulay, and Zisk 1970). A large number of mathematically oriented urban models which can be simulated have been developed in the last quarter-century. They include intervening opportunity models (Stouffer 1940), gravity models (Hanson 1960), trend models (Hamburg and Sharkey 1961), input-output models (Isard Langford, and Romanoff 1966–68), economic base-multiplier models (Lowry 1964), and growth models (Ashby 1964), to mention only the major types.[1]

Many urban simulation models are the results of constant revision by large teams of researchers. Lowry's pioneer urban development model (1964) was used as the basis of TOMM (Time Oriented Metropolitan Model), which was revised into TOMMII (Crecine 1968) and TOMMIII (Crecine 1969). These use sequential processes to focus on spatial interaction (Crecine 1964). EMPIRIC, which was developed at the same time, recognized the possibility of both sequential and simultaneous urban processes but handled spatial interaction implicitly. POLIMETRIC was slightly later to use differential equations but was actually a refined revision of EMPIRIC (Irwin and Brand 1965). It was within this context that Forrester more or less contemporaneously

148

gathered together teams of researchers to focus system dynamics on industrial, urban, and world temporal interaction. A few years afterward, more sophisticated studies were completed. Batty (1972) has a balanced dynamic simulation of an urban area. Unlike Forrester's, it does not emphasize spatial interaction at the price of spatial aggregation. Forrester's model is both temporally and spatially disaggregated. In short, as we have seen, Forrester's model, though widely known, is neither the most sophisticated nor an unprecedented urban simulation.

Archaeologists have made important empirical and theoretical contributions toward understanding urbanism. First, they have collected large amounts of data on early sedentary life and early cities. From such sites as Askili Huyuk, Jarmo, Jericho, and Ali Kosh, such scholars as Kenyon (1957), Braidwood (1975), Solecki (1959), Perrot (1966), and more recently Smith (1975), Mortensen (1972), and Flannery and Wright (1966) have created a tradition of excavating early villages and examining the developmental patterns of early village life. Simultaneously, Braidwood (1975), Lamberg-Karlovsky (1971), Adams and Nissen (1972), and others have examined such early cities as Uruk, Tepe Yahya, and Susa in considerable detail. The empirical contributions were not limited to the Old World. In the New World, one may point to such analogous village sites as La Venta and Ocos and to analogous cities such as Cuzco and Teotihuacan. Corresponding scholarly works are those by MacNeish (1961), Flannery (1976), Sanders (1968), and Millon (1967), to note only a few.

Archaeologists have also devoted considerable effort to the development of explanations concerning the origin of urban society. Redman (1978) has enumerated many of these theories, including Wittfogel's hydraulic hypothesis, Childe's craft and irrigation specialization hypothesis, the Rathje-Wright-Flannery interregional trade hypothesis, the system ecology model, and R. M. Adams's combination theory.

Far less theoretical emphasis has been placed upon how cities operated and how their operation changed over time. There are no groups of archaeologically derived theories that explain the workings of early cities in the same sense as the above theories purport to explain their origin. Forrester's model accordingly addresses archaeological interests in the origin and development of urbanism but differs from archaeological analysis by examining the actual mechanisms of urban operation.

149

Forrester's Model: A Brief Description

How does one describe an urban area? Forrester believes that at any particular instant, a city consists of a series of inventories. One determines the stocks of population and land, capital and production, transportation and utilities, as well as private and public sector administration. But a synchronic description is insufficient to attain an understanding of an urban area; one should be able to discern how these inventories change over time and relate to a changing environment.

Forrester has developed a time-dependent model in which complex matrices of variables and data are functions of each other and of time. His theory is a series of equations that describes the interaction of economic inventories and their environment in a sophisticated manner. The core of his model consists of nine major inventory variables and their interactive controls. These variables in the vocabulary of systems theory are called state or level variables. In the production set, new enterprise, mature business, and declining industry are the state variables. The set of variables concerning shelter is made up of premium housing, worker housing, and underemployed housing. Finally, there is a demographic grouping which includes managerial population, labor, and the underemployed (Figure 6.1). The basic unit is the productive member of the society. Dependents and households are calculated as secondary variables.

Each variable may be affected by the size and rate of change of every other variable or by its own size or rate of change. Thus, the theory is segregated into level and rate equations as well as feedback loops. The level equations describe some magnitude or relationship among magnitudes associated with a state variable or with an inventory at a particular point in time. The rate equations define the rates at which the levels change through time. For example, a level equation might state that the amount of underemployed housing is a function of obsolescent worker housing, housing demolition, and low-cost-housing construction. A related rate equation would delimit the rate of unemployed arrivals as a function of the perceived attractiveness-for-migration multiplier and the ratio of labor to underemployment.

These rate and level equations are related through the various feedback loops. The feedback loops consist of a structure in which a decision point, the rate equation, determines the flow of a particular stock. This stock is accumulated (integrated) to generate a system level or a

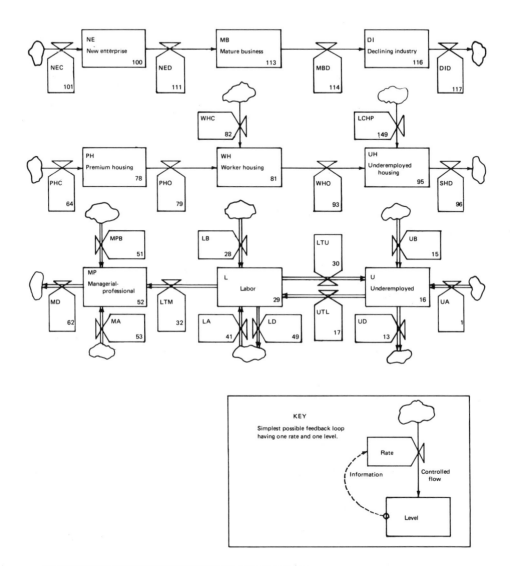

The major levels (rectangles) and rates (value symbols) for the model of an urban area.

FIGURE 6.1. The essential structure of Forrester's model: the major levels and rates (source: Forrester 1969: Figures 2.2 and 2.4, by permission of the M.I.T. Press).

state variable in a level equation. Information about the levels of the state variables is the basis on which the flow rate is controlled.

Unlike other dynamic modellers, Forrester does not use differential equations. Instead, he divides time into a series of sequential segments which are the basis of difference equations. He labels these segments 0,1,2,3, . . . J,K,L. One may think of them as a nonrepetitive calendar consisting of day 1,2,3, . . . or year 1,2,3, ... A variable labelled DT specifies the time interval. This is the solution interval between the successive evaluations of the equations. The length of time is given by a variable named LENGTH. If LENGTH is set to 200 years and DT to 1, then the equations are computed once per simulated year and solved for every year for 200 years. If LENGTH is set for 300 years and DT to 2, the equations are solved biannually 150 times. In other words, they are computed for year 2,4,6, and so on to the 300th year.

Forrester's model consists of literally hundreds of equations. In addition to the 20 level equations and the 22 rate equations (see Lists 6.1 and 6.2 and Table 6.1), some 195 auxiliary equations compute values for 108 auxiliary variables which influence the rate and level equations. Clearly, we cannot consider all of them here. Instead, let us consider a few exemplary equations.

Urban Dynamics should be commended, for it presents all the mathematical relationships of the model. Somewhat unfortunately for archaeological readers, the equations are presented without translation in DYNAMO II, a computer simulation language. Although DYNAMO II is reasonably well known and quite easy to use if a computer center has a compiler, most archaeologists will be more familiar with standard mathematical notation or FORTRAN IV. Therefore, these exemplary equations are presented with illustrative transactions.

Consider the following sample equation in DYNAMO II: $U.L. = U.K. + UA.KL$. Verbally, it states that the level of unemployed (U) at time L will be equal to the level of unemployed at the previous time K plus the number of unemployed arrivals per time unit (UA) multiplied by the number of time units between K and L. A standard mathematical translation using differential equations would be:

$$U(t+r) = U(t) + \frac{dU(t)}{d(t)} \, r,$$

where r is the time interval between K and L and t is K. However, as Cooke and Low pointed out during the Advanced Seminar, the DYNAMO II representation only approximates the mathematical

LIST 6.1. Level Equations

$AMMP(2) = AMMP(1) + (DT/AMMPT)*(AMM - AMMP(1))$
$DI(2) = DI(1) + DT*(MBD - DID)$
$L(2) = L(1) + DT*(UTL + LB - LTM + LA - LD - LTU)$
$LAMP(2) = LAMP(1) + (DT/LAMPT)*(LAM - LAMP(1))$
$LMMP(2) = LMMP(1) + (DT/LMMPT)*(LMM - LMMP(1))$
$LRP(2) = LRP(1) + (DT/LRPT)*(LR - LRP(1))$
$MAMP(2) = MAMP(1) + (DT/MAMPT)*(MAM - MAMP(1))$
$MB(2) = MB(1) - DT*(NED - MBD)$
$MP(2) = MP(1) + DT*(LTM + MPB + MA - MD)$
$NE(2) = NE(1) + DT*(NEC - NED)$
$NEA(2) = NEA(1) + (DT/NEAT)*(NE(1) - NEA(1))$
$PH(2) = PH(1) + DT*(PHC - PHO)$
$PHA(2) = PHA(1) + (DT/PHAT)*(PH(1) - PHA(1))$
$TRNP(2) = TRNP(1) + (DT/TRNPT)*(TRN - TRNP(1))$
$U(2) = U(1) + DT*(UA = UB + LTU - UD - UTL)$
$UH(2) = UH(1) + DT*(WHO - SHD + LCHP)$
$UMMP(2) = UMMP(1) + (DT/UMMPT)*(UMM - UMMP(1))$
$UTLP(2) = UTLP(1) + (DT/UTLPT)*(UTL - UTLP(1))$
$WH(2) = WH(1) + DT*(PHO + WHC - WHO)$
$WHA(2) = WHA(1) + (DT/WHAT)*(WH(1) - WHA(1))$

LIST 6.2. Rate Equations

$DID = DIDN*DI*DIDM + DIDP$
$LA = LAN*L*LAMP$
$LB = L*LBR$
$LCHP = LCHCD*LCR$
$LD = LDN*L*LDM$
$LTM = LMN*L*LMMP + LTPG$
$LTU = L*LLF$
$MA = MAN*MP*MAMP$
$MBD = MBDN*MB*BDM$
$MD = MDN*MP*MDM$
$MPB = MP*MPBR$
$NEC = NECD*LCR$
$NED = NEDN*NE*EDM$
$PHC = PHCD*LCR$

LIST 6.2 *(Continued)*
$PHD = PHDN*PH*PHDM$
$SHD = SHDN*UH*SHDM = SHDP$
$UA = (U + L)*UAN*AMMP$
$UB = U*UBR$
$UD = UDN*U*UDM$
$UTL = UMN*UW*UMMP + UTP$
$WHC = WHCD*LCR$
$WHO = WHON*WH*WHOM$

TABLE 6.1
INDEX OF VARIABLES

AMMP	Attractiveness-for-Migration-Multiplier Perceived
DI	Declining Industry
L	Labor
LAMP	Labor-Arrival Multiplier Perceived
LMMP	Labor-Mobility Multiplier Perceived
LRP	Labor-job Ratio Perceived
MAMP	Manager Arrival Multiplier Perceived
MB	Mature Business
MP	Managerial-Professional
NE	New Enterprise
NEA	New Enterprise Average
PH	Premium Housing
PHA	Premium Housing Average
TRNP	Tax Ratio Needed Perceived
U	Underemployed
UG	Underemployed Housing
UMMP	Underemployed Mobility Multiplier Perceived
UTLP	Underemployed-To-Labor Perceived
WH	Worker Housing
WHA	Worker Housing Average
DID	Declining Industry Demolition
LA	Labor Arrivals
LB	Labor Births
LCHP	Low Cost Housing Program
LD	Labor Departures
LTM	Labor-To-Manager
LTU	Labor-To-Underemployed
MA	Manager Arrivals
MBD	Mature Business Decline
MD	Manager Departures
MPB	Managerial-Professional Births
NEC	New Enterprise Construction
NED	New Enterprise Decline

TABLE 6.1 *(Continued)*

PHC	Premium-Housing Construction
PHO	Premium-Housing Obsolescence
SHD	Slum Housing Demolition
UA	Underemployed Arrivals
UB	Underemployed Births
UD	Underemployed Departures
UTL	Underemployed-To-Labor
WHC	Worker Housing Construction
WHO	Worker Housing Obsolescence
AMMPT	Attractiveness-For-Migration Muliplier Perceived Time Lag
DIDN	Declining Industry Demolition Normal
LAMPT	Labor-Arrival-Multiplier-Perception Time
LAN	Labor Arrivals Normal
LBR	Labor Birth Rate
LDN	Labor Departures Normal
LMMPT	Labor Mobility Multiplier Perception Time
LMN	Labor Mobility Normal
LRPT	Labor/job Ratio Perception Time
MAMPT	Manager Arrival Multiplier Perception Time
MAN	Manager Arrivals Normal
MBDN	Mature Business Decline Normal
MDN	Manager Departures Normal
MPBR	Managerial Professional Birth Rate
NEAT	New Enterprise Averaging Time
NEDN	New Enterprise Decline Normal
PHAT	Premium Housing Averaging Time
PHON	Premium Housing Obsolescence Normal
SHDN	Slum Housing Demolition Normal
TRNPT	Tax Ratio Needed Perception Time
UAN	Underemployed Arrivals Normal
UBR	Underemployed Birth Rate
UDN	Underemployed Departures Normal
UMMPT	Underemployed Mobility Multiplier Perception Time
UMN	Underemployed Mobility Normal
UTLPT	Underemployed-To-Labor Perception Time
WHAT	Worker Housing Averaging Time
WHON	Worker Housing Obsolescence Normal
AMM	Attractiveness-For-Migration Multiplier
BDM	Business Decline Multiplier
DIDM	Declining Industry Demolition Multiplier
DIDP	Declining Industry Demolition Program
EDM	Enterprise-Decline Multiplier
LCHCD	Low Cost Housing Construction Desired
LCR	Labor Construction Ratio
LDM	Labor Departure Multiplier
LLF	Labor Layoff Fraction
LMM	Labor Mobility Multiplier
LR	Labor/Job Ratio
LTP	Labor Training Program
MAM	Manager-Arrival Multiplier

TABLE 6.1 *(Continued)*

MDM	Manager Departure Multiplier
NECD	New Enterprise Construction Desired
PHCD	Premium Housing Construction Desired
PHOM	Premium Housing Obsolescence Multiplier
SHDM	Slum Housing Demolition Multiplier
SHDP	Slum Housing Demolition Program
TRN	Tax Ratio Needed
UDM	Underemployed Departure Multiplier
UMM	Underemployed Mobility Multiplier
UTP	Underemployed Training Program
UM	Underemployed Working
WHCD	Worker-Housing Construction Desired
WHOM	Worker-Housing Obsolescence Multiplier

equation if DT is sufficiently small. This is a problem to which we shall return. The FORTRAN IV equivalent would be $U(L) = U(K) + (UA*(K-L))$. This is a return to the difference equation form. Forrester's actual level equation is

$$U.L = U.K + (DT)$$
$$(UA.KL + UB.KL + LTU.KL - UD.KL - UTL.KL),$$

which translates into FORTRAN as

$$U(L) = U(K) + ((DT)*(UA*(L-K)) + (UB*(L-K))$$
$$+ (LTU*(L-K)) - (UD*(L-K)) - (UTL*(L-K))),$$

where, in addition to the above definitions, $UB.JK$ is the number of underemployed "births" (really births less deaths) (men/year) rate in the period J to K; $LTU.JK$ is the labor to underemployed mobility rate (men/year) in period J to K; $UD.JK$ is the number of underemployed departures (men/year) rate in the period J to K; $UTL. JK$ is the underemployed to labor mobility rate (men/year) in period J to K. Forrester's first rate equation is

$$UA.KL = (U.K + L.K) (UAN) (AMMP.K), \text{ or, in FORTRAN IV,}$$

$$UA*(L-K) = (U(K) + L(K))*(UAN)*(AMMP(K)).$$

It states that the number of arrivals of underemployed into the urban area from given time K to L is equal to the product of the summation of the previous underemployed and labor populations at time K with a scaling parameter and a perceived attractiveness multiplier $(AMMP)$ calculated at the previous time in a separate function. The scaling parameter, normal unemployed arrivals (UAN), is construed as a fixed percentage of the labor and unemployed populations.

156

In order to determine the perceived attractiveness of an urban area for migration, two more functions must be solved. One must calculate the objective attractiveness of an area and then the relationship between objective and perceived attractiveness. Forrester's equation for the attractiveness of a given urban area for the underemployed is a product of six terms, each concerned with a different dimension of attractiveness. Most of these values are time specific and all are the result of the evaluation of other equations. Thus, the attractiveness of migration for the underemployed at time K is the function of the underemployed arrivals' mobility factor $(UAMM)$ at time K, the underemployed housing multiplier (UHM) at time K, the public expenditure multiplier (PEM) at time K, the underemployed job multiplier (UJM) at time K, the underemployed housing program multiplier $(UHPM)$ at time K, and an attractiveness-for-migration scaling factor which is a constant parameter used in calibrating the model. In DYNAMO II this relationship is stated $AMM.K = (UAMM.K) (UHM.K) (PEM.K) (UJM.K) (UHPM.K) (AMF)$.

Of course, there is a time lag between the objective and perceptive changes in the attractiveness to migration. A growing city with high employment will gain a reputation as a potential location for employment. However, it takes time for news of the subsequent flooding of the job market to reach an unemployed migrant. Thus, an immigrant may move to an urban area fully expecting to find employment on the basis of his information when none exists. Or, vice versa, jobs may exist but insufficient time has passed for potential employees to be made aware of them. Forrester calculates this type of time-lag phenomenon in the following equations:

$$AMMP.K = AMMP.J + (AAM.J - AMMP.J)/AMMPT,$$

or, in mathematical notation,

$$AMMP(t+r) = AMMP(t) + \frac{AMM(t) - AMMPT(t)}{AMMPT},$$

where AMMPT is the attractiveness-for-migration-multiplier-perceived time lag.

For Forrester, all of the above discussions and equations represent a partial explanation of the net propensity to migrate. The multipliers act in a manner similar to utility functions, for they do not produce unique solutions but degrees of preference among alternatives. Actually to determine the values of these multipliers, Forrester often uses table functions. These are look-up functions with a standard form as exemplified in DYNAMO II by the following equation: $UAMM.K = TABLE(UAMMT, UM, K, O, .15, 025)$. In FORTRAN IV, it has a similar form: $VAR = (TABLE(NO, X, XO, XF, DX))$, where VAR is the variable, NO is the number of the table to be entered, X is the value of the input to the table, and XO, XF, DX specify abscissa points corresponding to the stored ordinate values. The table functions are used in a linear interpolation between a set of ordinate points for every abscissa value given to it.

The simulation of Forrester's urban model is simultaneously simple and complex. As we have seen, it is relatively simple when beheld from an overview. Only nine major state variables and their interactive controls constitute his simulation (see Figure 6.1). However, if one specifies in detail the technical aspects of the model, it becomes quite intricate. There are 310 variables, as well as some 350 equations, in the original DYNAMO II transcription. In my version, which is written in FORTRAN IV, the simulation contains slightly over 650 equations. (Incidentally, this is a comment on the difference in power of the two languages.) A complete analysis of Forrester's program needs to be quite sophisticated and is beyond the scope of this paper. The reader may gain a partial insight into the level of complexity by considering the various interrelationships traced out for the premium housing sector of the city in Figure 6.2.

Forrester's Assumptions

Forrester's model is constrained by certain restrictive assumptions, each of which significantly affects the design and operation of the model. They are areal, systemic, distributive, attractiveness, environmental, and noncompetitive assumptions. The areal assumption states that the city is limited by its geographic boundaries. Within this area of central concern, economic activity and stagnation, construction and obsolescence, birth and death, as well as trade and migration, take place. The systemic assumption suggests that the urban area is an economic, social, ideological, and geographic system. It interacts within an environment with which it can communicate. Furthermore, cultural, economic, and educational interchange is possible among its component populations. The distribution assumption divides population enterprise and housing each into three categories on the basis of economic value. Although each of the categories is mutually exclu-

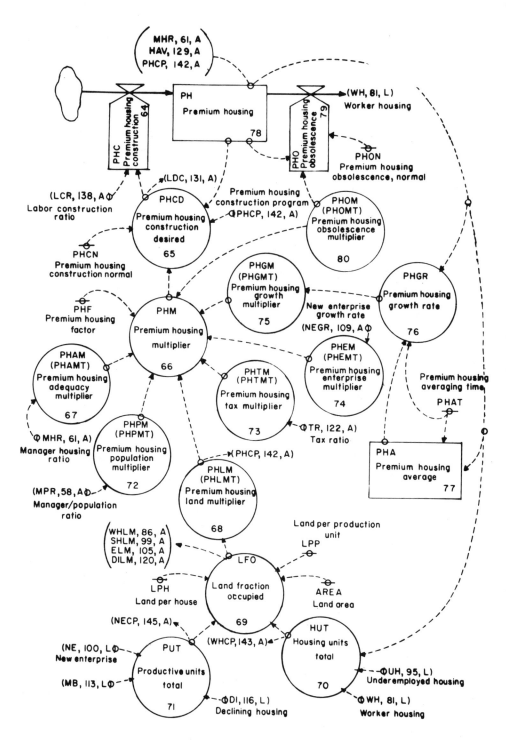

FIGURE 6.2. Forrester's flow chart of his premium housing sector (source: Forrester 1969: Figure A30, by permission of the M.I.T. Press).

sive, there is mobility among the classes. For example, members of the underemployed may become part of the labor force. The attractiveness assumption is somewhat reminiscent of the moth-and-light-bulb relationship. It determines the direction and the flow of goods and services within the urban core and between the city and its environment. If the urban area is more attractive to labor than the environment, one can expect labor to be drawn to the city from the country in a manner proportional to the attraction.

The environmental assumption is important for growth, for it states that the environment is an infinite resource base. It is capable of supplying people and goods to the city as long as the urban area is more attractive. This assumption corresponds to the opinion of many scholars that urban areas are demographic and economic sinks. The human and real costs are too great to be borne solely internally. The environmental assumption also includes the converse: the countryside can absorb people and goods as they leave the urban area. Thus for Forrester the environment is limitless. Finally, there is an assumption of noncompetition. Forrester's city exists in truly splendid isolation. There are no cities within the environment with which Forrester's city has to compete for limited resources.

In short, Forrester's city is not meant to be real. At best, these assumptions span a simplified city. It is an ideal city in the same sense that Plato's Republic is an ideal state. As in the case of Plato, the utility of the model is related not only to its congruence with reality, but also to the clarity and appropriateness of the simplification that is created by the assumptions.

Forrester's Conclusions

Forrester's conclusions concerning the nature of urban dynamics may be quickly summarized: the life cycle of the modern urban area is one of boom growth and gradual decline (Figure 6.3). Each period has its own set of idiosyncratic relationships among the components. During the growth phase, economic activity has a high intensity, and such concomitant indicators as employment per unit of productive land are high. Or one many find overcrowding and abandoned housing in the same neighborhood at the same time during the decline phase.

Urban megalopolises are complex systems, and complex systems are counterintuitive. They provide indicators for action, but if followed,

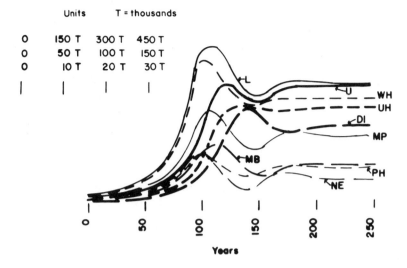

FIGURE 6.3. The life cycle of the modern urban area is one of boom growth and gradual decline (source: Forrester 1969: Figure 3.1a, by permission of the M.I.T. Press).

the results are at best ineffective and more often adverse. The reason is that cause and effect are not closely related in either time or space. Furthermore, numerous intervening variables can mask the actual chain of events. Remedies to cure the symptoms of urban blight which ignore the underlying causes often create greater problems than the ones with which the urban physician began. Forrester believes one problem builds upon the next and a destructive spiral becomes established. Attempts to create corrective programs are far fewer than expected, for rather than supplementing existing systems, they tend to replace corresponding internal processes.

For Forrester, time and human mistakes have a chance to wreak havoc. The urban process is characterized as having (a) a high failure rate; (b) a high probability for stagnation and decline for most cities most of the time; (c) very short pulselike periods of boom growth; and (d) some potential but a low probability for evolution.

Incidentally, this viewpoint is quite different from that held by most archaeologists, who have a general tendency to see cities as centers of innovation, cultural change, and other symbols of success. That the end product of the urban revolution in most places most of the time is failure does not sit well with the materialist nature of archaeologists. We expect most cultural changes to create improvement as exempli-

161

fied by Wittfogel's irrigation hypothesis or Childe's agricultural revolution.

For complex systems such as cities, Forrester believes that the ultimate equilibrium and gradual decline values are independent of the starting point. By this he means they are independent of the initial values of the variable.[2] Among the three types of variables—system rates, system levels or states, and variable constants—he ranks the first as most important and the last as least important. In addition, he has made the rates the most difficult variables to change. Thus, the system essentially is insensitive. This lack of sensitivity even extends to policy changes.[3] Once change does take place, it may be only short-term, and the system rapidly returns to equilibrium. However, sometimes these short-term changes are opposite in direction from the desired or designed long-term effect. These "it's going to get worse before it will get better" sequences make it particularly difficult for a leader trying to revive a stagnant city.

Commenting on these aspects of Forrester's model, Boulding (1972) notes that the results of these "under the counter-intuitive assumptions" are dismal, indeed—similar to Malthus's original work. Forrester's urban areas have poverty which cannot be relieved in the short run if it is to be relieved in the long run. If the poor are supported in a way that encourages propagation, the result is not to decrease but to increase poverty. First stagnation and then abandonment ultimately bring the city to its knees.

In short, Forrester's cities are insensitive behemoths, sleeping Brontosauri whose general tendencies are to move slowly toward a condition of increasingly poor performance and eventual extinction. The inevitable process can only be reversed by stimulation of a very few ganglia or influence points in the head or tail. The death of one creates the conditions for the existence of another.

The Rationale for the Application of Forrester's Model to Early Cities

Any simulation requires the suspension of disbelief; the assumptions always oversimplify and the relationship to reality is never exact. To make an analogy between modern cities and prehistoric urban areas, one must ignore local variation and paint with a very broad brush indeed. One may always find differences among cities in different areas and at different times. It is only in the most basic characteristics of urbanism that one finds universals, and these, of course, have priority for study.

The analogy can be justified five ways. In December 1977, Sabloff and I discussed the possibility of applying Forrester's simulations to prehistoric situations. It appealed because here was a well-known, reasonably sophisticated, and truly dynamic as well as potentially interactive simulation. The various subsystems and components enter and leave the general system depending upon thresholds being surpassed or changed according to logical conditions being fulfilled. It further appealed since, as we have noted, the problems of urban growth and decay have long been central to the study of archaeology. I was aware that Hosler, Sabloff, and Runge (1977) had already combined a model of the Classic Maya collapse with part of Forrester's methodology to create a simulation. Therefore, in some sense this simulation was an extension of ongoing work.

The second justification rests with the simplicity of Forrester's model. The central nine levels correspond in many ways better to earlier cities than to the present megalopolises. Many phenomena which exist in modern metropolitan areas cannot be assimilated by Forrester's model. For example, the effects of image saturation, political manipulation, financial red-lining, or stock market speculation cannot be monitored.

Third, the reality of a functionally infinite environment and non-competitive city is closer to early cities than today's crowded urban landscape. Today there is competition not only for such basic resources as labor and power, but for such ephemeral resources as style and tourist attractions. Early cities, with more primitive transportation and smaller populations, simply had less competition for a greater amount of resources.

Fourth, the essential nature of cities has not changed that much with respect to function or structure. Functionally, cities have been and continue to be aggregates of population providing markets and the redistribution of goods, technological development and production, as well as communication networks and equipment. Structurally, cities have been the traditional warehouses for administrative hierarchies and the military power by which the structure is enforced.

Forrester's model is unique in that it claims to be generic. The first sentence of *Urban Dynamics* is, "This book is about the growth processes of urban areas" (Forrester 1969:1). The implicit generality of the model indicated by the title and first sentence is made explicit throughout the book with confidence. For example,

> When first modeling a social system it is usually best to model the general class of system rather than a specific system. Here, this means a model to represent the central processes common to all urban areas rather than to represent those of a specific area. (Forrester 1969:14)
>
> Urban growth and stagnation do not appear to require changes in the world environment as a cause. The urban problem is not limited to any single country, society or historical era. (Forrester 1969:15)
>
> When structure is properly represented, parameter values are of secondary importance. Parameter values must not be crucial because cities have much the same character and life cycle regardless of the era and the society within which they exist. Similar patterns emerge in cities having quite different economic constraints and social traditions. (Forrester 1969:114)

One major class of early urban areas is an exception, that is, not similar functionally or structurally to the modern city. This is the ceremonial center, which we will consider briefly later.

Finally, given even a loose correspondence between the model and reality, the simulation will be heuristically useful if we learn new ideas and create new research problems.

The Chronological Saga of a Simulation and Some Methodological Insights

Forrester published his *Urban Dynamics* model and simulation in 1969; the following year, I became aware of the model. I was a graduate student at the University of Arizona, and one of the class projects for a systems engineering graduate seminar was to translate Forrester's original DYNAMO II source program into FORTRAN IV for a CDC 6400 computer. After my initial exposure to the model under the tutelage of D. Thompson, now of Electronic Data Systems, my interest lapsed into a passive curiosity. I read occasional publications as they appeared until Sabloff rekindled my interest in December 1977.

In January 1978, I began rewriting the program for the CDC Cyber 173 system, modifying the variables and logic to make it more appropriate for early cities. By June 1, I had all the bugs out of the program, had added my own graphics routines, and had made the system partially interactive in a time-sharing sense.

164

By early August I had completed some 50 simulation runs. This may not seem a significant landmark if the reader is new to simulation studies. However, I had been forced by reams of output to move out of my office, out of my study, and into my attic in order to house the results. There were slightly over 8,000 pages of completed output and some 50 graphs. This does not include an equal number of materials from irrelevant or error-filled runs. By late August, with 75 runs completed, I was writing this chapter.

Out of this morass of paper and after eight months of work, I gained several useful methodological insights. First, develop and program your own model rather than modifying someone else's, for modification is more difficult than it appears on the surface. Other simulators' documentation is never sufficient, and to "get into their minds" is difficult, if not impossible. Second, if possible, do your own programming, for minor changes in style, logic, and equations may make significant differences in the results. Third, since simulations are addictive, do not enter into them lightly, for they require larger expenditures of time, finances, and space than you are probably willing to commit initially.

Data

One's quantitative results are clearly dependent upon the interpretation of the qualitative evidence. There is a wider latitude in acceptable data if, as in our case, one's interests are in the qualitative rather than the quantitative results. In either case, to quote an old computer adage, "garbage in, garbage out." So it is appropriate to ask what kinds of data were input and what quality control has been exercised. My strategy was a curious one. I began testing my version of Forrester's simulation with his data. I did not accept my program until I produced his results with his data and my program. The data were slowly modified to determine operational limits. Only then did I presume to use appropriate prehistoric data files; I chose some data from Rome and from Mesoamerican ceremonial centers which I thought contrasted the range of prehistoric data. As an example of the data used, I have included in Table 6.2 some of the estimates from Rome. These estimates are based upon the considerable literature of classical economics. It should be noted that they are primarily based upon secondary sources and archaeological reports rather than on the original Latin documents.

TABLE 6.2
EXEMPLARY INITIAL ROMAN DATA FROM THE PERIOD OF AUGUSTUS

Variable and Variable Value	Comments	Reference
Population = 650,000		(Chandler and Fox 1974:81)
Area = 3,244.7 acres	This is the area within the Aurilean wall.	(Chandler and Fox 1974:81)
Labor = 78,000 slaves and 156,000 free men = a total of 234,000		(A. M. H. Jones 1974:244)
Labor = 143,000 slaves	This is using the Galen coefficient.	(R. D. Jones 1974:273)
Labor = 286,000 slaves and free males		(R. D. Jones 1974:273)
Labor = 260,000 slaves	At a coefficient of 40%	(R. D. Jones 1974:273)
Labor = 520,000 slaves	At a coefficient of 80%	(Frank 1962:330)
Labor	One should note all of these values to be changed if one assumes slave families.	
Labor	There is a free-to-slave ratio of approximately 1:8.	(A. M. H. Jones 1974:243)
Labor	Slaves are most often employed in small groups of 1 to 2.	(A. M. H. Jones 1974:244)
Land per housing unit = 0.3 acres	Decurions' house needs 1,500 roofing tiles by law. Roofing tiles are approximately 1 foot square.	
Land per housing unit = .01 acres	The house at Caranis is 60 square meters derived from the plans. However, the house is actually on more than 1 floor.	(Rostovzeff 1957:287)
Land per housing unit = 1,760 square feet	From plans of a small house	(Rostovrzeff 1957:312)
Land per housing unit = 5,600 square feet	From plans of a medium size house	(Rostovrzeff 1957:315)
Land per housing unit = 8,547 square feet	From plans of a large urban home	(Rostovrzeff 1957:403)
Land per housing unit = 3,300 square feet		(Rostovrzeff 1957:422)

166

Land per productive unit = 9.4 acres	Brutus gave 15 iugera of land to 100,000 loyal soldiers (15 iugera = 9.4 acres)	(Frank 1962:354)
Population housing density	Today one thinks, on the basis of our own society, of population housing density as inversely proportional to wealth, but for Roman society, if one counted servants and slaves, it was directly proportional. Thus, one should note that in societies with well-developed labor-intensive service industries, the population housing density is the opposite of what is expected.	(Frank 1962:354)
Premium housing population density = 3 and hundreds of slaves		(Rostovzeff 1957:565)
Premium housing population density = 3 and 18 slaves		
Premium housing population density = 3 and 10 slaves		(Tucker 1928:201)
Worker housing population density = 5 and 10 slaves		(Tucker 1928:201)
Worker housing population density = 5 and 2 slaves		(Tucker 1928:201)
Under- and unemployed housing population density	10–12 examples of apartment living are known.	
Family size		
Managerial professional family size = 3	Many managerial families are becoming extinct.	(Tucker 1928:303)
Labor family size = 6		
Under- and unemployed family size = 8	For this estimate and the one above, no data exist, but one knows elementary systems existed	

167

TABLE 6.2 (Continued)

Managerial professional family = 3 Labor family size = 4 Under- and unemployed family size = 4	to fund and subsidize children for the purpose of encouraging an increase in birth rates.	(R. D. Jones 1974:317–18)
Labor distribution in productive industries Mature business managers = 2 or 3 Declining industry managers = 1 or 2	The three values noted here are based on the suggestion that family size is low in all classes.	(Balsdon 1963:195)
	In later centuries we know that management decreased due to the high liabilities put upon managerial failure, as well as general economic distrust. These liabilities included corporal punishment.	
Mature business labor = scores to hundreds of workers	In bakery	(Rostovrzeff 1957:485)
Mature business labor = 41	Zubrow's count of the number of workers on funeral monument of M. Vergilus Eurysaces	(Rostovrzeff 1957:32)
Mature business labor = 13	Cato's count for an ideal olive plantation	(R. D. Jones 1974:328)
Premium housing assessed valuation = HS* 100,000	Based upon HS 20,000 per column	(R. D. Jones 1974:125)
Premium housing assessed valuation = HS 100,000	Based upon the property qualifications of a decurion	(R. D. Jones 1974:147)
Worker housing assessed valuation = HS 1,500	This is based on 1,500 tiles per decurion's home and the known cost of HS per 1 tile	(R. D. Jones 1974:125)
Under- and unemployed housing assessed valuation = HS 567	This is based upon plans and tile prices	(Rostovrzeff 1957:288)

168

Industrial assessed valuations	These figures are based upon known Italian and African building and construction costs R. D. Jones has compiled; the prices of 859 Italian items and 438 African items.	(R. D. Jones 1974:90–114, 157–224)
New and appraised assessed valuation in Africa = HS 85,000	An average figure	See above
New and appraised assessed valuation (Italian) = HS 103,163	Mean data	See above
Mature business assessed valuation = (African) HS 56,800	Mean data	See above
Declining industry assessed valuation (African) = HS 84,312	Mean data	See above
Mean Italian building construction, road construction, and misc. construction costs = HS 213,712	Mean data	See above

*HS = housing in sesterces

169

Results

Once I had developed a simulation and found that data, I began a series of tests to answer a group of questions. We know that early cities differ in scale from modern megalopolises. I wanted to analyze how and if early cities also differ in form and structure. What are the sensitive parameters that caused urban change and what parameters are insensitive and could be safely manipulated by early political leaders? In addition, I found myself formulating two sets of more specific questions while running the simulation under changing conditions.

The first group of questions corresponds to the various causes suggested for the weakening of Rome. For example, it has been claimed that Rome fell partially as a result of insufficient capital-intensive industry. It was clear that although industry with large capital and large-scale labor could have been created, it never was. The labor supply was so cheap (there being no cheaper labor than slaves) that capital-intensive industry was never allowed to develop. When the supply of cheap labor was cut off, capital-intensive industry could not develop under conditions of contemporary competition. This significantly impaired the economy. Similar arguments have been made that increasing taxation was the underlying cause for the weakening of the Roman megalopolis. Conversely, the claim has also been made that the taxation rate could not be increased sufficiently to make up for the government expenditures.

The above explanations based on the insufficiency of capital or taxation may be contrasted to explanations of surplus. We are all familiar with the image of the Roman circus, where the emperor rules by entertaining and feeding the masses. Given surplus production and slavery, there was little demand for increased levels of employment or consumption. When conquest slowed, not only was there no alternative economic foundation, but also Rome's production and trade position had been weakened competitively.

In order to examine these problems, I first computed a Roman baseline using my FORTRAN version of Forrester's model (Figure 6.4; also see Table 6.3). This baseline simulation run had the variables set to the best estimates that I was able to obtain from the literature. It and all of the other Roman simulations begin at the time of Augustus, which I arbitrarily set at A.D. 0. The Augustan period is usually dated at 30 B.C. to A.D. 14. This figure shows each of the state variables plotted through time for ease of differentiation. It is the baseline in that it is

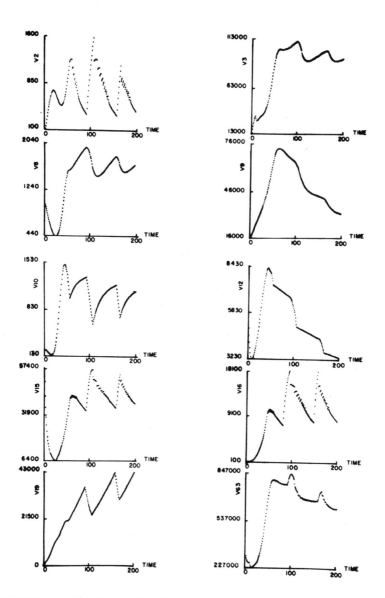

FIGURE 6.4. The Roman Baseline; nine levels and population.

TABLE 6.3
VALUES FOR FIGURES 6.4–6.13

v2 = declining industry	v3 = labor
v8 = mature business	v9 = managers
v10 = new enterprise	v12 = premium housing
v15 = unemployed	v16 = unemployed housing
v19 = worker housing	v63 = population

the product of applying Forrester's model to the best literary estimates of Rome's economic conditions at the time of Augustus. The figure shows what happens to these nine variables over the next two centuries.

To examine the effect of increased slavery, I began systematically to increase the labor sector of the model. In other words, the initial value of labor was changed without altering any other variables. In Figure 6.5, labor has been increased to twice the size of the labor force of the Roman base. And it no longer corresponds to the best estimates. In Figure 6.6, it has been increased twice more. Similarly, in later runs I systematically increased taxation, worker housing, and under- and unemployment.

Let us compare the results. Run 19 (Figure 6.4) is the Roman base. From it one may draw the first heuristically useful conclusion. An early city appears to have more potential for oscillation than modern cities. Compare Figure 6.3 to Figure 6.4. Disregarding the quantitative differences, which could be attributed to scale, there are considerable qualitative differences, which are shown by the forms of the curves. There is a multiple-cycle structure, approximately three cycles in 200 years. This is particularly obvious for six of the nine state variables—declining industry, mature business, new enterprise, underemployment, underemployed housing, and worker housing. It is less marked but still noticeable in labor and total population. Even where this business cycle is not apparent, as in the upper-class state variables of managerial population and premium housing, one may see its effect as slight bulges. In this particular case, it is clear that labor and population follow each other quite closely.

What kinds of heuristic conclusions may be reached by systematically changing the values of the state variables as mentioned above? I will pass over numerous intermediary cases and report only the more significant results. If one compares Figure 6.5 to Figure 6.4, that is, a simulation in which the labor force has been doubled to the original Roman base, one sees minor quantitative changes and no qualitative

172

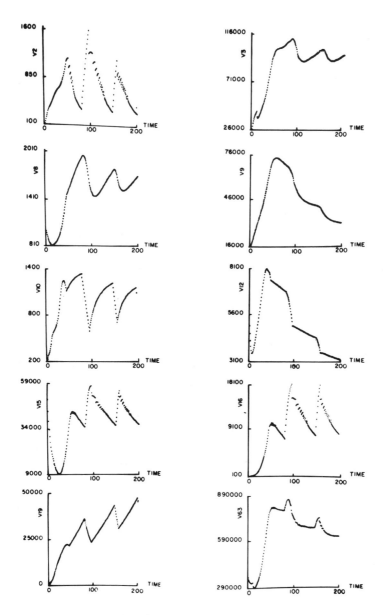

FIGURE 6.5. The results of increasing labor 100 percent; nine levels and population.

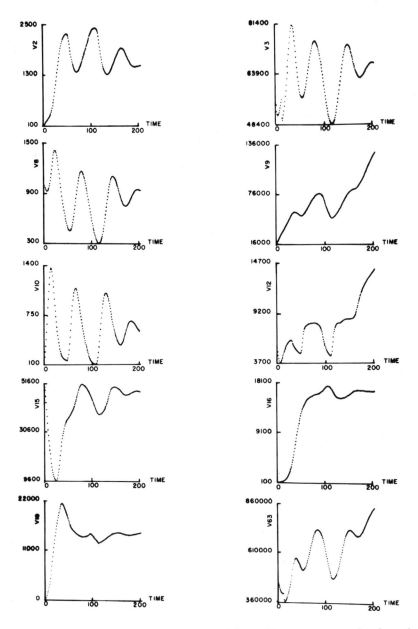

FIGURE 6.6 The results of increasing labor 200 percent; nine levels and population.

changes in terms of the shape of the curves. If, however, we double the labor force again so that we now have four times the original labor force, there are major changes in both the quantitative and qualitative aspects of the city (Figure 6.6). Structural changes occur in labor, managers, premium housing, workers' housing, and population, indicated by fundamental changes in the shape of the curves.

The size of the multicyclical structure increases for new and mature production while it decreases for declining production. Underemployment falls and then rises; managers and population increase with a dampened cycle while labor has a new, strong, multicycle oscillation. Worker and underemployed housing have boom growth and reach an equilibrium of sorts, but premium housing oscillates unevenly and finally follows the managerial population into a continuous growth phase.

Clearly, there is a threshold in the labor parameter. Until it is passed, no real change in Roman society is reached. Once it is passed, however, the society is drastically and irreversibly moved along a different path of development.

Rome as portrayed in the Roman baseline was a society developed through the labor of the poor for the benefit of the wealthy. It had a high demand upon extremely limited housing facilities, particularly in the middle and lower classes. What happens if we relieve this demand and decrease the cost of worker housing? Figure 6.7 shows the effects of relieving worker housing by increasing it 100 times. As one can see, even this huge construction project creates no change in the life path of the Roman economy.

Figure 6.8 shows increased taxation by 100 percent. There are minor quantitative changes and very slight qualitative changes in terms of the general structure of all ten variables. In the production and housing sectors, the amount of time per cycle generally increases. In the population sector, the cycles tend to oscillate around a more constant value. But as in the case of labor, if we increase taxation another 100 percent (Figure 6.9), the structure of all parts of the society again is changed irreversibly. One of the most notable changes is the new lack of a multiple-cycle structure in any of the variables. The numerous and multiple oscillations, which often reach three or four complete cycles in many of the state variables, are now reduced to a single cycle, or sometimes even less. Rapid boom growth is seen in all the variables, and for premium housing, as well as managerial and total population,

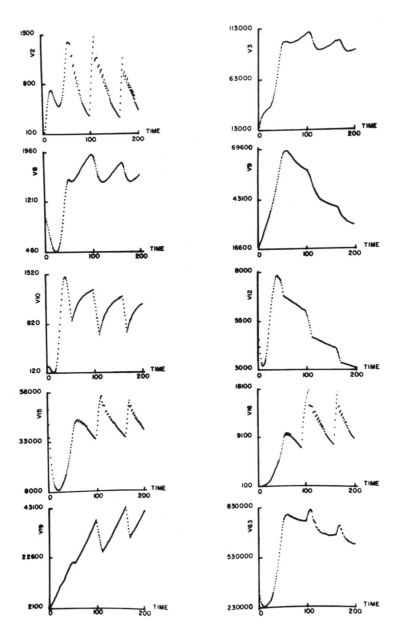

FIGURE 6.7. The results of increasing worker housing by 100 times; nine levels and population.

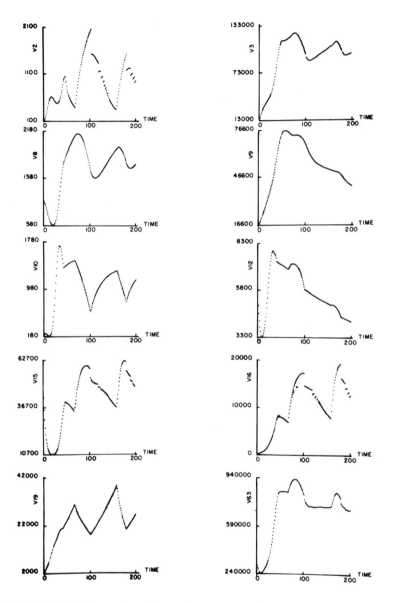

FIGURE 6.8. The results of increasing taxation 100 percent; nine levels and population.

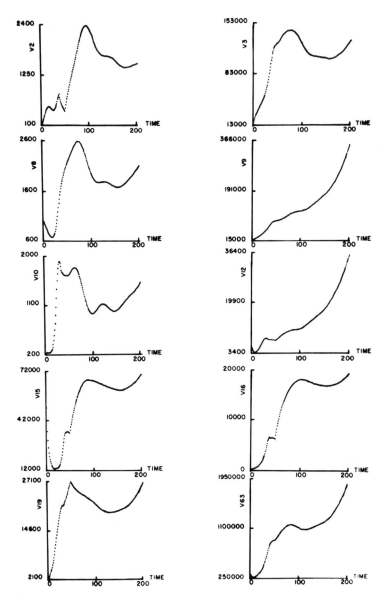

FIGURE 6.9. The results of increasing taxation 200 percent; nine levels and population.

this growth is essentially continuous. Discontinuity is most noticeable during the growth phases, while long term equilibria do not seem to be capable of being maintained in all the variables.

Figure 6.10 shows what happens to the nine state variables and the total population if underemployment is increased by 100 percent. Major quantitative changes occur as do changes in the structure and form of the curves.

But a second 100 percent increase (four times the baseline) does not bring significant further change to the curves (Figure 6.11). These increases, compared to the baseline, may be characterized as increasing the size of the oscillation in the multiple cycles of the productive sector. The demographic and housing sectors show primarily a mono-cycle structure which sometimes reaches equilibrium values. The major exceptions are the elite variables of managerial population and premium housing, where boom growth replaces the equilibrium section.

If we compare the four parameters above that have been systematically changed, it is clear that underemployment is the most influential. It creates massive structural change most rapidly (that is, change in the shape of the functions). When the initial values are increased between 0 and 100 percent, only underemployment undergoes significant change. Labor and taxation need to pass a much higher threshold, while worker housing seems to be functionally irrelevant.

A more detailed analysis of these simulation runs could provide a large number of interesting as well as useful conclusions. For example, in all these runs, the increase in taxes does not change labor or under-employment nearly as much as it changes the shape of the managerial class. An increase in taxes either creates the conditions for or is created by the movement of a large proportion of the total population into the managerial class. This is not a surprising conclusion. Today we are used to thinking of the managerial population running from or even changing occupations because of taxation. Yet if one looks in developmental terms, the increasing bureaucratization and expansion of the government sector has been made possible by the increase in taxation. In the United States today one out of seven people in the labor force is employed by the government. Government employees are paid by average taxes of over 35 percent. In Roman society, the entire managerial professional population in the governmental and private sector was far less than 10 percent of the total population, while taxation levels were between 5 and 10 percent.

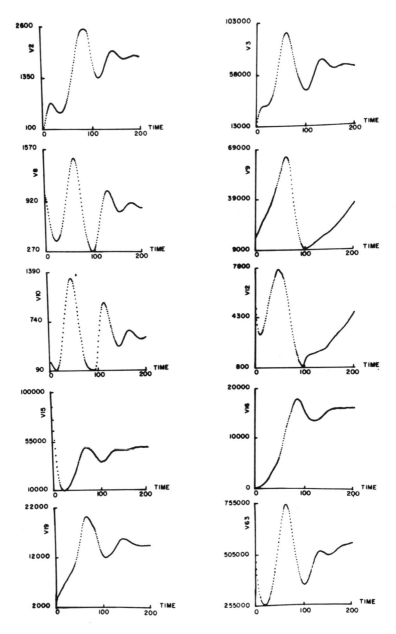

FIGURE 6.10. The results of increasing under- and unemployed 100 percent; nine levels and population.

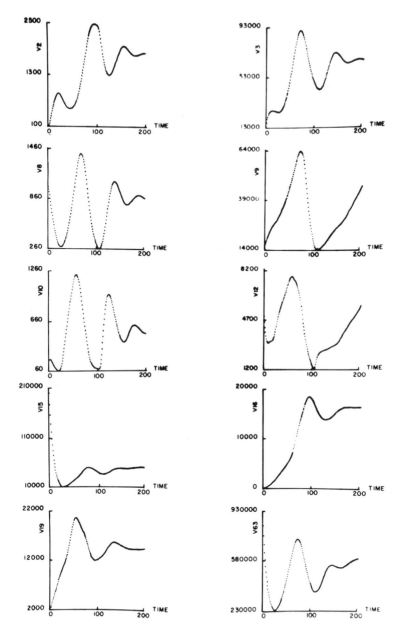

FIGURE 6.11. The results of increasing under- and unemployed 200 percent; nine levels and population.

One may look carefully at the temporal relationships among the various parameters. For example, the systematic increase in underemployment creates larger, slower, and less discontinuous oscillations. Thus, although underemployment creates massive change, it is essentially comprehensible. Since it has a reasonably high degree of continuity, one may expect trends from the past to continue through the present into the future.

Let me turn briefly to that anomalous settlement phenomenon, the Mesoamerican ceremonial center. Culbert (1973), Sabloff (1973), and others have been interested in the fall of the Maya and the collapse of the ceremonial center. Erasmus (1965), Rathje (1971), and Freidel (1979) have examined the construction of the centers. Few have considered the issue, How did the ceremonial center operate normally after construction but prior to destruction? Ceremonial centers contrast with early cities particularly in that they lack large residential areas, residential labor forces, and "urban-style" production and marketing. They are similar as centers of administrative, political, and financial power. In particular, I want to focus on the problems of operational normalcy for a ceremonial center.

Figure 6.12 is exemplary of several simulations of ceremonial centers after construction. Data were obtained from secondary sources, and initial parameters, rates, and levels were adjusted to conform to the above characteristics.

Several differences between the Roman and Mayan cases are immediately apparent. At best, Mayan ceremonial centers appear to be one-cycle structures. In other words, equilibrium is reached very rapidly after a single increase and/or decrease in one of the parameters. This is clearly in contrast to the Roman multiple-cycle structure. Equilibria are sometimes reached in the Roman case as well but may take considerably longer (see Figure 6.13). In the ceremonial center all changes occur initially and rapidly. After the first forty years, equilibrium is reached, and subsequently only minor changes occur. Moreover, this life cycle is not Forrester's boom growth and gradual decline of the entire economic production sector complemented by the increase in the managerial classes. Rather, there is rapid growth and rapid decline or sometimes just a decrease in these state variables.

Finally, there is a labor vacuum which is very rapidly filled. It is difficult to keep labor out of a center of power, wealth, and administrative organization. No matter how I changed the parameters, I was

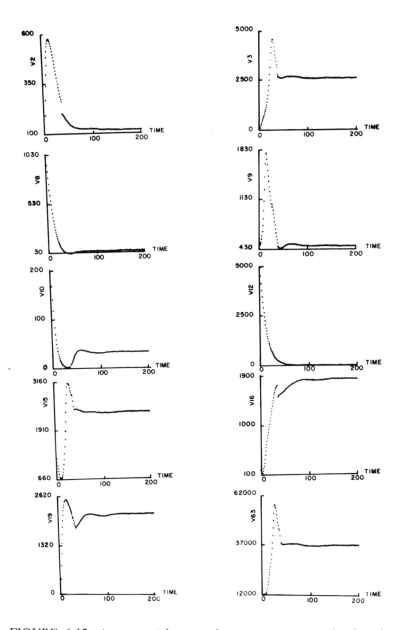

FIGURE 6.12. A ceremonial center after construction; nine levels and population.

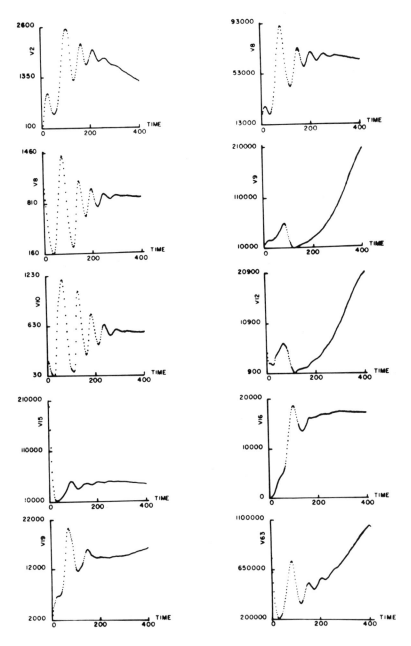

FIGURE 6.13. Results of increasing unemployment 200 percent and increasing time to 400 years; Roman data, nine levels and population.

unable to determine a set of variables which would allow for the continuous existence of a ceremonial center without a labor influx. Either the Mayan and other ceremonial centers had mechanisms for keeping labor out, or we have been unable to find the material indicators of large labor forces living and operating within the ceremonial centers.[4] What are the mechanisms to exclude labor? These would include ideological sanctions, laws, and eventually military or police force. But it should be noted that these same factors have been remarkably unsuccessful in modern times.

The most recent example of a new ceremonial city is Brazilia. It corresponds to the ancient centers in the administrative, financial, and monumental functions. As a national capital, it has limited residential and small industrial and trade components. In this case, labor entered the vacuum rapidly as the demand for services provided employment opportunities. The perceived higher standards of living caused large-scale rural migration into the town creating the now famous barrios of Brazilia. The squatting upon land even took on the character of a quasi-military operation. On the appointed day, thousands of people rushed into the barrio and on arriving immediately put up shelters as fast as possible while lookouts and guards kept out land owners and police. Only a major political event could move the population out.

Given the growth of rural as well as ceremonial center population, what prevented rural-to-urban migration and the rise of shanty towns throughout the Maya world? To paraphrase the old song, once people have seen Paris, it is hard to keep them in the country.

The Issue of Stability

As previously noted, Forrester believes that all cities as complex systems have boom growth followed by gradual decline and long-term stability in which equilibria are maintained. This trend is irrespective of the initial parameter values. As we have seen, our data from early cities do not confirm this position. A close examination shows that changing the initial parameters does affect the shape of the curves for state variables. Furthermore, the state variables rarely reach equilibrium. If we define equilibrium generously, only one out of every ten variables plotted ever reached anything like equilibrium during the 200-year Roman simulations. This corresponds to the data presented in the figures, with equilibria being reached for worker and underemployed housing twice and for labor and underemployed population once. As we increase the length of time the simulation operates, the stability issue becomes more complex. More variables, though never all or even a significant majority of the total, reach equilibrium (Figure 6.13). Once reached, furthermore, these equilibria may last several decades or centuries and then frequently break down. We can index the degree of instability of the various simulations by grouping them into three sets on the basis of increasing amounts of oscillation. They are Figure 6.9; Figures 6.4–6.7; and Figures 6.8, 6.10, and 6.11.

We speak of a system being asymptotically stable when $\lim x(t) - \bar{x} = 0$ as $t \longrightarrow \infty$ where $x(t)$ is the state vector, and $\bar{x}$ is the equilibrium position of the system variables. System stability means that the rate of change of all system components must reach 0 when equilibrium is reached and must persist without further change. Most systems are designed to react to change in two ways. For transient changes, the system reacts with variants of its internal components and then returns to its stable form. For permanent changes, the system may have to reorganize its basic structure, components, and relationships in order to achieve a new stable form.

What are some of the factors that influence the stability or instability of systems? Makridakis and Faucheux in "Stability Properties of General Systems" (1973) show that

(1) the probability of a system being stable is inversely related to the number of elements and the size of the system;

(2) the larger the system size and the more important the elements which are internally changed, the smaller the probability that the resulting system will be stable;

(3) the larger the system size and the smaller its stability, the smaller the probability that when expanded the resulting system will be stable;

(4) the probability that a system will decompose into stable subsystems is greater if the original system is stable; and,

(5) the probability that a system will decompose into stable subsystems is no greater if the original system is expanding.

I performed a series of tests in order to determine whether the instability might be an artifact of the methodology rather than an aspect of the structure of the model. One might expect with difference

186

equations that the instability might be the result of the time unit used to solve the equations. Like Forrester, I used a time unit of 1 year for the value of *DT*. All the figures in this paper use that value. However, at the suggestion of the Advanced Seminar's mathematician, Cooke, I varied *DT* for each run from .25 to 5. It made no significant difference in the degree of stability. Second, I asked if the lack of stability could be a result of the length of time the simulation was run. Perhaps equilibria and resulting stability would have been revealed in the next 100 years. Although the data presented only represent two centuries, we ran tests at 300-, 400-, 500-, and 1,000-year time spans. Increasing the length of simulated time increases the number of variables reaching equilibrium for a period of time without any major patterns of stability appearing.

How does one interpret the difference in results regarding stability between Forrester's tests and my own? I do not question the validity of his results. Rather, it seems to me that his results are based upon the model's operating within a wide but limited set of parameters which makes up the modern urban experience. Early cities and ceremonial centers may operate with parameters beyond these limitations, and thus instability is created.

CONCLUSIONS

It has been stated in this chapter that simulation requires the suspension of disbelief in order to create new problems and new views of old problems. Prior to closing, it is appropriate to take stock. If simulation is to be a heuristic device, what new insights have been gained? For me, they can be briefly summarized even though they are contradictory and, I know, incomplete.

First, I found Forrester's concept of most cities as insensitive, counterintuitive failures an intriguing contrast to most archaeological theory. Second, there are clear indications from this study that early cities are far more sensitive to change than are Forrester's modern cities. Third, the simulations showed the multicyclical nature of the early city in many of its components and under a multitude of conditions; not only was there a business cycle, but a housing, a labor, and numerous other cycles. Fourth, a remarkable degree of discontinuity could occur in certain variables in early cities, making predictability extremely difficult. Fifth, there is no correspondence between, on the one hand, the length of time needed for the early city to reach equilibrium and, on the other, that needed for either Forrester's modern city or the Mayan ceremonial center. Sixth, there appear to be large labor vacuums in ceremonial centers immediately after their construction. The simulations indicate that labor abhors a vacuum, and thus these locations rapidly fill with migrant laborers. Seventh, changes in the structure of the early city are most radical when thresholds in taxation and labor are surpassed.

Simulations are heuristic devices even though they are a step removed from reality. They allow us to explore problems too complex for usual analysis, and the interpretation of their results often provides not only new insights but also new ideas and new questions about the nature of the phenomena being simulated. For example, what structural causes are responsible for the development of urban areas? These causes generate not only the rapidly changing unicyclical ceremonial centers, but also the multicyclical early city and the boom growth and gradual decline of modern cities. Preliminary indications suggest that the answer lies in the areas of labor and taxation.

Many simulators try to test causation and confirm reality. In this simulation we have done neither. Over 200 years ago Hume showed that the truths of reason are true by definition, but that the truths of the world we live in are based upon experience rather than logic. The recombination of what Hume split asunder is an important task.

If we cannot ask "why" in the real world of experience, perhaps we can get answers in the artificial world of simulation.

NOTES

1. Ironically, the urban simulation tradition originally developed out of interests in the processes that destroy urban areas. Beginning with war games (Goldhamer and Speier 1957) and progressing to the practice of nuclear holocaust (Kahn 1965), the techniques were extended to more peaceful studies. International diplomacy was tried by INTERNATION (Guetzkow 1959), national economies by the WHARTON and NATIONAL models, and urban studies represented by the New York Metropolitan Regional Study (Berman, Hoover, and Chinitz 1961).

2. He may be wrong for early cities.

3. Policy change is a change of the rules that describe how information is used to determine variable or parameter action.

4. According to some experts, there is recent evidence for ceremonial centers' having much larger residential and local labor forces than previously thought (P. Harrison and J. Sabloff, personal communication).

7

Dynamic Systems and Epochal Change

RICHARD H. DAY

University of Southern California[1]

There may have been a time when archaeologists were primarily concerned with discovering and describing fossils and artifacts. If so, that time has surely passed, for data have by now been assembled that form the basis of bold and sweeping hypotheses concerning human evolution, culture change, and economic adaptation.[2] Inevitably, theory must now flourish, for theory flourishes best when significant collections of fact present themselves for explanation and interpretation. At this point, it is natural that mathematical models be developed to illuminate archaeological facts and hypotheses. This is not because mathematics can ever replace traditional investigative techniques or broader means of description and analysis: it cannot. But mathematics does provide a language of precision, analytical convenience, and symbolic simplification for delineating cause and effect and for demarcating those zones of knowledge about which scholars can agree and those still subject to doubt and controversy.

As an economist who has only an amateur acquaintance with (and naive enthusiasm for) the discipline of archaeology, it cannot be my task either to survey the current state of mathematical archaeology or to project its future direction. I propose instead to survey some concepts that have proven useful in economics and dynamical systems

189

theory and which may be used to develop insights into the emergence, duration, and disappearance of distinct phases or epochs in socioeconomic evolution.

My remarks are divided into two parts. In the first part, several models of specific prehistoric or historic settings are presented. These examples involve (a) the switchover from hunting-gathering to agriculture; (b) instabilities in the transition from feudalism to capitalism; (c) the effects of civilization on a society whose balance is maintained by Malthusian mechanisms; and (d) overlapping waves of technology and the demise of economic classes defined by obsolete modes of production. Illustrated in these case studies are (a) state-determined dynamic models; (b) model solutions and simulations; and (c) comparative dynamic analysis. The four cases share a common theme: one phase is replaced by another through the impact of endogenous forces having more or less catastrophic dimension.

The second part of the paper outlines a general framework, for which the preceding examples are special cases. This framework incorporates adapative behavior and disequilibrium mechanisms into a theory of "adapting economic systems." These systems appear to make possible the rigorous study of endogenously generated switches in socioeconomic regimes. They may also help in understanding the basis for the evolution of changes in system structure, changes that are created to cope with problems of instability and internal inconsistencies that arise from time to time in the course of economic development and cultural evolution.

1. EPOCHAL CHANGE

Before we begin our discussion, it should be noted that our purpose here is not to assess the merits of a particular modelling study, whose assumptions may be subject to dispute and whose conclusions may be of debatable relevance. Obviously, we also do not have the leisure to present a thorough exegesis of each model and hence must run the risk of doing a given study a considerable injustice. Nonetheless, we hope to describe each example in enough detail so as to illustrate some basic concepts and procedures in the analysis of dynamical systems. For pedagogical reasons I have limited discussion to discrete time models, but for the present purposes, very little is lost and much is gained by avoiding an explicit treatment of their continuous time analogs.

From Hunting to Agriculture

The application of dynamical systems to the study of epochal change is cogently illustrated by V. Smith's (1975) economic analysis of the transition from hunting to agriculture. Smith presents a model designed to elucidate in the simplest possible terms the economic choice between hunting and gathering (later, agriculture) and the subsequent feedback effect this choice induces on abstract prey species. I shall here present a discrete time version of the model that will facilitate comparison with the other examples to follow and that incorporates certain principles of adaptive economics to be discussed in Part 2.

We consider an economy which, for simplicity, is assumed to have a fixed population of identical individuals. Each individual may allocate a portion of his total effort L to hunting H and a portion to agriculture or food collecting A. A single homogeneous prey species exists with biomass M. Hunting yields a per capita output of m per unit of time. Agricultural activity or gathering yields a per capita output of some homogeneous domesticated crop or wild food of c units per unit of time.

> The production function for corn is $c = g(\gamma A)$ and for meat $m = f(\beta H, M/n)$, in which it is assumed that increasing the stock of game and of hunters by the same proportion has no effect on the per capita output of meat. The parameters γ and β are efficiency parameters for labor in hunting and farming or gathering respectively. Thus, an increase in β increases the hunting efficiency of labor. The effect of a technological change in weapons, or the introduction of the horse into the Plains Indian culture, is assumed to be captured by an appropriate increase in β. . . .
> (V. Smith 1975:735–36)

Each of the n individuals is assumed to choose a mix of hunting and agricultural effort (H,A) so as to maximize a utility function $u(c,m)$ subject to the labor constraint $L = H + A$ and the constraints given by the production functions. By substituting $c = g[\gamma(L-H)]$, and $m = f(\beta H, M_t/n)$, the problem can be expressed as

(1) $\qquad \pi(M_t; \beta, \gamma, n) := \max_{H} u\{g[\gamma(L-H)], f(\beta H, M_t/n), \}^3$

in which the current biomass, M_t, plays the role of a parameter. This is equivalent to assuming that the generation in question makes its choice without reference to the consequence on the prey population or to the potential needs and desires of future generations.

Equation (1) expresses a "temporary equilibrium" condition on the social choice between hunting and agriculture which may be expressed in words as follows: the best current utility, $\pi(M_t;\beta,\gamma,n)$, given the current biomass, M_t, human population, n, and efficiencies of labor in hunting and agriculture, β and γ, is obtained by allocating effort to hunting (and thereby to agriculture) so as to maximize u. The solution of this problem may be denoted by H_t, the per capita allocation of effort to hunting, from which follows the per capita allocation of effort to agriculture, $A_t = L - H_t$. Evidently, this allocation depends upon all the parameters that enter the optimization so that we may write as the *decision operator* representing individual choice

$$(2) \qquad H_t := \psi(M_t;\beta,\gamma, n),$$

which satisfies the equation of local (myopic) optimality or temporary equilibrium (1), that is,

$$(3) \; \pi(M_t;\beta,\gamma,n) = u\{g[L-\psi(M_t\beta,\gamma,n), f(\beta\psi(M_t;\beta,\gamma, n), M_t/n]\}.$$

(Obviously, the problem solution could equally well be expressed in terms of A_t).

Upon substituting (2) into the production function $f(\cdot,\cdot)$, the economy's aggregate *harvest function* becomes

$$(4) \qquad H(M_t) := nf[\beta\psi(M_t;\beta,\gamma, n), M_t/n].$$

Now, assume a biological S-curve of population growth for the prey species, which, in the absence of predation and in discrete time can be written $M_{t+1} = M_t + F(M_t)$. One obtains, by subtracting off the harvest, the state transition equation of the prey population

$$(5) \qquad M_{t+1} = M_t + F(M_t) - H(M_t).$$

A graphic exegesis of this equation is shown in Figure 7.1. Three situations are illustrated, each of which represents a distinct relationship between the "natural growth function" of biomass $F(\cdot)$ and the harvest function for hunting $H(\cdot)$. They are designed to show how the evolution of hunting and agriculture (or gathering) varies according to differences in hunting efficiency as determined by different values of the parameter β given a fixed agricultural efficiency γ.

192

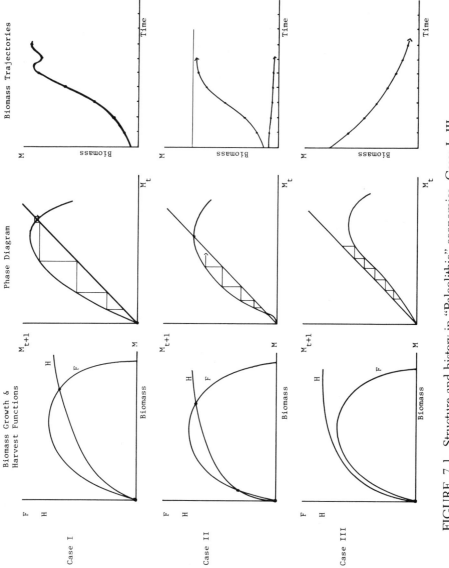

FIGURE 7.1. Structure and history in "Paleolithic" economics. Cases I–III: Progressive increases in hunting efficiency (β).

The diagrams in the first column of Figure 7.1 display the relationships between $F(\cdot)$ and $H(\cdot)$. Shown in the next column are the graphs of equation (5). These are the so-called phase diagrams of the model. The diagrams of the last column illustrate model solutions for the three situations. The smooth curves illustrate mathematical solutions of the model, while the discrete points represent simulations. One should note that all the relevant qualitative implications that can be derived from a given assumed situation can be obtained by a study of the middle "phase" diagram.

Case I shows a situation in which hunting is relatively inefficient compared to agriculture. Hunting efficiency rises somewhat in Case II and still more in Case III. In the first case, the biomass grows until oscillations around an equilibrium emerge. Such oscillations may converge to the equilibrium, to some period cycle, or, possibly, to a nonperiodic fluctuation.[4] When hunting is more efficient, the biomass declines, or, if the initial biomass is small, it grows, but to a lower equilibrium value, implying a greater role for agriculture or food gathering. A still further increase in hunting efficiency as shown in the bottom row leads to extinction of the biomass and complete specialization in agriculture or gathering.

The transition from one to another of these possibilities is not explained by the model described by equations (1)–(3). To provide a completely endogenous analysis, we would explicitly have to model changes in the parameters β, γ, and n. We will not do that here. We may observe, however, that the model appears to capture the possible consequences of the evolution of the hunting band and of efficient weapons such as spears and arrows and to show how such innovations might ultimately have led to a demise in the way of life they initially made possible. Likewise, we can imagine a situation in the Case I mode, in which agriculture (or food collecting) is extremely efficient relative to hunting so that after a period of growth in biomass, an extreme overshoot of equilibrium could occur with the result of a sudden extinction of the prey species.

Smith used the model to provide an explanation for the hypothesis that Paleolithic hunters decimated the large mammals some 10,000 years ago. This hypothesis is a controversial one. Certainly, a mathematical analysis can hardly settle the matter one way or the other. It can, however, show how purely economic forces can bring a transition between essentially different ways of life.

From Manorialism to Precapitalism[5]

After its invention and gradual diffusion, agriculture became organized according to a variety of systems including slash-and-burn cultivation, pastoralism, and the manorial organization characteristic of feudalism. The latter, our present concern, eventually gave way to capitalism after a transition through a period of mercantilist precapitalism. This last emerged from the manorial economy when (among other things) property rights and markets in land and labor were established. The transition, which took several centuries and preceded the process of massive capital accumulation characteristic of industrial production, was typified by various instabilities such as plagues, wars, and, what will concern us here, class conflict. My purpose now is to define a model that describes this development using a simple two-class model system that I call *Manoria*, which generates "class conflict," and which, in contradistinction to our preceding example, treats the *human* population as the basic state variable of the system.

Population is divided between peasants numbering P and aristocrats numbering A. Assuming (for simplicity) that the aristocracy contributes nothing to output, we have a production function $Y = f(P)$, which we shall suppose possesses ranges of increasing, constant, diminishing, and absolutely diminishing returns to scale. The aristocracy may be supposed (in view of the clergy's celibacy and the nobility's internecine warfare) to keep its population more or less constant at a number $\bar{A}$. Peasants, however, reproduce according to the Malthusian law,

$$(6) \qquad \Delta P/P = \min\{\lambda, (w-\sigma)/\sigma\},$$

illustrated in Figure 7.2a, in which w is the per capita share paid the peasants by their lords. The parameter σ is the per capita subsistence wage, and λ is the net birth rate in the absence of constraining economic forces. We now postulate the existence of a distribution function $w(P)$ that specifies for any given population the share to be allotted by the aristocracy to the peasants in accordance with their desire for present consumption and future income. It must have the property that

$$(7) \qquad Pw(P) \leq f(P) \qquad \text{all} \qquad P \geq 0,$$

which ensures that the total wage bill will never exceed the total product available.

What form should the distribution function assume in order to represent the feudal world? When decreasing returns prevail, the wage

195

should, according to neoclassical economics, be equal to the marginal product, for, from the aristocracy's point of view, to employ more labor would be unprofitable in terms of rent $R = f(P) - \omega(P) \cdot P$, and competition among peasants would prevent them from acquiring more. On the other hand, when increasing returns to labor prevail, a marginal-product wage would be impossible. We postulate, therefore, a *traditional share* of the average product τ such that $0 < \tau < 1$. In this case the distribution function can be written

$$(8) \qquad w = \omega_T(P) = \tau f(P)/P.$$

Multiplying by P we get the total wage bill under this scheme, $\tau f(P)$, as illustrated in Figure 7.2b. The distribution function itself is shown in Figure 7.2c.

Because of the assumption of eventual decreasing returns to scale, a marginal product wage is possible once population reaches a sufficiently high level. This level is exactly the point, P^*, at which the per capita output of peasants is at a maximum. If population grows beyond P^*, the marginal product wage becomes feasible; but because it would initially lie above the traditional share, it would not be in the interest of the aristocracy to exploit it. However, there exists a population, P^s, beyond which population growth brings down the marginal product below the traditional share. After this point, it is in the interest of the aristocracy to grant (or impose) a free market in labor.

Suppose, then, that the aristocracy can make good its monopsony power.[6] Instead of equation (8), the distribution function would be $\min\{\tau f(P), f'(P)\}$ which states that the smaller of the traditional share and marginal product attains. Because we have allowed for absolutely diminishing returns, there may exist populations for which $f'(P) < 0$. Of course, a negative wage cannot be paid, so to prevent this we specify that

$$(9) \qquad \omega_M(P) := \min\{\tau f(P)/P, \max\{f'(P), 0\}\},$$

the graph of which is shown by the heavy line in Figure 7.2c. The corresponding wage bill is also indicated by the heavy line in Figure 7.2b.

What we want to do now is examine the behavior of our manorial economy under the two distribution schemes (8) and (9). First, substituting (8) into (6) and setting $P_{t+1} - P_t = P \cdot P_t$, we get the difference equation for the progress of peasant population

196

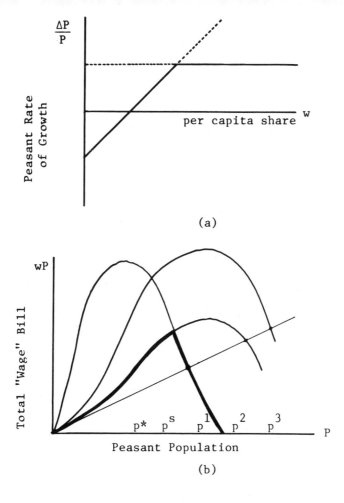

(a)

(b)

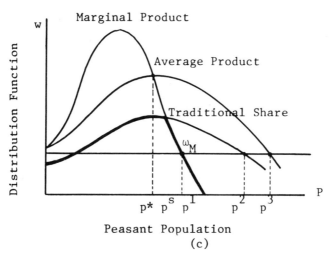

(c)

FIGURE 7.2. The structure of Manoria for alternative distribution schemes: (A) The peasant rate of growth function; (B) The total "wage" bill; (C) The distribution function.

(10) $$P_{t+1} = \min\{(1+\lambda)P_t, (\tau/\sigma)f(P_t)\}$$

whose phase diagram is shown in Figure 7.3, Case I. The middle diagram for this case shows the implied analytical solution of population growth with the "paper and pencil" simulated points superimposed. It is assumed that $f'(0) > \sigma$ so that the growth can occur for any initial population, however small. But, as can be seen in the diagrams, population must always be limited by the supply of "necessaries and conveniences." The example, however, shows the situation when the maximal biological growth rate operates between two periods of economically constrained growth, the first governed by increasing, the second by decreasing returns. The progress of real wages, shown in Figure 7.3, Case III, shows that a period of growing prosperity, reaching a level that could be sustained, perhaps for a very long time, is quite compatible with the model assumptions and the eventual role of Malthus's Iron Law of Wages.

Assume now the alternative, monopsonistic distribution scheme (7). By substitution, we obtain

(11) $$P_{t+1} = \min\{(1+\lambda)P_t, \min\{(\tau/\sigma)f(P_t), \max\{0, (1/\sigma)f'(P_t)P_t\}\}\},$$

whose phase diagram appears to the left in the Case II row of Figure 7.3. In the middle diagram is the implied "analytical solution," and to the right is shown the corollary progress in wages. Let us suppose that we begin with an initially small population well within the zone of increasing returns. Progress is exactly as before. Eventually, after P^* is exceeded, the marginal productivity distribution scheme becomes feasible. We could imagine that perceptive individuals, gradually becoming aware of this fact, would conceive the advantage to peasants of a labor market. We could imagine pressure from below for freedom from traditional feudal ties. Peasants would want to be paid what they are worth to the aristocracy, that is, their marginal product. The aristocracy, however, would resist, for such a change in the institutions of distribution would not be in its interest. Not, that is, until the further expansion in peasant numbers brings the marginal product of labor to the switch point P^s. Beyond this point the economic interests of the two classes reverse. A wage system is no longer in the peasants' interest, and, ironically, the aristocracy would now be willing to grant (or impose) a free labor market. Not only that, as the marginal-product wage bill is declining, an overshoot of equilibrium occurs, and an oscillation in population and in the resulting interests of the classes

198

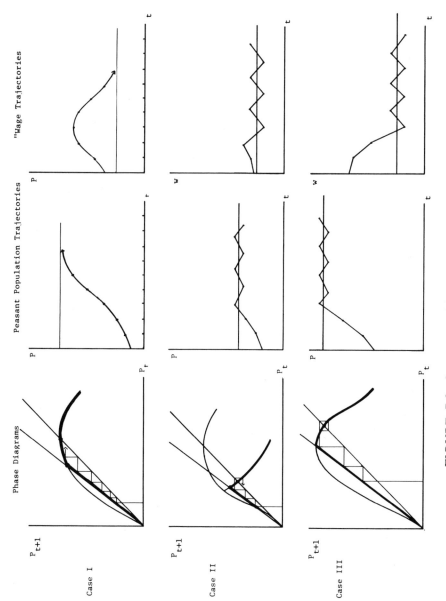

FIGURE 7.3. Structure and history in Malthusia: Case I: traditional share. Case II: switchover to a marginal product wage. Case III: egalitarian share and share alike.

ensues. Evidently, the emergence of a labor market has a destabilizing effect on this simple society, and a stationary state need not be brought about, or if it is, only after a period of oscillation.

In a real economy roughly approximated by our theory of Manoria, we would expect to observe a vigorously expanding manorial agriculture, with improving conditions for both peasants and lords, followed by a period of declining peasant welfare and a falling off of further increases in aristocratic rents. The relative desirability of alternative distribution schemes (traditional versus market competition) would oscillate from one to the other. The interests of the two classes would enter a stage of conflict after a period of harmony. This would be an age of peasant wars.

One may wonder at the fate of an agrarian society without a two-class structure which distributes the product in an egalitarian fashion. This is equivalent to a $\tau = 1$ and, we can assume, an $A = 0$. One possible outcome is that shown in the lower three diagrams of Figure 7.3, labelled Case III. Though the peasant population is much larger than before and no leisure class exists to antagonize it, its ultimate obedience to the Iron Law nevertheless is insured, and, as we have shown, the possibility of oscillation also exists.

Indeed, in Chapter 2 of his *Essay on Population*, Malthus argues that the Iron Law operates in a succession of retrograde and progressive movements, a history that can be generated, as in our illustration, if at the stationary population P^3, the marginal product of labor is negative, that is, if $f'(P^3) < 0$. As one can readily see from the phase diagrams, which are left to the reader to construct, converging, stable, or diverging population cycles are possible. If, like Malthus, we use 25 years as our time unit, then population would rise and fall twice in each century, periods of famine alternating with periods of plenty. Malthus had no doubt that this was a common situation, citing informal evidence and explaining that it was not more evident simply because in the societies whose histories could be explained in such terms, inadequate records were kept (Malthus 1817:Chapter 2).[7]

Ethologia

We have seen that the effect of a labor market in the manorial state is to restrict population growth and bring into existence an equilibrium which, *if attained*, maximizes the rental income of the aristocracy in perpetuity. Moreover, we saw that an egalitarian agrarian society did nothing to protect the long-run economic interests of the peasants, nor did the traditional wage structure. In every case, the Iron Law prevailed. Yet, it was clear in all of this that if numbers *could* be restricted *or* if subsistence could be raised above a biological level, then the well-being of the working class could be sustained. Recently, ethologists have pointed out the existence of behavioral mechanisms that control animal populations in such a way as to maintain an optimal sustenance per capita. Anthropologists have discovered similar mechanisms among primitive peoples. The mechanisms themselves are complex and sometimes bizarre. Yet their effect is simple. It is that of a simple homeostatic mechanism.

This theory has been comprehensively developed by Wynne-Edwards, who argues that "self-limiting homeostatic methods of density regulation are in practically universal operation not only in experiments, but under 'wild' conditions also" (Wynne-Edwards 1962:11). Building on the work of Carr-Saunders, he claims that the same can be said for primitive man, who developed territorial systems which led "not to overpopulation and starvation, but to a close control both of family size and exploitation of resources, (. . . these systems) evolved under natural selection, and (were) far beyond the wit of primitive men completely to rationalize or 'explain' them" (Wynne-Edwards 1962:118).

Such a homeostatic mechanism can be discussed within the present setting easily enough and serves as an interesting contrast to the ones described so far. First of all, we note that if income per capita in an egalitarian society is to be maximized, population must be at such a level that the marginal-product and average-product wages are the same. This is because $f(P^*)/P^* = \max_P f(P)/P$ implies that $f'(P^*) = f(P^*)/P^*$.

A negative feedback mechanism that brings such an optimum about would have the effect of operating according to the transition equation

(12) $$P_{t+1} = P_t + \alpha[f'(P_t) - f(P_t)/P_t]P_t,$$

where P_t is total population. This process is stable if $-1 < 1 + \alpha P^* f''(P^*) \leq 1$ or if $-2 < \alpha P^* f''(P^*) \leq 0$. Hence $f''(P^*)$ must be negative so that at equilibrium the marginal product of labor must be falling, but not too fast. Likewise the adjustment of population to existing disequilibrium conditions must not be too fast or oscillations would result.

The difference equation (12) describing evolution in Ethologia may be contrasted to the one for Manoria (11) in which both marginal-product and average-product wage bills also enter but in a quite different way. Clearly, to lead to an optimal per capita output, population adjustment must be made in reference to the best one can get (the average product) relative to what one is worth (the marginal product) and not merely to what one is worth relative to subsistence. Diagrams that show the evolution of (12) are displayed in Figure 7.4.

Obviously, equation (12) merely illustrates the possibility of homeostasis. It is not based on an empirically established dynamic mechanism, and one may wonder whether its real analog might exist even in the simplest cultural setting. A more realistic—and more complicated—model has been developed on the basis of a systematic description of a slash-and-burn agricultural group. As one might guess, this more complicated model implies more complicated behavior.

Civilized Interference in a Slash-and-Burn Culture

The study we refer to is Shantzis's and Behrens's (1973) system dynamics model of the ritual pig cycle of the Tsembaga that had been described in consummate detail by Rappaport (1968). The system state is described by human population H, pig population P, and by the yield of food F. Delays in human deaths from war D and delayed accumulation of information about food yields I are also included. The system consists of five difference equations,

(13)
$$
\begin{aligned}
H_{t+\Delta} &= H_t + \Delta h(H_t, P_t, F_t, D_t) \\
P_{t+\Delta} &= P_t + \Delta p(H_t, P_t, F_t) \\
F_{t+\Delta} &= F_t + \Delta f(H_t, P_t, F_t) \\
D_{t+\Delta} &= D_t + \Delta d(P_t, D_t) \\
I_{t+\Delta} &= I_t + \Delta i(F_t, I_t),
\end{aligned}
$$

in which Δ is the time interval used for "integrating the system." The functions h, p, and f describe the structure of production, consumption, and social interaction including the incidence of festival and war. They have a complex, highly nonlinear structure that cannot be summarized briefly enough to be explicated here, though some idea of the interactions involved may be obtained from the causal loop diagram shown in Figure 7.5 and the DYNAMO flow diagram shown in Figure 7.6.

The standard simulation of the model that mimics the festival-war cycle is shown in Figure 7.7a. A second run displayed in Figure 7.7b shows the influence of modifying the net birth rate—through Western health care—from 1.3 percent to 2.0 percent. The triggering of festivals and wars is speeded up. Eventually, all pigs are consumed, the cycle ceases, and population, after a period of rapid growth, declines, eventually reaching a new, extremely low equilibrium. The ritual cycle has vanished. The outlawing of war has the same effect though the demise of the ritual cycle comes still earlier.

These results clearly show how cultural ceremonies, conflicts, and war provide checks on population growth while, on the average, maintaining the nutritional standard well above the subsistence level to which it must sink in their absence. It is interesting also to note how, after an initial parametric perturbation, endogenous development brings about a marked cultural change, in this case causing the demise of the ritual cycle and its associated pig culture.

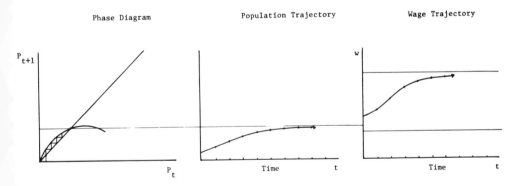

FIGURE 7.4. Structure and history in Ethologia.

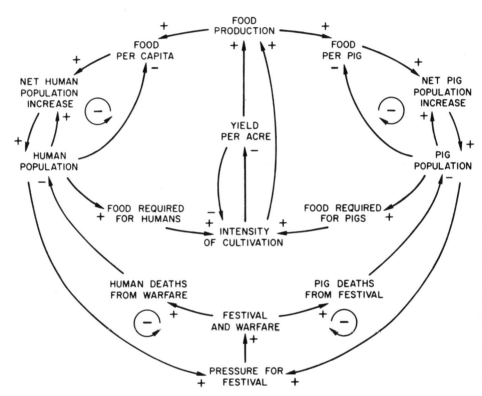

FIGURE 7.5. Causal-loop diagram of the Tsembaga system (source: Shantzis and Behrens 1973, by permission of the M.I.T. Press).

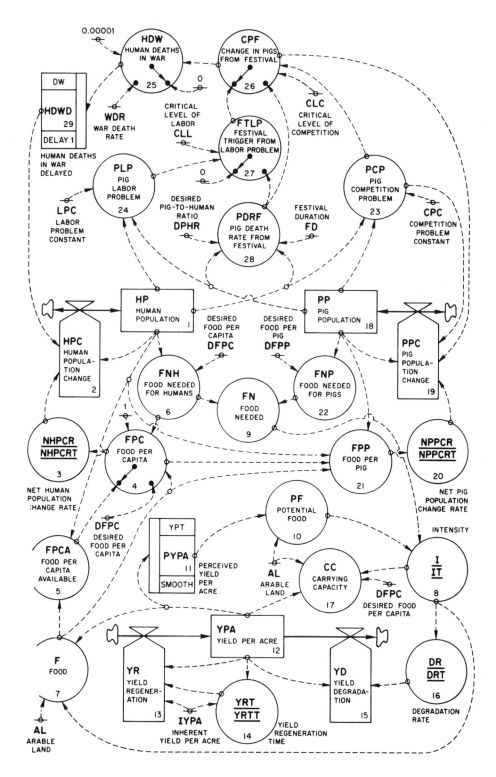

FIGURE 7.6. DYNAMO flow diagram of the Tsembaga model (source: Shantzis and Behrens 1973, by permission of the M.I.T. Press).

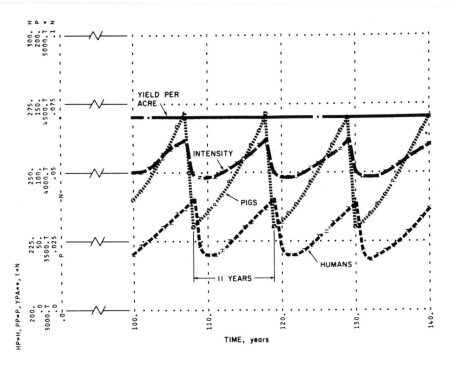

(a.) Standard simulation of the Tsembaga model

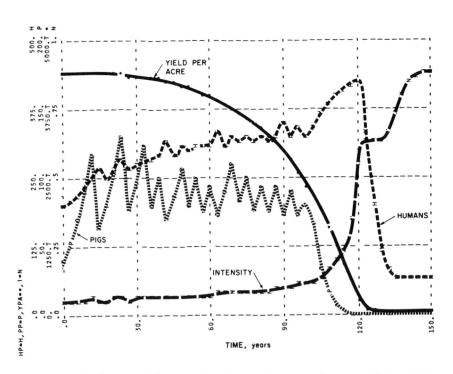

(b.) Model simulation of more improved health
(normal growth rate = 2.0 percent)

FIGURE 7.7. Comparative dynamics with the Tsembaga model (source: Shantzis and Behrens 1973, by permission of the M.I.T. Press).

Overlapping Waves in the Evolution of Technology

All of the above models may be said to be "coarse" or "highly aggregative" in that they summarize the essential features of an entire culture in a very small number (one to five in our examples) of state variables. Although we have used these relatively simple models to illustrate either "paper and pencil" or computer simulations, the full power of the computer can only be fully realized when we deal with models of microstructure in which the point is to identify and incorporate explicitly strategic details of technology, decision making, and institutional practice. For nearly two decades, I have been involved in the development of a particular class of such microdynamic models which I call recursive programming models, the general properties of which I shall review in Part 2 of this chapter. At this point, I want to call attention to several examples of this modelling approach that shed light on the behavioral economics of technological diffusion (Day and Singh 1977; Abe et al. 1978).

A nonmathematical summary of the model structure is shown in Figure 7.8. Technological resource, financial, and adaptive constraints implied by cautious behavior and current aspiration levels are determined on the basis of past experience and current data. Current decisions are regarded as potential (or necessary) departures from past actions. If a past action is not feasible, a search for feasible alternatives ensues. If none is found, the goal or constraints structure must be modified. If the past solution is feasible, it is checked to see if any high-order goals are satisfied. Then the next highest goal is maximized. When there is no further room for choice, a decision is made. A special case of the model occurs when there is only one dominating goal.

Models with this general structure may be thought of as behavioral models in the sense of Cyert and March (1963) but in which certain decisions are made on the basis of explicit economizing or optimizing calculations, as in the model of Pleistocene transition described above. Moreover, in empirical work, the optimizing component is usually represented by a linear programming submodel based on an activity analysis of technology. In this way, *activities* are regarded as the basic variables with production, supplies, and demands of particular artifacts as derivative variables.

Among the activities incorporated are those representing production of various commodities, with alternative technologies using varying

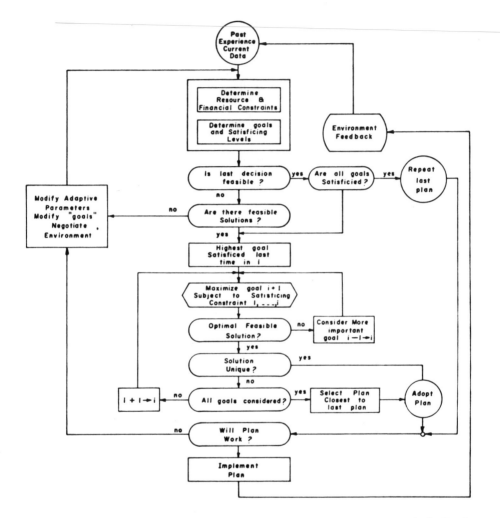

FIGURE 7.8. A behavioral model incorporating optimizing with feedback (source: Day and Singh 1977, by permission of Cambridge University Press).

commodity input mixes. Behavioral constraints, representing learning and caution, as well as capital and other resource constraints, limit technological choices in any given period. Such constraints are adjusted period by period in response to "experience" as represented by past optimizing "solutions."

Figure 7.9 presents three idealized pictures illustrating the results of three separate modelling studies. In each we have the displacement of an established mode of production by a "modern" one. Corollary to these trends is the demand for labor, which generally follows a pattern more or less like that shown in Figure 7.10. In some industries, like coal mining or farming, the consequence is a transformation of the population structure of the associated geographical region. In reality, well-established patterns of social behavior often accompany such demographic changes, leading to a growth in the behavior associated with the "modern" technology and to a decline in the behavior associated with the obsolete technology. One can imagine the corollary growth and decline in the labor and managerial groups associated with the distinct technologies.

Although these results in particular and the model structure in general explicitly allow for inertia or resistance to adaptation of new techniques, it is found that the phasing over from one technique to another often takes place quite rapidly, sometimes in less than a decade and often within a generation. In this way "mini-epochs" of very short duration are generated.

2. OUTLINE OF A GENERAL THEORY OF ADAPTING ECONOMIC SYSTEMS[8]

We have before us several dissimilar mathematical models, each tailored to a specific purpose of dynamic analysis. Each, however, illustrates a process by which the qualitative character of a culture or of an economic sector is modified by the internal forces of adjustment, that is, how ways of life associated with modes of production grow, flourish, then give way to succeeding types of activity, sometimes disappearing altogether as the overall state of the system develops. This kind of qualitative progression is an essential property of evolution. It is more or less analogous to the biological mechanisms of variation, competition, and selection that lead to successive occupations of environmental niches by evolving specific organisms. But because we are

209

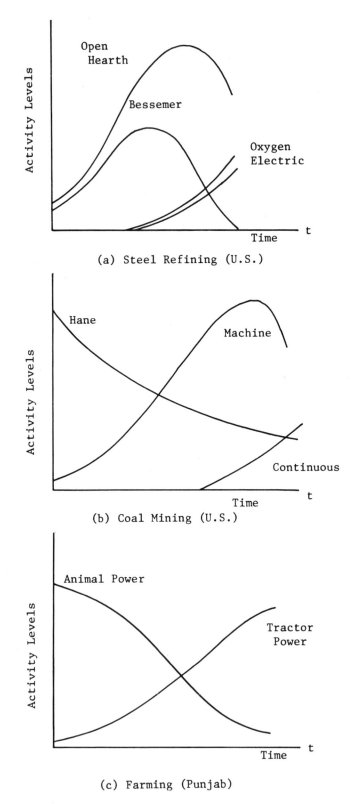

FIGURE 7.9. Technological diffusion in three different settings (the diagrams are highly stylized).

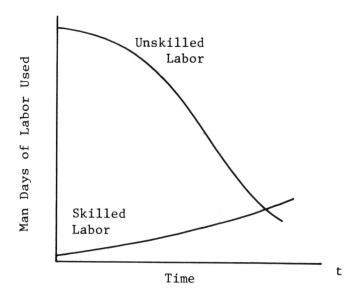

FIGURE 7.10. Effect of technological diffusion on labor utilization.

dealing with human economic activity and culture, it seems reasonable to suppose that much more than a naive transfer of Darwinian theory is needed to understand the process.

I now wish to describe a conceptual framework and modelling approach that I hope may offer important ingredients from which rigorous general theories and models of economic and cultural dynamics can be constructed. Specific studies of the kind summarized in Part 1 fall as special cases within its boundaries.

Adaptation as a Process

Reduced to barest essentials, standard economic analysis begins with structures of technology and individual preferences and proceeds to a derivation of equilibria that represents individual rationality, that equates supply and demand, and that exhibits social efficiency. It may then, following the method of comparative statics, ask how equilibria are modified by changes in parameters in the system, changes that are perhaps associated with "policies" or other factors that for purposes of the analysis are treated as exogenous.

Reduced to *its* barest essentials, dynamical systems theory begins with a specification about how rates of change in a system are governed by states of the system. It then poses and answers questions of whether or not and, if so, just how system histories (as described by the trajectories of the states) may evolve from various initial situations. Following the method of comparative dynamics, one may ask how trajectories, either in quantitative or qualitative terms, may be modified by changes in the parameters of the system (Samuelson 1947; Hirsch and Smale 1974). Quite naturally, we might define *dynamical economic systems* as dynamical systems that incorporate specific representations of technology and preferences. The studies of Part 1 provide quite varied examples of what we are talking about.

Much of the mathematical economic literature dealing with dynamics involves a straightforward extension of the static concepts of rationality and equilibrium to encompass intertemporal production and exchange. Such an extension both generalizes and preserves the standard economic paradigm. An alternative approach, however, has been developed that recognizes cognitive limitations of individuals, organization limitations within groups, supply and demand disequilibria, and social inefficiencies. Models of this latter type have been denoted *adaptive economic models* (Day and Groves 1975). Because their basic assumptions are plausible, they would appear to offer a compelling contribution toward understanding the actual outcomes of economic development and its broader implications in terms of epochal social change.

Not that theories of intertemporal optimality have no place! Certainly they are essential in defining what we mean by "adaptedness." Also, as we shall see, they have their place in describing the *process* of adapting. But, though economic events are not governed by the blind, profligate mechanism that governs biological evolution, they are also not guided by a benevolent, unseen hand that sees to it that humans in all their diversity and tragicomic change live out their lives and pass through their stages of history in the best of all possible worlds. Thus when we use the terms "adaptive" or "adapting" we do not have in mind, except in carefully delineated contexts, optimal environmental fitness; nor do we have in mind the Social Darwinist doctrine that competition and selection necessarily produce socially efficient states or histories. We have in mind, instead, the *process* of agent-environmental interaction that leads to change, development, and, more broadly, to evolution. It is the latter that essentially involves not only growth but decay and demise in rich, contrapuntal patterns of emerging epochs and disappearing regimes.

212

The Agent-Environment Interaction

Beginning, then, with the observation that economic events exhibit change and development, we take as our first axiom that economic experience is determined by a system of cause and effect in which change in the system at any time is governed by the system state. We proceed by decomposing the system into two parts, one representing the behavior of a part of the process of special interest which we may call—quite arbitrarily—the agent and the other representing all other parts of reality which we call—equally arbitrarily—the environment. Adaptation may then be defined as the interaction of agent and environment. The "agent" may be a person, a household, a group of firms, an entire economy, a culture, or a society depending on the purpose at hand. The "agent" must be understood here to be a purely formal entity. The "environment" may include not only the natural surroundings of the agent but also his technological infrastructure and the collection of other agents with whom he interacts. For simplicity here we shall use the terms "agent," "collection of agents," "group," "economy," "culture," and "society" as synonymous, though it should be clear that when we speak of adapting systems we have in mind complex interactions within groups as well as between individuals or group aggregates and their aggregate environment.

META–ADAPTATION

Adaptation as defined so far involves the interaction of agent and environment according to fixed rules of behavior for a fixed agent or population of agents. If we are to consider how a given process comes into being, or if we are to inquire how a system changes (or may be changed) from one structure to another, then we come to a more complex type of adaptation that may be called *meta-adaptation*, in which rules of behavior, or the population of agents, or both are variables.

Three forms of meta-adaptation may thus be distinguished. In evolution, the population of agents is a variable and is determined at any given time by the previously existing population's interaction with its environment through forces of competition, cooperation, and selection. This concept was of course developed to explain the progress of biological populations, but its application to socioeconomic organizations is of obvious relevance.

213

The selection or modification of adaptors for a given agent or population of agents through conscious effort may be called *cultural adaptation*, a type of meta-adaptation so important that society as a whole and many of its institutions set aside resources for the use of specialists in this function. Cultural adaptation enables agents to survive in the face of evolutionary forces that would spell their demise if they did not acquire new modes of behavior. It also enables them to improve their performance in the sense of some criterion or outcome measure, that is, to economize or socialize more effectively.

When both evolution and cultural adaptations are present, we have *cultural evolution* (Childe 1951), which allows for the response of agents to their environment, the modification of strategies or modes of behavior by given agents, and the modification of the population of agents (organizations) itself.

ADAPTORS

To carry the theory further, specific mechanisms of adaptation must be identified and provided with mathematical analogs. This must be done not only for the study of social behavior in general but also for economizing in particular. Economizing behavior as described, for example, by the neoclassical marginalist Marshall involved incremental, economically improving adjustments. Optimality of full equilibrium only would occur—if at all—through a converging sequence of marginal changes in behavior. Marshall's focus, however, like that of many of his contemporaries, was on the characteristics of the state of equilibrium, assuming it was brought about. But if one is to understand the adaptive mechanisms that underlie economizing, then one must study the process of marginal adjustment itself and ask whether and under what conditions it will bring about optimality, and at what speed. And, as explicit optimizing takes time, involves the consumption of other resources, and is far from easy, it must itself become a part of the economizing problem. When investigating such issues, therefore, one must think of economizing or rational decision making as adaptive in character.

It is important to note that any search for best or even good solutions must be preceded by a search for one that works at all. In other words, feasible choice is prior to optimal choice. It should be recognized that the resources and patience of even the most rational decision maker may be so exhausted by the search for feasibility that improving on it at least for the time being may be out of the question. These reflections lead us to the concept of *homeostasis*.

HOMEOSTASIS IN THE GENERAL SENSE

All living systems possess critical variables that must be maintained within the boundaries of certain critical sets if they are to survive. In general, these critical sets depend upon the current situation. The agent must possess a mode of adaptation (an adaptor) that leads to an action within the critical set. The agent survives so long as this set is nonempty and action falls within it. In this case I shall say that the agent exhibits *homeostasis in the general sense* (Ashby 1967; Day 1975). If either of these conditions fails, then the agent goes out of existence and the system collapses to a transistor that maps a given environmental state into a succeeding environmental state.

HOMEOSTASIS IN THE SPECIFIC SENSE

A mechanism for achieving homeostasis is the negative feedback control device or servomechanism that adjusts actions on the basis of an observed discrepancy between a desired or target value of the critical variables and their experienced values. Extensively developed by Canon (1939) in the context of human physiology, the idea was applied to economic behavior by Cooper (1951) and Simon (1952). Furthermore, it forms the basis of the flexible accelerator of Goodwin (1948) and Chenery (1952). Systems that behave according to such rules I shall say exhibit *homeostasis in the specific sense*. It may be noted that homeostasis in the specific sense is in essence an algorithm for minimizing the distance between target and observed critical outcomes and implies a preference for outcomes closer to the target than others. This distance can be thought of as a "disutility" so that this scheme has a kind of implicit rationality to it.

ADAPTIVE, MOTIVATED BEHAVIOR

March and Simon (1958) proposed a model of adaptive motivated behavior, that, like the flexible accelerator, possesses an adapting target. In this model, the object is to satisfy a goal by adjusting action

215

according to a (specific sense) homeostatic rule. The goal, as represented by an aspiration level, is adjusted upward or downward in direct proportion to the success or failure of previous action in terms of a reward or payoff. Forrester (1966) developed a similar negative feedback mechanism in which the goal to which behavior is adjusted is the weighted average of a traditional performance measure, a management goal, and a factor that reflects management's effectiveness in "projecting its goals." He specifies that this effectiveness depends upon the "effective size" of the organization in question.

SWITCHES, RULES, AND ADAPTIVE LEARNING

Closely related to the March-Simon-Forrester model of adaptive motivated behavior is the elementary adaptive learning algorithm. The canonical form for learning algorithms is a system of switches and rules in which the rules governing behavior at any time are determined when the performance measure belongs to the rule's associated switching set. A change in the performance measure sufficient to bring its value to a different set of values causes a change in action or a switch in the rule governing behavior. Simple examples can readily be constructed using four elemental principles of learning: (a) successful behavior is repeated; (b) unsuccessful behavior is avoided; (c) unsuccessful behavior is followed by a search for alternative modes of behavior; and (d) behavior becomes more cautious in response to failure. Well founded in psychological theory and experimentation, models incorporating (a)–(c) have been the basis of the behavioral theory of the form developed by Cyert and March (1963). In Day (1967) it is shown that behavioral learning models, augmented by failure response (d), can converge to the economist's traditional economic equilibria for individual agents or two-agent teams with stationary environments. Recently, empirical evidence has been assembled which indicates that businesses are actually governed by such learning rules (Crain and Tollison n.d.).

The essence of the behavioral learning model is an extremely simple local or approximate optimizing of marginal variations in action based on an extremely limited knowledge of past results. This characteristic is shared by mathematical algorithms for computing optima of complex, unconstrained, or constrained optimization problems. Optima for such problems cannot usually be intuited. They must be approximated by computational sequences involving suboptimization with feedback. Gradient methods are transparent examples of such algorithms in which search is directed along a locally steepest path of ascent (or descent). Here, increasing caution is represented by shortening step lengths as marginal payoffs decrease or local optima are overshot. The locally steepest path is the gradient (or constrained gradient) which solves a local maximization problem. The fact that optimizing algorithms have a learning structure suggests that learning, even of a limited kind, may constitute a powerfully adaptive device in stable environments; the fact that learning has a simple optimizing character suggests that the concept of optimality is an essential, irreducible concept in understanding adaptation when choice is perceived. Nonetheless, nothing in the structure of these algorithms implies that learning will be effectively adaptive in unstable environments.

OPTIMIZING WITH FEEDBACK OR RECURSIVE PROGRAMMING

The analogy between elemental learning behavior and optimizing algorithms exposes a fundamental duality between optimizing and learning. The solutions of complex optimizing problems *must be learned* by what are in effect elemental adaptive processes, and elemental adaptive processes that exhibit learning involve optimization in a simple way. This duality motivates a consideration of the class of all processes which represent behavior or planning computations by sequences of recursively connected, local, approximate, or behaviorally conditioned optimizations with feedback, or *recursive programming models*.

Such models appear in a great variety of special forms. These include highly simplified examples, such as Smith's model of Pleistocene transition with which we introduced our discussion of dynamical systems in Part 1. They include as well the rather complicated ones devised by Day and Singh (1977) and by Abe et al. (1978) that were summarized at the close of Part 1. These were designed to simulate detailed patterns of production and investment in various agricultural regions and production sectors. All of them share certain common features of mathematical structure.

From a purely formal point of view, these models are three component systems involving data, optimizing, and feedback operators. The data operator, which subsumes observation, storage, and processing functions, defines how the parameters or data entering objective and constraint functions depend upon the current state of the system as a whole. The optimizing operator describes the dependence of certain decision or choice variables on objective and constraint functions that in turn depend on the various parameters or data. The feedback operator, which subsumes implementation and environmental transition functions, specifies how the succeeding state of the system depends upon the current optimal decision variables, the data, and the current state. Given an initial state for the system, the data for an optimization can be generated, the optimization problem formed and solved, and the next state of the system evolved through feedback. In this way, a sequence of optimizations is generated in which parameters or data upon which any one optimization is based depend upon past optimizations and parameters or data in the sequence.[9] We emphasize that the behavioral learning models and gradient algorithms are simple examples of this general approach.

In recursive programming models of economic behavior, constrained maximizing is used to describe the plans or intended behavior of an economizing agent or group of agents, but with the added assumption that actual performance is determined by additional forces unaccounted for in the individual optimizations. These additional forces may act on the agent through environmental and behavioral feedback in the form of physical and financial accumulations (and decumulations), through information incorporated into estimates of current states and forecasts of anticipated states, and through behavioral rules. The latter must be able to make allowances for future decision making and to modify objectives on the basis of past behavior as a tactic for avoiding uncertainty.

The description of a decision maker who proceeds according to a succession of behaviorally conditioned, more or less myopic suboptimizing decisions corresponds reasonably well to behavior observed in many business firms and government agencies. Nonetheless, strategic considerations can also be incorporated by using optimal control or dynamic programming for the optimizing operator, in which the payoff (or expected payoff) of an anticipated sequence of future actions is maximized, subject to a simplified feedback operator that represents the decision maker's *perceived* environmental feedback operator. A plan consisting of optimal intended future behavior is derived, or, more

218

generally, an "optimal" strategy is derived which specifies how current behavior should be controlled given current information. When such a "strategic" optimizing (dynamic programming) operator is imbedded in a model of the "true" or "complete" feedback structure, the system as a whole becomes a recursive programming model that represents an agent or several agents who are forward looking and whose plans have strategic quality but whose actual behavior is conditioned by forces beyond those incorporated in the optimizing calculations. In such a model the "true" optimal strategy is not used unless the "true" world structure is assumed to be perceived by the agents.

ADAPTIVE PROGRAMMING OR DUAL CONTROL

When applying strategic considerations to the problem of adaptation the agent must, if he/she is to achieve global optimality, account for all the decision functions including observation, storage, processing, planning, and implementation. In choosing a course of action he/she must consider the advantage to be gained by allocating present resources to learning about the system through conscious experimentation as compared with their allocation for maximizing current performance, given the current level of knowledge of the system's operation. Formal models which embody these considerations are called adaptive control or adaptive programming models and seem to have been originated by Fel'dbaum (1965) in a generalization of Bellman's dynamic programming and of stochastic programming techniques (Aoki 1967). Extensively studied by control engineers, alternative models of this general type have been described in several recent surveys and need not be elaborated here (Aoki 1977).

Imagine now a process in which new aspects of the "true" environmental feedback structure are learned with the passage of time. Then the adaptive control model to be optimized depends recursively on the "true" external environment. A model of this complete system is a recursive programming model involving suboptimization with feedback as before, but in which intended behavior at each state is influenced by an attempt to learn as well as to control optimally.

The more inclusive the range of decision-making considerations explicitly incorporated within the adaptive control framework, the more complex, costly, and time-consuming is the implied algorithm for obtaining "optimal" decisions. Such costs indeed rise more or less exponentially with the level of detail accommodated so that the model must become an extreme simplification of actual operating decisions. Even so, it may involve taxing logical and computational difficulties.

The implication is that an adaptive programming strategy is simply one way of planning in a state of partial knowledge. In actual practice, it must involve substituting a complex and extremely costly computational algorithm for "real time" behavioral learning, servomechanistic procedures, or simple tactical optimizing. But if the decision maker has something to learn about the structure of the environment (and not just its parameters), then one cannot be sure that sophisticated strategies will, in fact, perform better than the simpler ones they replace. Whether or not and under what conditions they will perform better depends on how stable the decision-making structure is when plans roll and knowledge evolves in interaction with the "true" environment.

Evidently, a universal form of explicit optimizing does not govern evolution. Instead, the form of optimizing is itself a product of learning, that is, of adaptation, and as activity adds to the store of knowledge, the conception of what exists, what is possible, what is desirable, and how to make plans evolves. In adaptive economics, then, adaptive control models form merely one among several fundamental classes of techniques for describing the adaptive procedures by which humans and organizations solve their economic problems.

META-ADAPTATION

In cultural adaptation, in which rules of behavior (adaptors) are modified, one has a process more or less analogous to elemental adaptation except that change is occurring in a function space as well as in the agent's action space. The subsystem governing the selection (or modification) of adaptors or behavioral rules is based on an orchestration of activities in which the memory, data processing, and observation functions are called investigation; the planning function, which involves synthesizing new rules, is called theorizing or model building; and the implementation function involves education, training, indoctrination, and practice.

People's manners of responding to unfolding events change as they mature. The seeking of immediate pleasure, the direct avoidance of pain, and spontaneous curiosity become less apparent. Reflective activity emerges, and rational choice plays a gradually increasing role in some domains. Analogously, as organizations mature, rules of thumb make way for scientific management. In either case, however, rational modes of operation are limited in scope and content by habit, tradition, impulse, and imitation. Emerging behavior probably follows a weighing of rational and traditional rules in which the emphasis on one or the other evolves on the basis of experimentation and the knowledge of past results. The superiority and eventual dominance of rational behavior in this process cannot be assumed or taken for granted.

Agents must exhibit homeostasis in the general sense (defined above) if they are to survive. Evolutionary adaptation—as contrasted with the cultural adaptation just considered—occurs when actions carry critical variables outside their critical sets of values. Of course, humans are subject to ordinary biological selection mechanisms, and these are thought by some extreme advocates of evolutionary theory to have exerted a powerful influence on human development, even within the historical epoch (Darlington 1969). Economic organizations add wholly new and characteristically (if not uniquely) human modes of competition and selection that transcend the random variation and mindless selection of the biological world. Bankruptcy, for example, allows for the demise of firms and households while preserving the human participants. It is this kind of organizational evolution that is the special province of institutional economics (Commons 1924) and whose formal study has been launched impressively by Shubik (1959) and Winter (1964, 1971), among others.

Disequilibrium Mechanisms

These considerations of adaptation and evolution must lead to an emphasis on disequilibrium phenomena in adapting—as opposed to adapted—systems: disappointment of expectations, imperfect coordination of separately managed enterprises, inequation of supply and demand, inefficiencies in the allocation of resources, and declining as well as improving fortunes of some participants in the system. The extent of these phenomena may be greater at one time than at another. At all times they pose threats to survival. They virtually always bring about the demise of individual firms—the number of bankruptcies in the United States runs in the thousands per month, even in good times! They occasionally conspire to drive industries, regions, even entire nations to ruin. The primary concern of the economic organization, then, must be for its survival, while the institutional development of society must be guided to a considerable degree by the need to maintain viability in the face of disequilibrium.

For the individual as well as for the organization, caution is an element strongly influencing adaptive behavior, and a part of cautious behavior is the maintenance of stocks of unused resources and the existence of "organization slack" to absorb unpredictable divergences between plans and realization. Special organizations evolve whose functions are to mediate disequilibrium transactions and to sustain critical variables within homeostatic bounds. Stores, for example, function as inventories on display, mediating the flow of supplied and demanded commodities without the intervention of centralized coordination or of complicated and time-consuming market *tâtonnement*[10] procedures. Banks and other financial intermediaries regulate the flow of purchasing power among uncoordinated savers and investors and mediate the flow of credits and debits that facilitates intertemporal exchanges without the simultaneous bartering of goods. Ordering mechanisms, with accompanying backlogs and variable delivery days, together with inventory fluctuations, provide a flow of information that facilitates decentralized adjustments to disequilibria in commodity supplies and demands. To these mechanisms must be added insurance and other transfer schemes, such as unemployment compensation, that place resources in the hands of agents who would possess no admissible action without them.

Models of adapting economies will contain elements representing these and other devices for maintaining economic viability. In reality, the preservation of such devices is always threatened when a system is working relatively well, for they create unused stocks and apparent inefficiencies. Frequently, they are instituted *after* an economic or natural disaster and later abandoned if they should go unused for long, only to be reinstated after the next crisis. In this way society ineffectually reacts to experience. It is, of course, the existence of these institutions prior to the need for them that makes possible their effective contribution when disequilibrium conditions are running strong. In any case, whether in reaction to or in anticipation of events, their emergence is a central feature of the adapting economy.

Existence and Evolution: The Qualitative Issues .

Normally in mathematical analysis, the first step to be undertaken upon the specification of a particular system is to prove the existence of "solutions." The next step is to determine their number and how they may change in response to changes in parameters of the system. This process has been illustrated in Part 1 (to be sure, in a most informal manner). Now, after reviewing a more complete set of ingredients that may be part of the recipe for an adapting economic system, one comes to the realization that systems which do not possess solutions in the usual sense are of interest. Such systems possess finite viability (Day 1975:5). In them dynamic behavior is possible for a finite period of time, after which no model solution exists. Such a model may provide a hypothesis, in terms of endogenously generated contradictions, for explaining the demise of some particular economic activity or some general way of life. And, as we have emphasized throughout our discussion, demise is the counterpart of growth in every evolutionary process.

Still, our most satisfying and theoretically interesting models will be those which do possess solutions, but which maintain viability through the substituting of new, feasible activities for obsolete or obsolescent ones. In this way we can find, as we did in the several examples of Part 1, a coherent explanation for the progression of a culture through a series of epochs of distinctly different character. It is in the discovery of just how these changes in epoch are governed by the parameters and initial conditions of the model that we find a new understanding of economic development and cultural evolution.

Phases of Development

If economic development and cultural evolution are typified by a progression of epochs of distinct qualitative character, we might be tempted to revive the concept of immutable stages of growth so prominent in nineteenth- and twentieth-century economic history and in early archeological theory as well (Steward 1956). It should be clear from our examples as well as from the complicated nature of our general framework that this would be a mistake.

Indeed, there is nothing immutable about the epochs generated by an adapting economic system. Even systems with simple structures—as

223

we have seen—may exhibit quite varied developments, whose epochs unfold in varied order and character depending on the particular setting of time and place. As the models gain in complexity of strategic detail, the number and character of possible model evolutions grows.

To distinguish, therefore, the epochs generated by our models from the idea of immutably ordered stages, I call them *phases*. It is in the character of adapting economic systems to generate phases. Their number and order, however, are strictly functions of model structure, that is, the number and form of technological and behavioral interrelationships, of parameters, and of initial conditions.

Economic Development and Cultural Evolution

Let us summarize the theoretical considerations outlined so far.

Economic adaptation involves an interaction of people (decision makers or agents) with their surrounding environment, including their organizational milieu. The behavior of agents is, in part, rational and involves explicit choice, economizing, and, more generally, optimizing. But people's knowledge of environmental structures is incomplete, their store of data and memory is limited, and their powers of cognition and computation are severely circumscribed. Rational choice, therefore, involves problem simplification, and problem solution often must involve adaptive learning of an elemental kind. Because adaptive decision makers cannot solve problems perfectly, actual behavior involves a blend of rational choice, of traditional or standard operating procedures, and servomechanistic, negative feedback adjustment mechanisms.

It follows that coordination among the members of a group, economic organization, or culture is imperfect. Disequilibria should therefore typify actual situations. This means unfulfilled expectations, inequations in supply and demand, and worsening situations for some while others improve. Because of disequilibrium, survival must be a key concern in adapting economic systems. The specific homeostatic or adaptive motivated feedback behavior is one type of strategy evolved to bring about homeostasis in the general sense, the maintenance of critical variables within bounds that define the possibilities of survival. Learning and explicit optimizing models must also have come into being to serve this purpose. Needless to say, they do not always succeed. For this reason, one should expect to observe variation and selection in rules as well as in individuals and organizations.

224

Although equilibria, balanced growth, or stationary states may be brought about within a given dynamical system, even simple examples, such as those outlined in Part I, are capable of overshoot, oscillation, and more extreme forms of catastrophic change. These unstable modes of behavior are to be expected and may be the rule rather than the exception in adapting processes. Particularly when resource scarcities are involved, we must expect to find either deterioration and eventual demise of the resource-dependent culture or overlapping waves of technology as new methods, products, and resources replace old ones in a succession of technologically based epochs.

Such discernible epochs, identified by characteristic economic and social activities and by characteristic resource inputs, unfold typically in a progression of growth, maturity, decline, and more or less rapid and final demise. But the number of distinct, identifiable phases and the order of their progression will depend upon the empirical data of time and place, that is, upon the initial conditions. When distinct socioeconomic groups (classes) are identified closely with economic functions, as is often the case, the fortunes of these groups will be strongly influenced by the underlying activity-resource phase structure and evolution.

Instability and phase evolution are to be seen, then, as fundamental characteristics of long-run economic development. What implications does this have for interpreting cultural evolution?

First, we must imagine that people caught in a matrix of shifting fortunes, due at times to rapid, perhaps catastrophic shifts in economic opportunity and constraints, will not always stick with past organizations but will search for new or different rules of organization and behavior. They will as a result introduce new mechanisms to govern adaptations. Thus, as specialized production and exchange grow, new institutions or enterprises will be introduced to mediate the disequilibria in supply and demand. These institutions and enterprises will buffer imbalances in supply and demand. At the same time, they introduce new decision points—often requiring new decision makers (new agents), and new delays. These become new sources of potential instability and pose totally new problems of coordination and control.

In these observations, we may find the underlying basis of socioeconomic morphogenesis that explains the evolution of new forms of socioeconomic activity, the emergence of new hierarchies of organization, growth in cultural complexity, and a corollary growth in the tendency for unstable response to further development.

225

Model Complexity and Theoretical Relativity

Evidently, adaptive economic models can become awesomely complex. When details of technology or decision making and their impact on behavior are the focus of inquiry, there is little hope of avoiding this fact. Mathematical analysis may be possible but computer simulation will almost always be necessary. On the other hand, when only the most dramatic aspects of a socioeconomic situation are of interest, the modeller can allow himself to paint with a correspondingly broad brush, to create theoretical cartoons, as it were, that illustrate at the risk of exaggeration—but with great intellectual economy—some salient features of what is in truth an intricate and complex phenomenon.

There is, thus, a vast range of potential models for explaining dynamic processes in socioeconomic life, plenty to keep many of us occupied for a long, long time. In this endeavor, it seems unlikely that anyone will stumble across *the* theory or *the* model of cultural evolution. There will only be models of more or less complexity, of more or less realism, of more or less relevance, of more or less elegance. And models and theories, too, evolve in interaction with the state and dispersion of knowledge. They are the artifacts of contemporary life and some day may hold the key to some future archaeologist's scheme for understanding our epoch and how we understand ourselves.

At this point in time and from our point of view, it would appear that we have a new basis for understanding many of the striking patterns of emergence, growth, decline, and demise of discernible ways of life that constitute the epochs of economic development and cultural evolution. This new basis lies in the analysis of dynamic structures and in the derivation of their implications for the trajectories of state-determined systems. When strategic details of technology, preferences, and social organization are carefully and realistically modelled, we should expect to find emerging from their study an understanding of archaeological and historical data less in terms of ad hoc explanations and more in terms of coherent, endogenously generated forces.

NOTES

1. The author was a member of the Institute for Advanced Study, Princeton, on leave from the University of Southern California, when this chapter was written.
2. One example is the Classic Maya collapse (see Culbert 1973).

3. The symbol ":=" indicates a definitional equation.

4. The possibility of nonperiodic or chaotic trajectories was investigated by Lorenz (1963) for difference equations with a similar form.

5. This and the following sections are based on Day and Koenig (1974).

6. By *monopsony* is meant *single buyer*, which implies the ability, in this setting, of the lord of the manor to impose a "wage" on the peasantry whose labor services he "purchases".

7. These oscillations can also be aperiodic or irregular (see Day 1980).

8. In this part, I have drawn heavily on Day (1975, 1978), but extensive revisions have been made and new material incorporated.

9. It is essential to note that while each solution in the sequence of recursively generated optimizations satisfies certain optimality properties, the sequence as a whole need not and in general will not do so. Indeed, some models of this structure can be constructed that will generate pessimal performance, just as other examples can be shown to generate optimal performance.

10. *Tâtonnement* is used by Walras to refer to a process of price adjustment more or less like an auction.

PART 3

Commentaries

8

On the Construction and Evaluation of
Mathematical Models

KENNETH L. COOKE

Pomona College

ASPECTS OF MODEL CONSTRUCTION

A mathematical model should be regarded as an experimental tool to be used as an instrument in basic research. In order to use this tool, the modeller should be familiar with various kinds of mathematical or simulation models and how they have been used in exploring possible explanations or theories. In the physical sciences, many of the basic theories and relationships have been worked out in mathematical form and refined during the course of many years. Thus, for example, if faced with a new problem involving heat transfer, a physicist finds that his job is easier because he knows equations for the flow of heat that have been reliably used many times before. In archaeology, however, there is little tradition of the description of processes or creation of basic theory in mathematical form.

An important task for theoretical archaeology during the next decade is likely to be the creation of the beginnings of a tradition of mathematical investigation and theory building. At first, this will likely take the form of collecting a large number of case studies that address a variety of situations with a variety of methods. The case studies in

231

Part 2 illustrate four rather different kinds of models and are among the first in what will be a growing collection.

One of the weaknesses of modelling in archaeology to date has, perhaps, been the fact that only a small proportion of archaeologists have sufficient training in the basic tools of applied mathematics or experience with mathematics as applied in other fields. Among these basic tools are such subjects as calculus, differential equations, probability theory, and computer programming. Training in these subjects ought surely to speed the application of mathematical thought in archaeology. A brief introduction to some of these is given in Cooke (1979). In the rest of this essay, I shall offer comments and suggestions on several specific aspects of modelling and the mathematics of modelling. It is hoped that these will help clarify some points about models and assist in the difficult matter of deciding when a model has been properly constructed and validated. Specifically, I shall discuss the distinction between discrete-time and continuous-time models, methods of accounting for delayed effects, and methods for including spatial structure. I shall comment on how one explores the content of a model and how one may perhaps simplify it, with particular attention to sensitivity analysis. Also, some general thoughts on the case studies will be presented.

Discrete or Continuous Time

Frequently in archaeology, we wish to investigate the changes in a system, its evolution through time. A model of the system must therefore be *dynamic* rather than *static*. The mathematical representation of these dynamical systems ordinarily involves either difference equations or differential equations. If one thinks of time as advancing in a continuous way, we have differential equations. However, it is sometimes more convenient to think of discrete time steps, in which case we encounter difference equations. In discussions during the seminar, a question arose as to how to choose between these two kinds of models and whether the results will be equivalent. In an abstract mathematical sense, the two formulations can be almost equivalent, but in practice, caution is required. To guide our thinking on this, consider the differential equation

(1)
$$\frac{dN}{dt} = aN - bN^2 = N(a - bN).$$

This is the famous "logistic equation," and $N(t)$ could represent the size of the population of some organism or community at time t. The symbols a and b represent constants specific to the organism being considered and its environment. The usual interpretation is that a is the intrinsic net birth rate of the species, and bN represents a depression of birth rate when the population is large, owing to limitations on available resources. Day's first example (Chapter 7) includes a similar population equation.

What information about N, as a function t, can be inferred from equation (1)? If we let N_0 denote the size of the population at some initial time, which we may take to be $t = 0$, that is $N(0) = N_0$, then the differential equation may be solved to yield

$$(2) \qquad N(t) = \left[\frac{b}{a} + e^{-at} \left(\frac{1}{N_0} - \frac{b}{a} \right) \right]^{-1}$$

(provided $N_0 \neq a/b$). Here e is the symbol for one of the important special numbers in calculus and $e = 2.718$, approximately. Since a is positive, the term containing e^{-at} tends to zero as t increases indefinitely. Therefore, every solution $N(t)$ approaches the unique limiting value a/b as $t \to \infty$. The graph of $N(t)$ is the usual S-shaped or logistic curve. It has been found that many populations, be they bacteria or humans, follow a growth pattern generally of this shape under certain conditions. For an archaeological example, see Eighmy (1979).

From its definition, the derivative dN/dt can be approximated by a difference quotient. Therefore, we might expect that the difference equation

$$(3) \qquad \frac{N(t + \Delta) - N(t)}{\Delta} = aN(t) - bN(t)^2$$

would have solutions very similar to those of the differential equation. In fact, it can be proved mathematically that if we fix a positive number T, then the solution of the difference equation with $N(0) = N_0$ will converge to the solution of the differential equation as Δ tends to zero, for all t on the time interval $0 \leqslant t \leqslant T$. Unfortunately, the required smallness of Δ, in order to obtain a specified closeness of approximation, depends in some complicated way on the numbers a, b, and T and it is difficult to estimate this. In any case, in modelling, one often proceeds directly from the difference equation, and in the present case we shall see that this can lead to strikingly different results. Rewrite the difference equation in the form

(4) $$N(t + \Delta) = (1 + a\Delta)N(t) - b\Delta N(t)^2.$$

If we permit only the discrete times $t = 0, \Delta, 2\Delta, 3\Delta, \ldots$, it is convenient to let N_k denote the number $N(k\Delta)$, for $k = 0, 1, 2, 3, \ldots$, and then our equation is

(5) $$N_{k+1} = a'N_k - b'N_k^2,$$

where $a' = 1 + a\Delta$ and $b' = b\Delta$. This equation is often taken to be the discrete version of the logistic equation. However, it is no longer true that all solutions approach a limiting value as $k \to \infty$. It is known that if $1 < a' < 3$, all solutions converge to the limit $(a' - 1)/b' = a/b$. However, if a' is greater than 3, solutions can oscillate cyclically. That is, there are periodic solutions. Moreover, the number of distinct values taken on by N_k in this oscillation depends in an extremely complicated way on the value of a' and may be very large. Worse yet, for certain values of a', the solution does not display any discernible pattern, instead varying in what gives the appearance of random behavior. For more details, see May (1974) or May and Oster (1976). In the language of mathematicians, as we vary the parameter a', bifurcations occur at which the whole behavior of solutions of the difference equation is drastically changed.

One conclusion that can be drawn from this example is that one must be very cautious about assuming the equivalence of discrete-time and continuous-time models, even when they appear to represent the same phenomenon.

In the example that we have just discussed, the differential equation displayed a strong regularity in the sense that solutions could have only one mode of behavior: convergence to a constant limit. This is not always true. It is known that certain systems of three or more differential equations can exhibit behavior just as complicated as that briefly described above for the difference equation.

When should one select a discrete-time formulation and when a continuous-time formulation? Both may be needed or desirable. One advantage of using continuous time is that the concept of *rate* of change has a more precise definition. Also, if the model is to be a small one, containing only a few variables and equations, then differential equations are often easier to analyze by mathematics than difference equations. That is, the mathematician may have a better chance of extracting inferences from the model equations. On the other hand, if the model has many variables and equations, there is probably little chance of getting anywhere by mathematical analysis. In this case, if the original formulation is in terms of differential equations, it will be necessary to employ approximations by means of difference equations, and then to generate solutions of these by means of a computer. The study of the efficiency and reliability of such approximations is the subject matter of courses on "numerical analysis."

Practical considerations may also influence the choice of type of model. In economic models, difference equations are commonly used in modelling, largely because data are ordinarily collected on a yearly or monthly basis rather than continuously. Of course, in archaeology, data may be available only at widely scattered times. Moreover, as Day has said, it is not necessarily true that the data sampling interval corresponds to the natural dynamics of the process. It seems quite possible that too large a sampling interval could lead to a prediction of behavior that is an artifact of the difference equations, not really intrinsic to the process itself. For example, it is possible that some of the instability observed initially by Zubrow in his Roman model was due merely to the choice of too large a time step.

Delayed Effects

It often happens that the feedback from one part of a system to another does not occur instantaneously, but rather is delayed. Time is required for the transfer of materials or information. There are several ways to include this in a dynamic mathematical model. In a discrete-time model it can be done in a very simple way. For example, let us return to the logistic model, but now suppose that the effect of crowding or depletion of resources is felt only after a delay of one time unit. We might then replace equation (5) by

$$(6) \qquad\qquad N_{k+1} = a'N_k - b'N_{k-1}^2.$$

Our new equation is called a difference equation of *second order* since it relates the present or predicted state (time $k+1$) to the state at two previous times (k and $k-1$). Many economic models include such lagged effects.

How can such time lags be included in continuous-time models?

One of the ways, common in engineering literature, is to imagine that the flow of material or information must proceed through a sequence of stages in which the rate of output from one stage becomes the rate of input to the next stage. This method is also the one usually used by systems dynamics modellers and is explained in detail in Forrester (1961:86).

For example, suppose that the variable Q represents the quantity of some physical good held in warehouse or in transit, and let I be the rate of input and y the rate of output (see Figure 8.1). Suppose it is

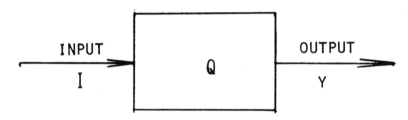

FIGURE 8.1. One-stage input-output diagram.

assumed that the output rate y is simply proportional to the stock level Q. Then $y = Q/\Delta$ where Δ is a constant. It can now be shown mathematically (by solving a differential equation) that if I is a constant, the output y will tend to the number I as $t \longrightarrow \infty$. The approach will be exponential and the rate of approach is fast if Δ is small and slow if Δ large. Forrester calls Δ the delay in the response, and many engineers call it the *time constant*.

More complicated delay patterns can be obtained by introducing a sequence of input-output blocks, as in Figure 8.2. However, if one

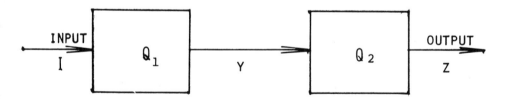

FIGURE 8.2. Two-stage input-output diagram.

wishes to include a pure time delay, in which there is a fixed time r between input and output but no change in form, this method is awkward since it requires a large increase in the number of differential equations. This *discrete delay* can be handled much more directly. For example, suppose that input I is fed into a box such as in Figure 8.1. However, assume that it takes a fixed time r to process the output, so that $y(t) = cQ(t-r)$. Then we get the equation

(7)
$$\frac{dQ\ (t)}{dt} = I - cQ\ (t-r).$$

An equation of this kind is called a *differential-delay* or *difference-differential equation*. These equations and their generalizations provide a direct way to include time delays, and a great deal of work has been done on their theory in the last few years (see Bellman and Cooke 1963 or Driver 1977). Many applications to models in biology, economics, engineering, and so on have been published, and applications may be found in archaeology.

Spatial Structure

The dynamical models of Day, Low, and Zubrow are all based on ordinary difference or differential equations. However, in an archaeological model, we may wish to take account of variations that occur from place to place as well as from time to time. For example, we may want to trace population growth or decay at several communities when, perhaps, there was migration among the communities. We can put this in a model simply by writing an equation for the population size in each community. A more complicated situation occurs when we want to model a quantity that is continuously varying in a spatial sense. Examples might be soil fertility, rainfall, or other physical variables that affect settlement patterns or population density. The density of population itself varies with location. Thus, we might want to examine a quantity $P(x,t)$, defined as the population density per square kilometer at the place x and at the time t, or a quantity $F(x,t)$, defined as a specified measure of soil fertility at place x and time t. In cases such as this, rates of change of P, F, and so forth, may be required with respect both to variation of time t and of location x. The resulting equations may then turn out to be what are called partial differential equations.

Rosen (1979) has explained in detail the derivation of such equations to describe the way in which a population distributes itself on a landscape under a variety of conditions.

Sensitivity Analysis

As Renfrew has pointed out (Chapter 10), when constructing exploratory models in archaeology, we shall often be seeking patterns or modes of behavior to replicate or simulate those in the real world. We seek a good explanation of observed phenomena rather than detailed predictive power. After one has a little experience with dynamic models or simulations, he has a feeling for what is meant by the phrase "modes of behavior." For example, the graphs of the variables in Zubrow's model of Rome (Figures 6.4–6.13) exhibit a number of qualitatively different modes. In some cases, the variable appears to approach a constant level and in others to show a cyclical structure. In Day's model of economic development in Manoria (Chapter 7), the population of peasants rises to a saturation level, whereas wages first rise to a maximum but then fall. It is difficult to offer a definition of the phrase "mode of behavior" that is general but mathematically precise. Usually, mathematicians speak in terms of *asymptotic behavior* of the solutions of their equations. That is, they classify equations in terms of the limiting behavior, such as approach to an equilibrium point, periodic oscillation, and so forth, that a solution may have as $t \longrightarrow \infty$. Some elementary aspects of this theory are outlined in Cooke (1979). Perhaps this can help the social scientist bring more exact meaning to qualitative analysis.

Sensitivity analysis is a very useful tool for exploring the modes of behavior of a given model and for building understanding of the circumstances that give rise to different modes. I shall illustrate the method by reference to a paper by Rose and Harmsen (1978), which contains a thorough and effective use of the technique.[1] This paper deals with the population dynamics of the forest tent caterpillar, *Malacosoma disstria*, an insect prevalent in North America that has dramatically fluctuating population densities. A few of the features of the model are as follows:

(1) Among the variables are the population of the caterpillar, the population of its parasites, and the population density of a virus that kills many larvae.

(2) There are two habitats. Between outbreaks, the caterpillar is confined to wet lowland forest at low densities. During outbreaks,

238

the caterpillar invades the uplands, where it is attacked by predation and parasitism.

(3) Females can fly from lowlands to highlands to lay eggs.

(4) Caterpillars can defoliate trees, causing shortage of food.

The model contains a variety of complicated interactions. In treat-
ing it, the authors used a systems dynamics approach and began by
"tuning" the parameters to make the model follow a known typical
pattern, exhibited here in Figure 8.3. They then conducted a variety of
perturbations of parameters to determine the sensitivity of the output of
the model to such changes. Among the perturbations performed were
the following:

(1) Each rate variable was increased to five times its nominal value
and decreased to one-tenth its nominal value.

(2) Rate variables to which the model was sensitive individually were
tested in combinations of two variables at a time.

(3) Random perturbations were imposed on all level variables and
on all rate variables.

During these experiments, the authors found that the simulated
population dynamics could be classified into one of six qualitatively
distinct types. For example, Figure 8.3 illustrates Type I, in which
there is a sharp outbreak of the caterpillar population occurring at
regular intervals. Figure 8.4 shows behavior in which the population is
ordinarily confined to the lowlands but varies irregularly, and there are
occasional small outbreaks into the highlands (Type IV). The other
types are not illustrated here.

The point of this discussion is that the sensitivity analysis produces a
variety of behavioral modes. There is no guarantee that all possibilities
have been found, but if this is done systematically, probably all will be
found that could occur under realistic conditions. Moreover in the
course of the analysis, one can observe which perturbations lead to
which modes and therefore obtain insight into the relative importance
of different parameters and the directions in which they tend to push
the system.

On Simplification of Models

Another important aspect is emphasized by Rose and Harmsen. In
their words, sensitivity analysis

enables the investigator to identify the variables and parameters
that determine the essential behaviour of the original mode . . . .

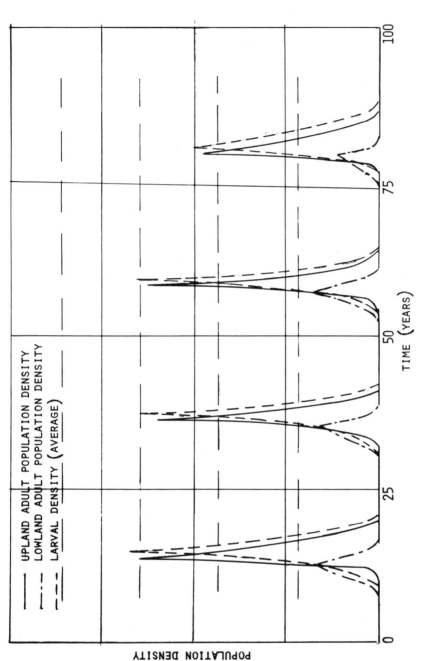

FIGURE 8.3. Population dynamics of the forest tent caterpillar. A typical pattern with sharp outbreaks at regular intervals (source: Rose and Harmsen 1978 © 1978 The Society for Computer Simulation [Simulation Councils, Inc.], reprinted by permission).

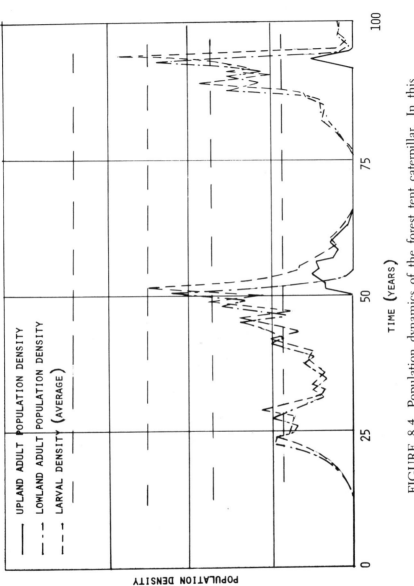

FIGURE 8.4. Population dynamics of the forest tent caterpillar. In this pattern, there is irregular variation and occasional small outbreaks into the highlands (source: Rose and Harmsen 1978 © The Society for Computer Simulation [Simulation Councils, Inc.], reprinted by permission).

With this information in hand, the investigator can devise a simplified model that exhibits the same essential behavior. (1978)

Such a simplified model might be achieved by dropping unimportant variables, aggregating variables that produce similar effects, and so on. The advantage of the simplified model might be that its behavior is more readily understood or more intuitive, or possibly more general in its applicability. As a matter of fact, Rose and Harmsen simplified their original model by a change of approach, replacing it by a cusp catastrophe model. That is, they demonstrated that the latter could produce the same kinds of aggregate system modes as the original model. The variables in the catastrophe model do not form a subset of those in the original model but may be interpreted as certain functions of some of the biologically relevant variables. The authors point out that the cusp model, like the original, can be used in explaining the gross features of the forest tent caterpillar ecosystem.

EVALUATION OF A MODEL

From the chapters of Aldenderfer and Bell (Chapters 2 and 3, respectively), we know how hard it may be to validate a model or to evaluate its adequacy. Among practitioners of simulation, validation means the matching of the model with the real system. Validation necessitates demonstrating that the model embodies an adequate representation of all aspects of the simuland pertinent to the objectives of the study. Usually selected data are used to test agreement between the model's behavior and the system it is meant to describe. The selected data might, in part, be artificially generated test data, but real-situation data should be collected and used if possible. Thus, validation has a fairly specific technical meaning. On the other hand, there is no one accepted procedure for validating a model. One approach is to use data-fitting techniques to choose parameters (the constants that enter into the various assumed relationships—for example, a and b in the logistic model) and initial conditions (N_0 in the logistic model) so as to obtain a best fit of model output to real world data. Best fit can be defined in terms of statistical measures. Even in physical systems such as are encountered in modelling of biochemical phenomena, environmental systems, and so forth, this may be a difficult mathematical problem because of the nonlinearities in the system and the large number of parameters.

242

Mathematical Models

The above concept of validation may be appropriate in the modelling of historical and archaeological processes when the structure of the system is well defined and ample data are available. On the other hand, archaeological data are often sparse, and, at present, many aspects of the real system may be incompletely understood.

What should validation mean in relation to exploratory models in archaeology? We would like to suggest several criteria:

(1) The model should be capable of generating patterns or modes of behavior that are qualitatively in agreement with the observed system. Of course, this does represent "data fitting," but only in the loose sense that the patterns are in qualitative agreement, or of the right quantitative order of magnitude.

(2) All possible modes of behavior of the model should, if possible, be determined. For example, for a systems dynamics model or model described by differential or difference equations, one should vary the initial conditions and parameters over all reasonable possibilities and observe the model output. An attempt should be made to explain the observed variations. Changes in the model may be necessary if reasonable input produces unreasonable output.

(3) The mathematical formulation should be self-consistent and as simple as possible while still providing the ends desired. No attempt will be made here to define what is meant by simple. One reason to seek simplicity is that it is then easier to check the consistency of the model. Another is that it may be easier to carry out the program in (2).

(4) The model should be robust. By this I mean that small changes in model structure result in small changes in output. Usually this means in practice that small changes in the parameters (constants) in the equations result in small changes in output. However, one must be careful in applying this criterion, for often what one is looking for is exactly the qualitative change that occurs when a parameter reaches a critical value. For example, the system may abruptly change from having one steady state to having two. Understanding such *bifurcations* may well give the greatest insight into model structure. Both mathematical analysis and sensitivity analysis are useful in this connection. I also want to point out that in complex models, for example in many of the systems dynamics models, the definitions of variables, assumed relationships, and feedback loops often have a certain

243

arbitrariness. It is important to check the robustness of such models against changes in mathematical functions and the introduction or deletion of some variables, feedback paths, and so forth.

(5) In the last analysis, perhaps the evaluation of an exploratory model in archaeology comes down to this: the model provides in some sense an explanation of a certain observation; it does so in a way that provides greater clarity or insight, and it behaves in a reasonable or explainable way when subjected to tests such as those I have just outlined. Underlying assumptions of the model as well as any of its limitations or uncertainties should be clearly stated.

Having suggested criteria for sound archaeological analysis, I now turn to the four case studies presented earlier in this volume to compare them with these criteria. In addition, I will comment on them further.

THOUGHTS ON THE CASE STUDIES

It was interesting to observe the almost universal desire among Advanced Seminar participants for parsimonious models, which I believe means models with structures that are in some sense simple but have great explanatory power as explained in criterion (3) in the previous section. However, it is likely that many archaeological models will contain many variables that are related in a complex way. Is there any way to simplify such models or to cut them up into smaller parts that can be understood more readily? An example of simplification of a model was given by Cordell in her case study. By computing correlations, she found several variables that were not relevant to site longevity and could be removed. Her work seems to satisfy all of the above criteria for validation quite well. Also, I have already described how sensitivity analysis was used in the caterpillar model to explore the relative importance of different factors. By varying one coefficient or one assumed relation at a time, the authors of the study were able eventually to understand the model as a whole.

The same problem of complex models arises, too, in the realm of physical science. It is not true, as some people think, that modelling there is simple or straightforward. Instead, it is frequently true that the final mathematical formulation contains many complicated equations (often, differential equations). One must then try to understand whether the model is a valid representation of the physical reality and also to understand the modes of behavior of the model and how it is that they arise as observed. To do this, it is standard practice to consider simplified versions of the model. For example, suppose that the problem involves a source of heat, which heats a fluid in a pipe. The fluid flows through the pipe and the heat is then captured from the fluid by some device and used to generate electricity. One can make simplifying assumptions, for example, that no heat is lost at intermediate points in the pipe, or that temperature change in the fluid does not change its flow properties. Each assumption yields a problem that may be easier to comprehend. Or, we may study an idealized problem of, say, an infinitely long pipe with fluid flowing at constant speed and heat inserted in a stretch of finite length. This problem might yield mathematical equations that we know how to solve explicitly. If so, we will have a problem that is extremely useful for comparison. In fact, if we then simulate a more complex version of the problem on a computer, the results should closely agree with those for the idealized problem when we choose parameters or conditions in the complex problem that make it close to the idealized problem. In other words, we can try to make a whole spectrum of models that describe the physical situation with lesser or greater verisimilitude. We can then build our intuition about the more complex from the simpler situations.

The effort by Zubrow to use Forrester's urban dynamics as the basis for a model of ancient Rome, and his difficulties in making this adaptation, suggest that several of my criteria for validation were not met. As already mentioned, some of this may merely be due to numerical instability caused by using a discrete model with a large time step. More importantly, Zubrow's work raises a number of interesting theoretical questions. Is there a generic urban model whose structure is invariant from century to century and continent to continent? Are there, at least, certain structures that are invariant? Is it possible to construct a classification scheme, each urban type being represented by a mathematical model? Perhaps if archaeologists were to construct models of various ancient cities *ab initio* and then to compare these models, essential structural differences and similarities might begin to emerge. I think that these models ought to be simple at first, for the most important contrasts may well occur at the grossest level of detail. If this has not already been done by urban theorists, then it seems to me that it would be a provocative study.

Aldenderfer's ABSIM model (Chapter 4) is an interesting example of a simulation conducted at a fine level of realistic detail, proving that my first criterion can be met in archaeological analysis. The problem is a specific example of a general class of problems in archaeology: how to infer as much information as possible from limited observations. This problem has been extensively treated in abstract form in the mathematical and engineering literature, and I shall briefly describe a formulation of it. Suppose that we know or can assume a particular model structure in the form of a system of differential or difference equations. These equations will describe the time evolution of the state variables, which I shall call $x_1(t)$, $x_2(t)$, . . . , $x_n(t)$. In the equations, there will be a number of rate constants or other parameters, the values of which are generally not well known. Now suppose that we cannot directly observe the state variables but only certain combinations of them, say $y_1(t)$, $y_2(t)$, . . . , $y_k(t)$. On the basis of these observables, can we determine the parameters? This is called the problem of *system identification* or the *inverse problem*. In certain cases, there is a theory of *observability*, which gives conditions under which the problem can be solved. Perhaps these theories could be usefully applied to some archaeological examples.

Chapter 7 (Day) contains several simple examples of mathematical models and a description of a very general framework for modelling. Day emphasizes the incorporation into the models of the economizing or optimizing motive in shaping human behavior. A second important idea is that these local or short-term optimizing principles are themselves changing in the light of changing conditions and newly acquired experience. These ideas are applied in simple examples and also explained in a very general and abstract way. The mathematical framework is very similar to the ideas of Bellman (1961) on adaptive systems.

Do Day's examples fulfill my criteria for validation? In one sense, criterion (1) is satisfied since the models generate patterns that are qualitatively in agreement with very large-scale societal shifts, as, for example, from hunting to agriculture. One is left with the feeling that the model is plausible, that things might have happened that way. On the other hand, some archaeologists may desire models with richer structure and greater possibility for checking against evidence in at least a semiquantitative sense. Singh and Day (1975) have constructed quite specific models of agricultural development. It would seem that such a modern-day model could be a useful guide or example for archaeologists in constructing models at a fairly rich level of detail.

246

SUMMARY

In this essay, I have tried to discuss a few ideas that might be helpful to archaeologists and anthropologists in understanding how mathematical and simulation models may be constructed, used, and evaluated. First, I emphasized the need for the creation of models of a variety of situations (case studies) in order to form a background of experience. I have also tried to create an awareness of the fact that applied mathematics contains many sophisticated devices for handling rates, flows, delays, patterns in space, and so forth. Social scientists should know of these and, to the extent feasible, should understand the mathematics involved.

The desirability of beginning with relatively simple models that may be amenable to exact mathematical solution has been pointed out. Two major ways to understand complex models have been presented. One way is to break the problem into several parts, each of which can be examined in isolation from the others. The behaviors of the simpler subsystems often provide insight into the behavior of the whole and benchmarks for judging the validity of the overall model. The second method employs sensitivity analysis in conjunction with a large number of computer simulation runs.

Finally, a set of criteria for validation models has been listed, and some comments made about the case studies in this volume.

NOTE

1. The author wishes to thank R. Harmsen and M. R. Rose for permission to use excerpts from their work, and the Society for Computer Simulation (Simulation Councils, Inc.) for permission to reprint Figures 8.3 and 8.4.

9

Using System Dynamics to Simulate the Past

GILBERT W. LOW

Albert P. Sloan School of Management
Massachusetts Institute of Technology

INTRODUCTION[1]

In Storm's *Seven Arrows*, a lyrical treatment of the Plains Indians, the great teachers were able to construct an orderly universe, indeed a "way of life," from a few stones scattered on the ground. According to some observers, the mystic teacher has been replaced in this age of technology and jargon by the systems analyst, who, like his predecessor, is expected to extract order from chaos and systems from scattered elements. For one who finds systems behind every bush, and feedback systems at that, a week-long conference consisting of five archaeologists, a philosopher of science, an economist, a systems analyst, and a mathematician was a great challenge. The challenge, which I shall try to meet in this commentary, is to gather up some of the diverse intellectual artifacts deposited at the conference and to mold them into a workable perspective that can enhance our understanding of the past.

The conferees shared an interest in the process of change and an inclination to seek structural, or systemic, explanations. The conferees agreed on the importance of systems and simulation, even though they did not always accept a common set of definitions. The purpose of this commentary, then, is to define a particular coherent framework for assessing the potential contribution of simulation to archaeology. The framework is system dynamics, an application of the principles of cybernetics to social science research (see Forrester 1961, 1968). Thus, I shall employ concepts like simulation, system, and structure from the system dynamics viewpoint.

Archaeologists and other anthropologists constitute the intended audience. Therefore, I shall treat some of the basic system dynamics concepts that may be new to this audience but that are covered more fully elsewhere (see System Dynamics Group 1979 for references). Much of the material, however, begins to fill gaps in the literature and, therefore, is aimed at a broader audience. As a system dynamics modeller, I have focused on what I know best. However, interpretation of archaeological literature and comments on presentations at the Advanced Seminar are included, without, I hope, exposing the naiveté of an enthusiastic neophyte.

FEEDBACK STRUCTURE AND SYSTEM SIMULATION

The title of this section is purposefully loaded with jargon. The literature is confusing, but to a system dynamicist, each term has a specific meaning. The major ideas follow from a claim that all change arises out of feedback structure. Accepting this view as an operational premise leads to a set of organizing concepts for constructing and using models.

Feedback characterizes causal interrelationships between system elements. If changing one element causes change in another, and that change in turn causes variation in the first, then the two elements are linked in a feedback loop. Hunger and eating, for example, are linked by feedback, where the act of eating changes the level of hunger which can feed back to the act of eating.

Portraying feedback with the conventional symbols of system dynamics tell us more about such a relationship. In Figure 9.1, feedback occurs between a condition, or state variable, that both affects and is affected by an action variable. The state variable (called a level) represents accumulation, and the action variable its rate of change (called a rate). Accumulation is a process that involves the passage of time, but at any point in time one can observe the quantity in the level. In Figure 9.1, this quantity affects its rate of change, which is not observ-

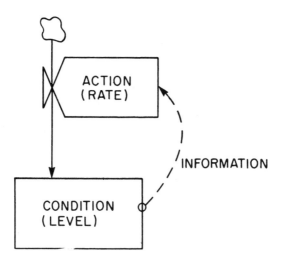

FIGURE 9.1. Basic feedback loop structure linking action and condition.

able at any instant in time, through an information like the dashed line. The action or rate variable controls the flow of material, information, or other quantity that accumulates in the level. As a general portrayal of information feedback, the structure produces change over time, because of the presence of accumulation within every loop, and encompasses every conscious or unconscious action.

Within the feedback framework, concepts of system and simulation take on particular meaning. A system, which Bertalanffy (1950) defines as a "complex of elements in mutual interaction," contains interaction of a particular type (feedback). Other aspects of a system and its boundary will be treated in later sections of this chapter. Any set of causal feedback loops constitutes a feedback structure, which can be portrayed quantitatively and solved to exhibit a trajectory for each element of the structure over time. Usually the solution involves non-linear relationships that are intractable analytically, so computer simulation is employed.

Simulation in this view consists of any operationally complete set of rules that links a set of elements to generate a history of events (Doran 1970:297). All of the models presented at the conference were simulations. *System simulation* in system dynamics terms has a narrower definition and encompasses the specific operating rules of feedback and accumulation. The models described by Cordell (Chapter 5) and Aldenderfer (Chapter 4) were not system simulations in this sense. System simulation solves over time, with or without a computer, a set of levels (accumulations) and their rates of change connected in feedback loops. As we shall see, only feedback systems, cast as interlinked states and actions, can simulate through time without being driven by exogenously imposed inputs. Both Zubrow's adaptation of the *Urban Dynamics* model to ancient Rome (Chapter 6) and Day's use of differential equations (Chapter 7) portrayed system simulation. Other anthropological examples are contained in Hosler, Sabloff, and Runge (1977) as well as in Shantzis and Behrens (1973).

Change arises from feedback structure. To explain patterns of change, one must identify characteristics of structure. Positive feedback, for example, can serve to amplify disturbances; while negative feedback is goal-seeking and can prevent a system from losing control. An example of positive, or self-reinforcing, feedback is given by Maruyama:

> Take, for example, weathering of rock. A small crack in a rock collects some water. The water freezes and makes the crack larger. A larger crack collects more water, which [freezes and] makes the crack still larger. (cited in Hill 1977b:79)

An example of negative feedback is the link between eating and hunger that was cited above. An increase in hunger causes one to eat, which, in turn, reduces hunger. Positive feedback can produce runaway growth or collapse, and thus tends to destabilize a system; negative feedback can provide control of a system.

Positive and negative feedback are essential distinctions whose importance is recognized in the systems literature. Hill, in his "Systems Theory and the Explanation of Change" (Hill 1977b), provides an interesting review of this literature. According to systems theory, an important characteristic of living systems is self-regulation, or homeostasis (Ashby 1956); without homeostasis, systems would not survive long enough for one to identify their characteristics. Self-regulation occurs because of negative feedback. Thus, survival implies feedback. Day calls the instinctive or conscious adaption of all surviving systems to a changing environment "homeostasis in the general sense" and refers to the particular negative feedback control mechanism as "homeostasis in the specific sense" (see Chapter 7).

Forrester identifies this specific mechanism as the goal structure that underlies all decisions (Forrester 1968: Chapter 4). As shown in Figure 9.2, individual actions aim to eliminate discrepancies between a goal for the system and the actual condition. Because a discrepancy cannot be eliminated instantaneously, an implicit or consciously recognized

252

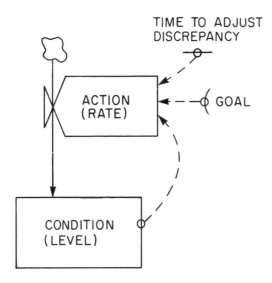

FIGURE 9.2. Goal structure governing individual actions.

"time constant" defines the intended speed of adjustment. The mechanism can be defined formally:

$$\text{Action} = \frac{\text{Goal} - \text{Condition}}{\text{Adjustment Time}}.$$

The goal formation process and its role in homeostasis is obscured by Hill's interpretation of systems concepts. While rightly objecting to the teleological notion of system goals, he fails to see goals as an essential part of individual action:

> I am not arguing that individuals and social systems never have goals. I do think, however, that such goals must originate in response to stress, rather than occurring in a vacuum. . . . It is only when certain critical variables are approaching or exceeding their tolerance limits, or are perceived to be approaching them, that individuals or social systems establish goals—and these goals are simply statements concerning possible solutions to the stresses involved. (Hill 1977b:75)

In contrast to Hill's view, it is the existence of goals, with or without any particular stress impinging on human actions, that keeps a system under control. Tight negative feedback between a particular system state and its rate of change, as shown in the equation above, will prevent the condition from moving far from the goal.

253

What makes a social system complex and interesting, however, is the frequent existence of conflicting goals in determining human action and the manner in which changes in a targeted condition can produce change elsewhere in a system that feeds back to affect future action. These indirect effects are what produce the unexpected results that computer simulations often reveal. Yet Hill, and perhaps Maruyama, whom he cites, seem to overstate the dichotomy between homeostatic mechanisms and deviation-amplifying positive feedback structures. Positive feedback can be goal-seeking (when the gain is less than unity); a negative feedback loop embodying goal-determining actions with two states can produce pure oscillations; and a system in which each individual agent is operating according to the goal structure shown previously can still contain positive feedback mechanisms that lead to major change or destruction. Thus, "homeostasis in the specific sense" (the individual goal-seeking mechanism) is a necessary component of human actions but is not sufficient to guarantee survival.

An interesting example of negative feedback, especially for archaeologists, is the continuous accumulation of information in an exponential delay that can produce slowly changing attitudes or traditions. The goal-seeking structure in Figure 9.2 precisely specifies an information-smoothing process, where "goal" is the value to be smoothed, "condition" is the smoothed or delayed value, and "time to adjust discrepancy" is the smoothing time constant. Information smoothing can be used to portray delayed perceptions of a changing physical environment, or delays in transmitting new technologies and other causes of social change. These delays in a model of prehistoric change would be on the order of generations and could easily produce instability in a rapidly changing environment.

The goal-seeking delay structure also can portray changing standards, values, and traditions. In his treatment of managerial goal structures, Forrester (1966) shows how the goal itself can become a variable that responds to past performance. The present assessment of past performance, in turn, is based on information smoothing. We see many examples of how tradition enters into our present goals. What is an acceptable inflation rate today was quite unacceptable fifteen years ago; the level of noise people will tolerate today was intolerable a century ago. As an adaptive mechanism, the floating goal is quite handy, for one way to eliminate the frustrating discrepancy between goal and condition is to change the goal. But the tradition-determined

254

goal structure is essentially an example of positive feedback (containing two negative feedback loops) that can produce long-term drift to vulnerability and extinction.

Recognition of the importance of feedback in one's everyday experience implies a specific approach to explanations of change and model simulation. A focus on structure forces one to identify feedback components when confronted with a problem involving change. One tends to look for relevant stocks (levels) and flows (rates) in any economic or cultural system. For example, goods (like cars) are produced, flow into a stock of inventory, and then are shipped (rate) to the consumer, who may hold the product in another stock while it yields a flow of services. From initial creation to final destruction or decay, the product moves through conserved channels.

Conservation is apparent in the physical world, and it means that forms of matter, like the car in our example, cannot enter a system or disappear from it except through explicit acts of energy transformation. The fact of physical conservation is generally accepted, but the need for its representation in formal models is not. This can lead to models of dynamic phenomena that yield unlikely, or at least suspicious, conclusions (see Low 1979 for an example from the economics literature). System dynamics models usually do observe conservation, if only because simulation of models with nonconserved flows often generates ridiculous behavior.

To generate realistic behavior, realistic feedback links must relate levels to their rates of change. The inventory of cars in our example must be linked to the shipment of cars, which is obvious at least when the inventory approaches zero. For without a link that would restrain shipments, inventory (in the model) would go negative, and consumers would, in essence, get something for nothing. The process of conservation, in fact, is what economics is all about; for scarcity involves the allocation and conscious management of stocks. The institutionalization of stock management, as Day showed in his fascinating treatment of the banking function, can lead to wide-ranging changes in social and cultural patterns.

Feedback was lurking implicitly or explicitly behind every model we discussed at the seminar. In some cases described by Zubrow, Day, and Sabloff (the Classic Mayan collapse), feedback and conservation were observed by design. Even in Aldenderfer's and Cordell's models, feedback was implied. For example, the aging of adzes and other tools

255

of Aldenderfer's hunter-gatherers requires negative feedback to capture the process of decay. And, of course, Aldenderfer's flow diagram (Figure 4.3) showed explicit feedback even if his discussion did not. In Cordell's model (Chapter 5), which correlates data on site abandonment with climatic changes, there is no explicit feedback, although the process of site migration implies movement that depends on site position.

Hunting for elusive feedback is hardly a rewarding sport unless it leads to useful insights and, perhaps, to more valid explanations of cultural change. To prove with an elegant application that explicit incorporation of feedback and conservation leads to improved archaeological explanation is beyond the scope of this commentary. But at least the issue can be raised. In Aldenderfer's study, for example, there is no link between the use of a·tool and the activities of hunter-gatherers. Use-life is based on probability distributions but not on a behavioral theory that tool formation, tool use, or migration would imply. The model represents state-determined processes but is not a state-determined model. This does not matter for the purpose of yielding a final assemblage of artifacts to compare with actual assemblages, but it would matter if we wanted to understand the dynamics of assemblage formation. I shall say more about the importance of behavioral process modelling in later sections.

The Internal Perspective

In system dynamics, a focus on behavioral process means that models generally portray explicitly the way people make decisions and affect their environment. The state-determined format of goal-driven actions implies direct representation of goals and actions as they occur at an individual level. These decisions, and the states with which they interact, together form a system for explaining some dynamic phenomenon of interest. Inside the system boundary, therefore, can be found all that one knows, or thinks he knows, about the behavioral processes required for explanation. Outside the boundary, by definition, lie the exogenous factors, some of which may influence what happens within the boundary but none of which interact with internal feedback elements. The useful explanatory information resides within a system boundary, thereby justifying what might be called an internal, as opposed to an external, perspective.

All of the Advanced Seminar participants seemed to share this internal perspective. Renfrew, for example, has stressed that the explanation of culture change involves a choice of mechanisms that generate the interaction of factors within a culture (Renfrew 1972). External events, such as earthquakes or invasions, are of less interest in explaining change than are the internal mechanisms that enable a system to adapt to outside developments unless, of course, a culture is simply wiped out by some outside incursion.

It is puzzling, therefore, that scholars concerned with the evolution and explanation of culture change take what I would call the external view. Athens, for example, writes that Renfrew is wrong to look inside a culture for explanation and suggests, mysteriously, that inquiry must extend "beyond the system under investigation" (Athens 1977:359). Yet the "system" is chosen as the locus of mechanisms necessary to explain behavior! Saxe devotes an entire paper to show that "the processes that result in systemic change for all systems are and must be initiated by extrasystemic variables" (Saxe 1977:116). The assertion is true only in the uninteresting sense that a system at rest cannot show disequilibrium behavior unless stimulated by something (unbalanced initial conditions, randomness, or changes in identifiable exogenous factors). Hill (1977b:75), in a similar vein, writes that societies "change in the process of failing to maintain stability. After all, why would social systems direct themselves to institute change just for the sake of change?" Yet it is precisely the *process* of change, meaning disequilibrium, that forces us to examine internal feedback mechanisms if we are to progress from description to explanation.

A few examples of the internal perspective will illustrate its importance. In the literature of economics, Frisch (1933) wrote years ago about the importance of internal structure to understanding the behavior of economic systems. He cites as an analogue the rocking horse, which when pushed continues to exhibit dynamic behavior long after the push, and which when pushed frequently in some random fashion displays a periodicity and a rocking motion that reflect its internal structure more than the input characteristics. Similarly, a business firm will exhibit dynamic characteristics that emanate from its internal management structure. Market forces, which influence corporate performance, are usually not enough to explain a company's behavior, for what counts in understanding dynamic response is how people inside the company make decisions when faced with both internal and external pressures. The perspective has an appeal in the management sciences and in public policy because it suggests that internal decision mechanisms as the source of problems are the very mechanisms that management can do something about, once their importance is understood. However, economists and managers often look to outside forces as the source of their troubles.

A third example of internal perspective is the Hosler, Sabloff, and Runge model of Mayan collapse (1977). Here the authors identify positive feedback mechanisms containing resource use and monument construction that eventually produce cultural extinction. The explanatory value, even before demonstrating validity, lies in showing how internal feedback mechanisms could lead to the observed collapse with *any* outside disturbance (change of trade patterns, invasion, drought, and so forth). A focus on the nature of such disturbance says little about how a culture might become dangerously vulnerable to environmental changes.

To explain observed patterns of change, the internal perspective requires that feedback mechanisms also be observable. That is, action variables in a quantitative model should represent behavior at the individual level even though the system produces behavior at an aggregate level. This explicit portrayal of "micro" decisions in "macro" models distinguishes system dynamics from other macromodelling approaches. In economics, for example, econometric models designed to explain changes in GNP and other aggregate phenomena statistically relate aggregate data and have a different appearance from microeconomic models of the firm. On the other hand, a system dynamics model of the economy currently being developed at M.I.T. (see Forrester, Mass, and Ryan 1976) centers around an explicit theory of the firm and contains no micro-macro distinctions. For example, supply and demand relate to price not in terms of the abstract supply and demand curves common to economic analysis, but in the explicit manner by which businessmen bring accessible information about supply (inventory levels) and demand (backlogs) into their pricing decisions. Thus, the decision variables are designed to portray recognizable roles of individuals in firms or households. The structure constitutes a role-playing model.

This role-playing, or micro perspective, has several important advantages, as well as attendant shortcomings. One advantage, as Bell pointed out at the Advanced Seminar and elsewhere (Bell and Senge 1979), is that modelling formulations based on direct observation of real decision processes introduce a point of contact with reality that is absent in other approaches. Internal model components, derived independently of the behavior they produce, are refutable by appeal to intuition, direct observation, experience, and expert advice. Bell's refutationist position claims a source of validation that cannot be found in the more widely used probabilistic and statistical models. Moreover, the refutable nature of model components severely reduces the inclination to "tinker" with a model in order to make it produce desired behavior, a temptation in most model building that particularly bothered conference participants. Validation at the direct component level, as well as through comparison of behavior, restrains ad hoc changes in structure.

The internal perspective permits the modeller to add any influence he deems important. In most models whose parameter values are determined by statistical data, this freedom is not available. Aldenderfer's model, for example, excluded social factors because no data were accessible, even though they were considered important to the problem at hand. A system dynamics model, in contrast, would include such variables, on the basis of intuition if nothing else. Giving an important relationship some intuitively reasonable value is superior to excluding the relationship altogether and thus attributing the precise value of zero. The advantage of including such variables may be especially significant to archaeologists, for whom good data are so sparse; although, then, the refutability of such intuitively based elements must rely on analogy with other known cultures.

The internal perspective permits one to develop model structures independent of formal collected data. System dynamics models, as Bell indicated, tend to be generic models whose implications can be tested against independent data. One does not try to extract conclusions from a particular set of collected data that have been used simultaneously to specify structure and estimate parameter values. This independence of model structure from the data used to test it seems to be an important goal of the "new archaeology" (Watson, LeBlanc, and Redman 1971:31–32). It also permits one to test the sensitivity of model behavior to selective changes in parameter values, for parameter estimates are not based on data drawn from the operation of an entire system. In a statistical model whose parameters come from historical data, one cannot test behavior by changing a particular set of parameters because in the operation of the real system, such a change would produce different behavior and thus different parameter estimates.

Finally, the internal, microlevel approach contributes to a model's explanatory clarity. One can relate model behavior directly to internal causal structure and thus gain understanding of why the model behaves as it does. These results may then be communicated to other people. Although a model's dynamic behavior is seldom easily understood, it is always at least possible to gain access to the black box interior. Analysis of the structure-behavior link is a critical part of model development, as we shall see later.

Models designed to represent actual causal processes do not overcome all problems and, indeed, have shortcomings of their own. For one thing, such models tend to contain many equations. This apparent complexity stems from trying to give each model component and its associated parameters an operational meaning identified with real decisions. But the result is often a confusing set of symbols on a flow diagram that make the basic set of equations look more complicated than they are. The *World Dynamics* model (Forrester 1971), for example, has 43 active equations, even though the whole structure can be boiled down to one 50-order differential equation. This reduced mathematical portrayal might look neater, but the refutationist content would be lost. Moreover, for archaeologists who deal with prehistory, as opposed to current policy issues, there are no direct experiences or "experts" who can verify a piece of model structure. The modeller cannot go to a Mayan monument builder and get information about his decision processes! Thus refutability at this level is pretty tenuous. On the other hand, the sparsity of useful archaeological data plagues all modelling approaches.

The internal perspective and its reliance on individual behavior mechanisms distinguishes system dynamics from much of the other systems literature, a point that Bell makes in connection with "reducing wholes to parts." General Systems Theory (GST), for example, claims that the whole, even after it is studied, cannot be explained in terms of its parts. This "holist" view is opposed by the "methodological individualists" who, like system dynamicists, look to the microcomponents to explain macrochange. One of these opposing voices, J. W. N. Watkins, writes:

> There may be unfinished or half way explanations of large-scale social phenomena (say, inflation) in terms of other large-scale phenomena (say, full employment); but we shall not have arrived at rock bottom explanations of such large-scale phenomena until

260

we have deduced an account of them from statements about the dispositions, beliefs, resources and interrelations of individuals. (Watkins, cited in Phillips 1976:40).

The system in system dynamics, unlike that of General Systems Theory, is known only because of our knowledge of its individual parts, and it is the relationship among parts that explains dynamic behavior. Phillips writes:

The case for system theory [meaning GST] rests to a large degree on the claim that a part cannot be removed from a system without becoming an artifact; it is fatal to ruin this foundation by admitting that useful information can be obtained by studying a part in isolation. (Phillips 1976:57)

The way one defines "system," perhaps the most confusing term in the systems lexicon, is colored by one's position on wholes versus parts. The internal perspective delineated here would be consistent with the definition offered by Hall and Fagan: "Why not simply select certain interrelated entities that happen to be of relevance to a particular investigation, and then call this group of entities a system?" (cited in Phillips 1976:62). "Relevance" to a system dynamicist generally means pertaining to some dynamic problem of interest, like the ritual pig cycle, the Mayan collapse, or the transmission of technology. System, then, has a meaning that goes beyond just a collection of interrelated parts to include the role of one's theory about what's important and how things interrelate. This view, unlike GST, implies that one can usefully bound a system to deal with a particular problem and that the knowledge necessary for drawing a boundary comes from a problem statement and component interactions even before we have knowledge of the whole. "System," then, is seen as artifact of the modeller defined with the modeller's purpose in mind. It is refutable by comparing its parts to real relationships and total behavior to real behavior; and it focuses our attention on the internal feedback structure or individual actions as the causal explanation of social change.

Linking Structure and Behavior

So far I have discussed mainly the nature of structure in system dynamics models. In this section I shall focus on the link between structure and dynamic change, for it is change that should be the focus

261

of systems research. As Hill (1977b:102) observes: "[Most] of the systems literature does not deal with *change* in enough detail to be of much use. Systems research has been much more concerned with what systems are, how they can be described and classified, and how they are regulated." My comments will first distinguish a static feedback structure from the dynamic behavior it produces and then attempt to justify the importance of that distinction.

There is considerable confusion about whether or not structure can transform itself; in other words, whether structure is conceptually a static or dynamic idea. In system dynamics, one generally thinks of feedback structure as being static. Static structure, in which time has no causal significance, generates dynamic behavior. This view, however, apparently is not accepted by all people sympathetic to systems concepts. In writing about technological change, for example, Renfrew (1972:37) says:

> The growth of human societies is not always subject to the law of diminishing returns precisely because the underlying structure is itself changed in the growth process. . . . Innovations arrest or negate the operation of the usual limiting factors. This change of structures of the systems with which he deals do not generally transform themselves into something different.

The difference here may be semantic, but it points to a fundamentally important view about systems. The notion of system as an artifact of the modeller bases internal structure on whatever is sufficient to handle a particular dynamic problem of interest. If one wants to explain change that occurs over a relatively short time, one does not include variables that require a long time to change. For example, to explain the ritual pig cycle, with a period of ten years, Shantzis and Behrens (1973) assumed basic cultural attitudes as fixed. But to explain culture change over centuries, one would have to include time-varying traditions and attitudes.

Similarly, in the production system that aims to control inventory levels, the goal in the decision structure would depend on the duration and type of behavior one wishes to analyze. If one were looking at some short-lived phenomenon, a fixed desired inventory would be appropriate. A longer time horizon where growth or decay enters the picture would call for a desired inventory that varies but is based on a fixed number of months' worth of business activity. A still longer perspective, one that might incorporate changes in communications technology, would formulate desired inventory on the basis of a variable

coverage time which, in turn, would depend on some more fundamental fixed quantity. In each case, the dynamic mode of interest and
its relative time horizon determine the appropriate static structure.

What people think of as self-generated structural change may really
involve variation in the strength of different feedback loops over time.
In the same context as before, Renfrew (1972:37) writes: "After a period
of sustained change or growth, further change (for example, further
investment increase) no longer has so large an effect as before (for
example, on output). A kind of saturation is reached, and the growth
ends. The feedback, in other words, is no longer positive." This statement is consistent with the notion of static structure, as the underlying
feedback loops (the structure) remain unchanged, but their importance
varies as the system moves along its trajectory through time. The
well-known sigmoidal (logistic) growth curve cited by Cooke (Chapter
8) provides a good example of what is called "changing loop dominance." Goodman (1974: Chapter 14) shows a level/rate portrayal of
the logistics curve equations, demonstrating how positive feedback
produces the initial exponential growth, which, because growth has
occurred, puts the system more and more under the control of negative
feedback constraints. Growth eventually ceases when negative feedback dominates positive feedback. The positive feedback loop (the
structure) is still intact; but it is no longer effective in producing growth.

Viewing structure as static means that one can master an understanding of basic system structures and apply them to many different
historical phenomena. For example, knowledge of simple positive and
negative feedback structures and some basic combinations can be
applied to a wide variety of fields, where certain behavior modes reflect
common elements of structure. If structure were not static but were
somehow dependent on the history it generates, then this transferabil-
ity of structure across disciplines or historical periods would be impossible. Moreover, being able to translate knowledge of structure into
knowledge of particular fields may also permit the useful transfer of
knowledge about current or historically known change to the explanation of prehistoric change. Clarke (1972:30) seems to allude to trans-
ferability of structure when he states that general systems properties
enable one to compare systems which may share elements of what he
calls "deep structure" but which appear dissimilar on the surface. This
approach, he says, may open up new realms of classificatory possibilities.

The behavior generated by static structures, particularly nonlinear structures, can be extremely complex. This is where system dynamics, with an explicit operating methodology, can contribute much-needed clarity to the existing systems literature. Hill's discussion of dynamics, for example, does not really shed much light by saying that social change is the process of failing to maintain stability (1977b:75). All systems that survive long enough for us to be interested in them are basically stable in Hill's sense of containing strong homeostatic mechanisms. Hill's definition of change as instability leaves out some of the most fascinating issues. On the other hand, change defined as disequilibrium (where the state variables are not constant) includes instances of recurrent ("stable") behavior patterns, long-term drifts in attitudes and expectations, and the relative amplification, phase relationships, and frequencies exhibited by a system as it responds to perturbations in the environment. Again, the internal perspective makes us relate complex behavior to structure so as to understand just what internal mechanisms are acting to prolong or cut short survival.

Understanding the connection between system behavior and internal feedback components also reveals how a system as a whole can lead to trajectories unintended by any of its individual actors. In constructing a system dynamics model, one never would include unknowable, implied system "goals." Rather, one would include information as individuals are able to perceive it. In such systems, individual rational actions can, and usually do, lead to suboptimal system behavior. Optimality is not a necessary condition to survival, despite some assertions to the contrary (see, for example, Hill 1977b:94). Dawkins (1976), for example, shows that the evolutionary stable strategy (ESS) suggested by Maynard-Smith can lead to suboptimal payoffs for a society of competing individuals. By producing behavior unintended by its individual actors, systems do, indeed, have a "life of their own," but it is one that results from internal decision structures that are accessible to the modeller.

Linking accessible structure to observed behavior is an essential aspect of building confidence with models (Forrester and Senge 1979). One cannot claim validity for model conclusions if the behavior being generated cannot be explained in terms of model structure. Dynamic behavior modes, whether expected by the modeller or not, are convincing only if they lead to some inference about real feedback structures; and that inference cannot be drawn until the modeller understands the structure/behavior link. It is tempting to produce a set of simulations without really dissecting them properly. Yet the process of constructing and validating models in some ways begins at the simulation stage. Thus Zubrow's attempt (Chapter 6) to apply the *Urban Dynamics* model to ancient Rome would be more persuasive if his varied oscillatory behavior modes, unlike any found with the original model or its other applications, were rigorously explained in terms of model structure. One's disbelief cannot be held in tow for long if the black box, whose insides *are* accessible, is not opened up.

Part of establishing explicitly the link between structure and behavior is the need to maintain control of a model. A widely accepted view among conference participants was that system dynamics models are exercises in cavalier, perhaps roughshod creativity. But good modelling requires both creative leaps and tight controls, though probably not simultaneously. One does not just build a model and then "let 'er rip." Tight control of the effort, if not exercised up to the "take-off" phase, will be forced on the modeller if he/she wants to be persuasive.

Even analytical, mathematical models seem to take on a "life of their own." The conferees discussed, for example, the use of differential equations and their equivalent difference equation formulations (see Cooke, Chapter 8). A striking distinction between the two forms was in their behavior, with difference equations yielding greater dynamic variety. For example, Day (Chapter 7) demonstrated the oscillatory behavior that a first-order difference equation can produce, and Cooke (Chapter 8) showed that a difference equation portrayal of the logistic curve can produce just about any behavior imaginable, including "chaos." However, these interesting behavior modes, which cannot be generated by differential equation counterparts, appear to be little more than mathematical artifacts that yield limited insight into the operation of real systems. A first-order differential equation cannot generate overshoot, but a difference equation can generate overshoot if one chooses a sufficiently long time interval. Moreover, convergence, divergence, and periodicity all depend upon a time interval that has nothing to do with real system relationships. Thus the behavior being generated cannot be linked back to internal feedback structure.

Renfrew presented a much more elaborate mathematical construct in the form of catastrophe theory (Chapter 10; see also Renfrew 1978). Despite its elegance, it is unclear how one might use the theory to simulate social change. The presentation of how internal continuous processes can give rise to apparently discontinuous change is powerful

265

and important to the process perspective. But the catastrophe-producing equations contain no structure of decision rules. The link between model structure and behavior that permits inference about real feedback structures is missing. Moreover, the cusp phenomena that Renfrew treats require knowledge of a system-wide quadratic utility function that is maximized across the system. As suggested earlier, we have no assurance that system-wide utility is ever maximized, even assuming attempts to maximize utility at an individual level are being made. Without some refutable contact between individual components in a model and their actual counterparts, one cannot easily use a model to do more than demonstrate (as opposed to explain) the process of change.

THE PURPOSE OF SIMULATION

Formal models serve several purposes, including heuristics, explanation, policy exploration, and pedagogy. Heuristics and explanation can contribute the most to archaeology, where the study of policy alternatives is not directly relevant; therefore I shall focus on these two aspects and say little about the other functions. Emphasis will be placed on how heuristic and explanatory purposes can be achieved through the modelling process.

The Webster definition of heuristic is "serving to guide, discover, or reveal; specif: valuable for stimulating or conducting empirical research but unproved or incapable of proof—often used of arguments, methods, or constructs that assume or postulate what remains to be proved or that lead a person to find out for himself' (*Webster's Third New International Dictionary* 1961).

In the study of prehistory, as Zubrow pointed out (Chapter 6), simulation models may be used primarily to guide the development of theory and to reveal the gaps in knowledge that must be filled through the acquisition of data or application of deductive logic. Zubrow gave several examples of the heuristic value of computer simulation that result from the process of construction and simulating models. With respect to the construction phase, he described an exercise in which students in a computer systems class were required to quantify specific rules for an ancient ball game. The process of model construction quickly revealed significant gaps in knowledge about the game that had to be filled before the model could be run on the computer.

266

Other examples of the heuristic process at the stage of model construction can be cited. In developing a state-determined feedback model, one is constantly forced to fill in gaps even where theory is well established. For instance, in constructing the System Dynamics National Model at M.I.T., we have constantly had to think "from scratch" about how consumer or producer decisions really are made in a world of conserved flows. Representing the explicit accumulation of money, order backlogs, or product inventories requires a theory of how they affect economic decisions, for we know that such quantities must be controlled in reality through their feedback on people's actions. Yet theories about these links are not well developed in the vast economics literature. Similarly, in building model structure, conservation forces one to maintain strict dimensional consistency. Order backlog accumulates the flow of orders, money accumulates the flow of money. Links between different flow channels are made with parameters of dimensionally correct as well as operationally sensible values.

Parameters in the conserved flow context have an operational meaning that often differentiates them from parameters obtained from statistical estimation. One must look directly at the decision processes to find their values. These values are frequently not available in empirical or theoretical literature and have to be filled in by the modeller. Thus, modelling as a heuristic at the initial construction stage obligates one to come up with basic structural feedback links as well as specific parameter values to specify those links. Even before running the model, one has to think through the relationships, ask new questions of the available data, and, perhaps, seek new sources of data.

Simulating the model provides new heuristic opportunities. While models can be fabricated out of pure intuition, simulation provides the "moment of truth," often in the early stages, by yielding ridiculous results. A quantity that must be conserved in reality goes negative, thereby implying the strong possibility of a controlling feedback in the real system. Adding the control that we know must exist may produce different dynamics. Model behavior may come closer to observed behavior, or it may reveal new problems elsewhere in the structure.

An example of the heuristic process at work can be related to an article by F. Plog (1977b:54–56) in which he discusses the negative feedback loop shown in Figure 9.3.

The phenomena of differentiation and integration in Plog's feedback structure require basic changes in attitudes and social organization,

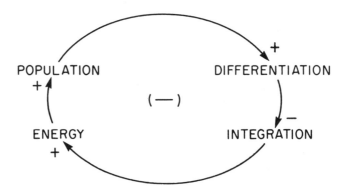

FIGURE 9.3. A negative feedback loop linking energy, population, differentiation, and integration (source: S. Plog 1977:56).

changes that may take centuries to evolve. If the structure were cased in a model of conserved flows and stocks, one might find that the available energy source depletes well before these long-term sociological and cultural changes have occurred. Model simulation, then, could produce nonsense (negative energy?) that would imply the need for a new feedback link that was originally neglected. When Plog writes, "The relationship between population and energy is well known" (1977b: 54), he is thinking, apparently, of the one-way causality shown in Figure 9.3. But clearly a reverse negative link between population and energy is also likely. This link introduces a tighter negative loop wherein available energy resources permit population growth, but a high population requires and thus depletes available energy.

The behavior reflecting this structural addition differs from the original behavior and could lead to new theories for which one would seek corroboration. Similar links between population, resources, and monument building are described in the Mayan collapse model of Hosler, Sabloff, and Runge (1977). Some of these links were not described in the written theory underlying their model but were undoubtedly necessary to produce the observed collapse mode.

While model simulation can lead to discovery of new theories, it can also reveal new behavior modes that actually exist but have not been documented before. In this case, the modeller may have enough confidence in his model to look for support in the data rather than immediately to modify or discard structure. The National Model work

268

provides an example of how simulation may reveal a mode of behavior that was previously unknown to the modellers. While the model contains decision structure appropriate to explaining short-term business cycles and the longer "Kuznets cycle," one of the model's configurations produced a much longer cycle, with about a fifty-year period. A search of data and literature relating to this "long wave" behavior unearthed evidence that such a mode has actually been observed. An attempt to explain the behavior in terms of model components followed its discovery.

A third heuristic purpose is served by embodying several apparently conflicting or fragmented theories into one model and then exploring the circumstances to which they may or may not apply. One is frequently confronted with different people building theory around different aspects of the same system, while ignoring the interrelationships between each aspect and other parts of the system. With a dynamic model that embodies alternative theories, one may find that each theory has a role in influencing behavior. However, such influence extends only over particular parts of the observed behavior mode. In a cycle, for example, one set of forces may be instrumental in producing the upswing, while another may come to the fore during the downswing. Mass's book on business cycles (1975) provides an example of the theory-testing approach by exploring all of the important business cycle explanations in the context of one model. The system model used in this manner can be a powerful tool for integrating seemingly disparate views.

A fourth heuristic aspect of model simulation comes even later in the process of confidence building. Once we apply a generic model to a variety of similar circumstances, we may then try to see if the same model applies to a greater range of possibilities. Since Forrester's urban model, for example, has been applied to numerous cities with some success, Zubrow (Chapter 6) asks whether it might not apply as well to ancient Rome or even to Mayan ceremonial centers. For ceremonial centers, he suggests that we accept the generic model long enough to see what internal forces might have counteracted the "attractiveness" of such centers so as to keep them from becoming heavily populated—a good illustration of modelling heuristics.

Finally, model simulation may be used to identify the formal data we need to collect. Theory building can proceed to formal simulation before any statistical data are processed, a practice decried by inductivists

269

as unscientific. Bayard (1969), for example, criticizes the tendency to formulate theory without adequately basing it on data. He writes, "It is my belief that theory is developed through generalization from the data, and it is not imposed upon them" (1969:380). A system dynamics model is not data-free (see next section); but, like any theory, it can help organize data gathering. Feedback modelling, perhaps more than other approaches, can greatly reduce the data-gathering effort.

System dynamics models repeatedly show substantial insensitivity of behavior to large changes in parameter values. Parameter insensitivity arises from the manner in which interacting feedback loops tend to compensate for parameter changes by transferring pressures from one part of a system to another. Little is written about this compensation phenomenon (see Forrester 1969:107–14 for a brief comment), but it occurs in just about every state-determined model. The phenomenon of feedback compensation vastly reduces the number of parameters for which precise estimates need to be developed. Most parameters for which large changes produce little variation in behavior can be accepted as good enough for the purpose at hand. The smaller number of sensitive parameters may require better estimates.

In summary, system dynamics modelling can serve an important heuristic function. In constructing a model, even before running it on a computer, one is forced to fill in gaps of knowledge about structure and about the parameters that specify feedback links. In simulating a model, one often discovers (a) new theories; (b) unknown modes of behavior that subsequently can be found in data; (c) the relationship among alternative theories; (d) insights from applying generic structures to particular situations; and (e) knowledge about whether or not a set of parameters needs further refinement.

Explanation in system dynamics modelling is usually viewed in the context of policy analysis. A dynamic problem (for example, instability in employment, declining market share, or urban growth) is specified as a "reference mode" that the model should produce and appropriate policy design should alter. The reference mode of behavior defines the problem; model feedback structure explains it; changes in decision rules constitute the policy interventions designed to alleviate it. In the context of policy analysis, one constructs a model of a *problem*, which then specifies the system of interacting elements that produces the problem. Without a dynamic problem statement, one has little guidance for drawing a system boundary, achieving an appropriate level of aggregation, or knowing when the model is producing the "right behavior."

In attempting to explain prehistory, one is generally not engaging in policy analysis. One does not use the Mayan collapse model to improve monument construction while averting disaster. And if there are present-day analogies to which "Mayan policy analysis" could be applied, they are probably unimportant. However, for many purposes, the lack of policy intent is not a constraint on developing explanatory theories. Mayan collapse or ritual pig festivals are documented well enough to provide useful reference modes. Models can be validated in part against documented behavior.

For much archaeological research, however, well-established reference modes are nonexistent. We have, instead, a record of artifacts and features that reside in what Schiffer (1976:28) calls the "archaeological context," as opposed to a "systemic context" in which materials of a culture are part of an ongoing behavioral system. For the archaeological context, systems models play an uncertain role. Using them to explain a record of artifacts, for example the assemblage of Aldenderfer's hunter-gatherers, is not very satisfactory. Lack of a reference mode of behavior removes one source of validation (Forrester and Senge 1979), and it is well known that any simulation model can be forced, through ad hoc changes in parameter values, to match a set of observations at some particular point in time.

Schiffer, like other process archaeologists, thinks that the systemic context can be used to explain archaeological data and that it provides a useful context for generating explanatory laws. He proposes four strategies for explanatory research.

If archaeological research were confined to pursuing Schiffer's Strategy 1, which says that one answers questions about past societies by examining past material cultures, system dynamics models would have little use. Analogies between past and present, which would be necessary to establish internal decision structures independent of observed behavior, would be absent, as would an observed reference mode. Without either of these major points of contact with reality, one would not have adequate means for model refutation.

The other three strategies, however, do offer useful possibilities for feedback process models. Strategy 2 looks at present material culture in order to acquire laws useful for studying past human behavior. It offers direct, observable physical relationships that can be incorporated as

271

components of internal structure. Strategy 3 examines past material remains to derive behavioral laws applicable to present societies. Strategy 3 does not directly provide the information for building components of internal structure. However, it is more likely to provide observable behavior with which to compare model output. Strategy 4, which studies present material objects to produce insights about past or present systems, comes closest to the use of system dynamics for policy analysis and offers the best possibilities for model validation.

Clearly, the four approaches are related, and one does not usually stay strictly within one cell of the matrix. But the division is helpful for understanding the potential contribution of system dynamics to archaeological research. By relying on direct observation of both causal relationships and dynamic behavior, system dynamics does best when the empirical resources are available. Thus a fifth strategy is also suggested. This strategy differs from the other four in relying on observed human behavior to explain material cultural artifacts. Here one might build a model around observed social interactions and assume similarity between those interactions and what must have occurred in prehistory.

System dynamics models serve relatively well both the heuristic and explanatory purposes of formal modelling. In the case of heuristics, one can develop a good foundation for building explanatory laws. In this sense, I would disagree with Aldenderfer's observation that simulation should be used only as a "last resort," for simulation may well provide an opening wedge for discovering explanation.

SYSTEM DYNAMICS PRACTICE

Throughout this chapter I have brought out elements of system dynamics practice to show how the heuristic and explanatory purposes of modelling are realized. In this section I shall consider the modelling process. The treatment will not be comprehensive but is intended to show how one might use the approach in archaeological research. For illustration, I shall consider the abandonment of settlements on the Colorado Plateau. Contrary to Doran's (1970:295) contention that cybernetics offers no specific techniques, the embodiment of cybernetic principles in system dynamics does provide precise rules for organizing and evaluating a simulation study. However, as with all social science modelling, applying those principles to real situations remains largely an art form.

A system dynamics study entails a number of phases which may occur simultaneously and may be repeated numerous times in the process of model development and confidence building (Randers 1973). These steps include (a) problem definition; (b) conjecture of basic explanatory hypotheses; (c) model construction; and (d) model testing.

Problem definition consists of identifying the major variables of interest and a mode of behavior for those variables. This "reference mode," as indicated earlier, may be quite simple, consisting of a plot against time of one variable (market share, population, and so on); or it may relate the behavior of several observed variables together (for example, population and settlement aggregation). When several variables are involved, relative dynamic characteristics such as phasing, amplitude, and frequency may be of interest. The object of defining a problem in this fashion is to identify the behavior that the computer model should reproduce. If the model cannot generate problem symptoms, it cannot be trusted as a source of explanation or policy recommendations.

The process of locating adequate data to support a reference mode can involve considerable effort. In a corporate setting, a manager may know what has happened qualitatively to sales and profits but may have to confirm his assumptions by analyzing company data. In an archaeological setting, one will have to consult incomplete records and uncertain data just to get some feeling for the dynamics to be explained. The researcher may conclude at this point that he can only speculate from vague evidence about what occurred over time and proceed to model what he thinks might have happened.

To establish an explanatory hypothesis for the reference mode, the modeller identifies major organizing concepts and important variables. For example, to explain changes in urban population, Forrester (1969) focused on the concept of "attractiveness"; the major model variables then became people, jobs, and housing. To explain Mayan collapse, Hosler, Sabloff, and Runge (1977) emphasized resource depletion and need for prestige; important variables then included resources, people, and monuments. To develop an underlying explanatory hypothesis, one might trace out a few basic feedback mechanisms, such as the negative feedback loop portrayed earlier in Figure 9.3.

Fleshing out the basic concepts requires more detailed structure,

273

with level and rate variables and dimensions carefully specified. Structural variables and the parameters linking them are determined on the basis of hunch, intuition, observation, expert advice, written description, and statistical data. In other words, all available data, including the most informal kind, are used to create a model that the computer can simulate. One is not forced to rely on formal statistical data to enter an influence that he thinks is important.

Model testing, what I identified above as the fourth phase of the process, is really an inherent part of model construction. At this point, though, the modeller has moved from thorough experiments about the kind of behavior his structure will yield to precise, quantitative results that show the implications of proposed model assumptions. The computer is merciless. Early results may show embarrassingly where the conservation principle has been ignored, where some absurd assumption produces nonsense, or how a carefully considered, simple model structure gives results that are totally contrary to expectations. Testing, then, encompasses exploration of internal logic as well as consistency with observed behavior. As the process continues, parameter values will be tested for their importance to model behavior, and whole feedback structures will be weakened, strengthened, or eliminated to determine how important they are to one's conclusions.

This experimentation phase can lead to modifications of structure, parameters, and initial hypotheses, or even to reexamination of assumed reference modes. Thus a study may iterate through all four stages many times before converging on a version considered acceptable for the purpose at hand. The effort can be time-consuming and frustrating, for the process of explaining why a certain phasing or amplification exists in even small models is an exercise without standard rules of thumb. With nonlinear systems, almost anything can happen as one presses into extreme regions in search of explanatory validity.

Now let us consider the site abandonment issue that Cordell examines in this volume and elsewhere (Cordell 1972, 1975, Chapter 5). She is interested in explaining the abandonment of Anasazi sites through a 600-year period of occupation of Wetherill Mesa, Colorado. A computer model with rules for site location in response to climatic changes proves highly accurate and indicates "that many abandonments may have been due to decreased crop yields caused by local variation in rainfall and length of the growing season" (Cordell 1975:189). However, her simulation does not model the internal system structure so as to derive causality from the processual dynamics of that structure. Nevertheless, under these circumstances, a process approach such as system dynamics may not yield better insights. But by way of illustration, one could treat the site abandonment issue by applying the four steps outlined above.

What, then, is the problem? Cordell focuses on site abandonment over five archaeological phases. Thus, we could trace the reference mode as the number of sites over time or, with much less certainty, the population over time. I shall use people rather than sites, on the assumption that our behavioral model will be concerned directly with people and their decision processes. Figure 9.4 shows one set of population estimates for the Wetherill Mesa (Cordell, personal communication), with each point except the first and last plotted at the end of a particular archaeological period. The first point is a guess, derived from Hayes's (1964) survey data. The last point reveals the documented abrupt decline in population that occurred at the beginning of the fourteenth century. It is mainly the perturbations after A.D. 900 and

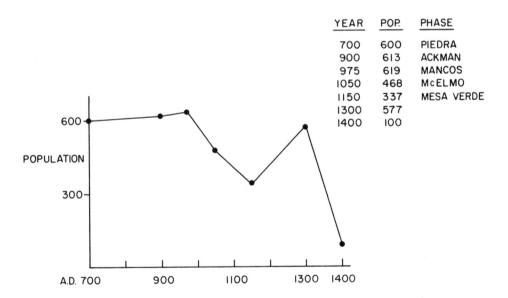

YEAR	POP	PHASE
700	600	PIEDRA
900	613	ACKMAN
975	619	MANCOS
1050	468	McELMO
1150	337	MESA VERDE
1300	577	
1400	100	

FIGURE 9.4. Population estimate for the Wetherill Mesa during A.D. 700–1400 (source for points 900–1300: Cordell, personal communication).

subsequent collapse that are of interest here. Our process model should produce this qualitative mode of collapse.

The reference mode is both very specific to one small area and much more aggregated than Cordell's data. The specific data are of interest because one assumes that they reflect the general population pattern of a much larger area. Therefore, process rules for these data should help to explain population movements elsewhere. The more aggregated nature of our reference mode reveals both a shortcoming and a somewhat different intent of system dynamics models. System dynamics cannot reasonably deal with considerable disaggregation. Connecting the 755 10-acre cells in Cordell's grid by means of conserved flows and explicit feedback mechanisms would produce an impossibly big model. Hence, our purpose must be confined to explaining generalizable dynamic phenomena (population change and collapse) rather than specific numbers of people or sites over many small areas. I would suggest that explaining basic patterns is most important, but others may pursue a different goal.

Given a reference mode of population collapse, what are the basic concepts that constitute a dynamic hypothesis? Here I shall rely on only a scant exposure to relevant literature, a caveat that appears justified because I am primarily concerned with illustrating an approach to seeking explanation rather than with the explanation itself. Most of what follows will draw from Martin and Plog's *The Archaeology of Arizona* (1973).

Three organizing concepts appear to be most important—population growth, environmental and social stress, and population aggregation (nucleation). During the first half of the 600-year period, up to about A.D. 1000, the Anasazi population of the Colorado Plateau apparently grew and spread into marginal growing areas, evolving from hunting and gathering for subsistence to more sedentary agricultural pursuits. By the year 1000, population pressures on the agricultural land began to produce considerable social stress, accompanied during the next century or so by expanded technoeconomic experimentation (Martin and Plog 1973:208). About this time, the population began to coalesce into large villages, thereby merging the formerly localized lineages into larger clans. Technological advances and aggregation may have staved off the growing stress, but by A.D. 1200 or 1225, environmental conditions appear to have worsened, stress became more evident, and population began to decline. "By A.D. 1400 all the towns in northern

Arizona, in the Mesa Verde area, and in the Chaco Canyon were abandoned" (Martin and Plog 1973:209).

This hypothetical framework can accommodate most of the major theories that have been offered to explain site abandonment, including aggregation and the extension of population into marginal areas. One argument that is not included focuses on the impact of erosion on settlement patterns, although this view is not strongly supported by the evidence (Martin and Plog 1973:322–23). The role of climate, on the other hand, was undoubtedly important. Was it as dominant as Cordell's simulation suggests? Or was it one of those exogenous influences that keeps a dynamic system out of balance and thus follows an evolutionary trajectory dependent more on internal structure than on characteristics of climatological input? The systems approach would stress internal feedback structure rather than climate as the "cause" of eventual collapse.

Pursuing this approach, I have taken the verbal description of Anasazi settlement patterns contained in Martin and Plog (1973:208–10, 318–33) and have traced out what appear to be the basic feedback relationships (see Figure 9.5). This step constitutes the beginning of model construction, which would evolve into precise equations that could be simulated and tested. Lines in Figure 9.5 indicate causal links, with the arrows specifying direction of causality, and the "+" and "−" signs showing whether a change in one direction produces pressure on the other variable in the same (+) or opposite (−) directions. Dashed lines indicate the exogenous influences of fixed land area on crowding, or variable, interacting climatic impacts on stress. Some evidence appears to exist for each of the hypothesized links. In most cases, I have simply used Martin and Plog's descriptions and indicate the relevant page reference in parentheses. A few of the connections are clearly controversial, and their verification would require more knowledge than I possess.

Population and net birth rate reflect a clear biological relationship. Births normally increase with population, and in turn, cause further growth. Population expansion leads to crowding, which results from the encroachment of even a sparsely settled population on marginal agricultural lands (1973:328). Crowding seems to produce greater stress:

> Increased strife leading to the need for defense would have been a probable effect of ecological factors such as population increase.

277

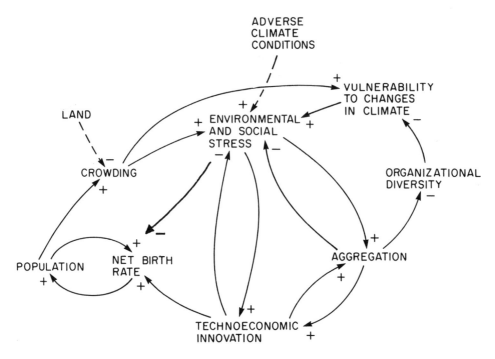

FIGURE 9.5. Feedback loop structure of Anasazi settlement patterns.

. . . Eventually, some of the population would have been obliged to relocate in defensible positions (cliff shelters) or ecologically marginal areas where more stress may have resulted. (1973:208)

Environmental and social stress has an important place in the proposed model because of its direct interaction with several other variables. Most of these interactions are homeostatic, although most are likely to require considerable time to produce their regulating effect. The link back to population closes the Malthusian subsistence loop and also suggests that social strife, through its encouragement of warfare, could reduce population growth. Stress is also linked to technoeconomic innovation, as "marginal populations adopt innovations at a more rapid rate than nonmarginal ones" (1973:328), presumably because stress at the margin causes an incentive for experimentation that is lacking in nonmarginal areas. These creative developments, in turn, probably served to offset the stress for some time (1973:208), as suggested by the negative feedback link to stress. Third, sociocultural experimentation, in the form of aggregation, was also encouraged by growing stress, both because of the need for defense and because of the relative advantages of larger villages for agricultural development (1973:329–30).

Like the burgeoning of technoeconomic creativity, aggregation, which developed largely because of stress, in turn seems to have alleviated some of the stress (1973:208).

Stress also links directly with vulnerability to changes in climate. Environmental stress clearly increases, for example, when adverse climatic conditions are coupled with growing vulnerability to these conditions. Climatic conditions lie outside of our model boundary. However, vulnerability to climate change is part of the system and, it is claimed, increases as a result of both greater crowding and expanded aggregation. The crowding link seems quite straightforward. Crowding leads to expanded use of marginal land. Martin and Plog write,

> Any given environmental variation will have a greater effect on marginal than on nonmarginal areas. Factors that are no more than normal variance in a secure environment may constitute major stresses in a marginal one. . . . Even if environmental conditions had not changed one whit from A.D. 1100 to 1300, crises could have resulted from the use of areas that were not really appropriate to agriculture. (1973:331)

Here the internal perspective that looks to endogenous causal structure for explanation of cultural change is clearly expressed; for the characteristics of climatic change are not considered responsible for social crises in the same way as are population pressures on a limited environment.

The causality linking aggregation and vulnerability is more uncertain than the connection between crowding and vulnerability. The link is based upon the assumption that aggregation tended to reduce social and agricultural diversity and, thereby, increased the society's vulnerability to changes in climate. The link between diversity and vulnerability is called the "Law of Requisite Variety," which suggests that "populations living in situations where critical environmental variables are either spatially or temporally varied must be capable of adjusting their organization and/or their subsistence practices to meet these exigencies" (1973:328).

The negative link between aggregation and diversity seems reasonable but is not certain. The Hopi Indians, who never relied significantly on large-scale agricultural technologies that accompanied nucleation, could adapt more easily to variations in climate.

> You can't move a canal to catch the rainwater. And hundreds of acres of·irrigated land or terraces built either in the upland or

lowland areas would fail to produce successful crops in some years. Thus, a system like that suggested by the Hopi would have been far more adaptive given the environmental variability that existed at the time of abandonments than one based on irrigation or terrace agriculture. (1973:329)

Two other direct feedback relationships in Figure 9.5 require justification. Aggregation and technoeconomic innovation are linked in a positive feedback loop. The enhanced communication and joint effort that characterized larger villages accelerated innovation, while innovations (for example, in agriculture and in construction techniques) that were initially developed in marginal areas would be adopted in less marginal settings and permitted continued aggregation to occur. Evidence suggests that innovation and aggregation occurred simultaneously; arrows in the figure suggest a causal relationship. The arrow connecting technoeconomic innovation to population, again, "makes sense." It has always been through technological advance that people have pushed out the limits defined by crowding and by other aspects of a finite environment.

As a reader familiar with prehistoric settlements in the Southwest will know, I have incorporated a number of different theories into one framework for systemic analysis. One reason for this approach was suggested earlier, namely, that an important heuristic function of modelling is served if we can show how different theories tie together and become more or less important to behavior as one moves through different dynamic modes. I also was looking for some positive feedback relationships that would serve to augment known deviations in climate and, thereby, eventually produce a population collapse. Without such positive feedback structures, only drastic environmental changes (like a volcanic eruption) would have caused this result. With positive feedback links, even mild perturbations in climate could have resulted in collapse.

The important positive feedbacks seem to involve population growth. Technological stimulus to net births, for example, may have permitted populations to push too far into the marginal areas that were most vulnerable to climatic change. Thus, stress, which would normally suppress an expanded population through Malthusian pressures, also led to innovations in technology (agriculture) and living patterns (aggregation) that both alleviated stress and permitted more population growth to occur. Aggregation, moreover, may have supported, as well

280

as depended upon, technoeconomic innovation and, at the same time, increased the population's vulnerability to environmental changes independent of the crowding effect. This independent influence reveals another positive link that one would want to examine. Greater aggregation increases vulnerability, which leads to more stress and, in turn, encourages accelerated aggregation.

As it stands, the model could not lead to acceptance or rejection of the theories it embodies. The next step, then, would be to develop explicit model structures to represent aggregation, innovation, and other processes. Delays in adapting to environmental and social stress through technological advance or aggregation would be included. Clearer evidence for some of the less certain links would be sought. Parameter values would be determined, largely without much data, on the basis of intuition.

An initial simulation can be produced once a complete set of equations is written. Then the important process of analyzing alternative theories can proceed. We might find that this structure with any reasonable set of parameter values cannot generate the reference mode. This result might lead to our rejecting some of the hypotheses that have been offered for site abandonment. Inability to produce the reference mode might lead to the discovery of neglected feedback loops that, when added, yield reasonable behavior. Alternatively, we might find that one subset of relationships, combined with what we know about climatic change, is sufficient to explain observed behavior. The rest of the structure would be considered superfluous.

Even without accurate data, then, much could be gained by simulating the model and testing the impact on behavior of large variations in parameter values. New paths for research could result. One might narrow the range of uncertainty for parameters to which model results are most sensitive. One could try to apply the proposed model to other situations for which better data exist. One could seek evidence for the relationships that appear most significant in reproducing recorded events. Equally important, the model could reveal research paths that are nonproductive.

In this section, I have suggested a procedure for performing system dynamics studies and have illustrated the procedure with an initial attempt to model Anasazi population collapse. The approach differs from "explanations" based on climate or on invasions from outside the area. As Martin and Plog write, such arguments "do not point in the direction of explanation. They embody no stated regularities that render this event or any class of events predictable" (1973:326). A feedback simulation model builds upon causal hypotheses to explain observed data. Such models can lead to new theoretical discoveries and perhaps even to the formulation of laws governing the process of past and present change.

NOTE

1. Editor's note: This paper is the second draft of the manuscript which Low prepared after the Seminar. Low had planned to make additional revisions in August 1979. His tragic death earlier in the summer made such revisions impossible. Cordell and I have made some minor editorial changes in order to clarify points in the paper we know Low himself would have worked on had he lived to do so. The aid of Prof. Peter Senge and his colleagues in the System Dynamics Group at M.I.T. in the preparation of Low's illustrations is greatly appreciated.

10
The Simulator as Demiurge

COLIN RENFREW

University of Southampton

Demiurge: (Greek *demios*, for the people, *ourgos*, work): 1a, a Platonic subordinate deity who fashions the sensible world in the light of eternal ideas; 1b, a Gnostic subordinate deity who is the creator of the material world; 2, something that is an autonomous creative force or decisive power
    —*Chambers Twentieth Century Dictionary*

Systems thinking has increasingly been regarded as an essential component of archaeological theory since its introduction to the subject nearly two decades ago (Binford 1962).[1] Yet despite the undoubted attractions of simulating the past, usually within some appropriate systems framework, simulations in this field have so far been rather few in number (Thomas 1972; Cordell 1975; and Zubrow 1975 being among the first). Only very recently has system dynamics modelling been applied to past cultural systems (Hosler, Sabloff, and Runge 1977; Shantzis and Behrens 1973).

The Advanced Seminar was therefore a timely one, and I learned a great deal from it. Its success was partly due to Sabloff's skillful inclusion in the discussion group of a philosopher of science, a mathematical economist, a systems analyst, and a mathematician specializing in differential questions, as well as three archaeologists actively concerned with simulation studies. As a discussant, my task is to discuss rather than to summarize, and in what follows I shall try to indicate how

283

effective I believe the meeting to have been in clarifying what systems thinking and simulation are, and in clearing up some of the confusions and misconceptions that surround their use. The participants, despite their different standpoints, found themselves in considerable harmony about the main issues discussed and departed with a reinforced optimism that this particular approach is an exceedingly promising one for the elucidation of the behavior of complex systems in the past.

The chapters in this volume, taken together, should give a timely statement on the nature and promise of simulation studies in archaeology. Yet I believe they may do more than this; they may initiate an examination of the position within the logic of science of systems explanations and of simulations in general. It was particularly appropriate that the first paper at the seminar was from a philosopher, Bell, rightly concerned with criteria of refutation and verification. For explanations involving dynamical systems often seem, at first sight, inimical to the spirit of Popperian falsification: "goodness of fit" can be a very flexible criterion for rejection.

It is the very essence of simulation modelling that the simulator creates a device which will produce some representation of reality. A good simulation mimics reality closely. But a successful simulation is rarely achieved at the first attempt. If at first you don't succeed you try again, modifying or tuning the device to give a better—that is, closer to real—output. The simulator proceeds in some senses very much like an inventor, trying to get his infernal device to work. The theoretical content of his creation is often not altogether clear, being sometimes implicit in the structure of his invention, rather than set out in advance, neatly and explicitly, in the form of a number of theoretical relationships.

These two aspects—the frequent necessity for successive attempts before it 'works,' and the deliberate anticipation of 'unexpected' behavior—often combine to make systems modelling seem a very creative process, in which the new creation has behavior, indeed, almost a life, of its own. It is this aspect, which often makes systems modelling seem such an exciting undertaking, that prompts the title to this paper.

Some time ago I pointed out that "the logical structure of a system model . . . differs fundamentally from that of a hypothetico-deductive explanation" (Renfrew 1973:1929), and, as several commentators have stressed (Flannery 1973:51; Perlman 1977:321), it is important not to become caught up too readily in any preconceived notion as to what logical form a scientific explanation *must* take. Recent excessive emphasis on one specific explanatory mode, the Hempel-Oppenheim covering law model, has risked elevating to dogma what should be no more than informative precept. As Binford (1977:6) states of theory building: "This is a creative process for which there are no methodological rules to ensure success."

Bell rightly emphasizes the importance of being aware of the procedures by which our models may be compared with reality, thus allowing them to be verified or refuted. Such procedures are the hallmark of empirical science, providing the criterion which distinguishes it from mere metaphysical speculation. Yet problems remain here which still await clarification. That is, indeed, one of the fascinations of this field, which is clearly at a very creative stage of development. Perhaps the most successful feature of our discussions was the manner in which these important theoretical and philosophical issues were kept in view, without their obscuring or impeding good practical discussion about how to make dynamical systems models work.

SYSTEMS AND SYSTEMS THINKING

The systemic approach has been widely advocated in archaeology (Wood and Matson 1973; Munton 1973; Hill 1977a), and a number of optimistic claims have been made, many with good justification. But there have been evident confusions so that terms like Systems Theory, General Systems Theory, System Dynamics, and Systems Thinking are employed almost interchangeably. That perhaps in part excuses the almost entirely negative critique, "What can systems theory do for archaeology?" recently contributed by a philosopher (Salmon 1978), who does not make these relevant distinctions.

In discussing the systemic approach to archaeology, it may be useful to try to distinguish between

(1) *Systems Thinking:* A general philosophical approach to the subject, an *intuitional framework* within which specific problems may be tackled;

(2) *General Systems Theory:* A consideration, initiated by von Bertalanffy, of the various properties and behaviors shared by a wide range of superficially very different systems;

(3) *Mathematical Systems Theory:* An explicit body of mathematical

theory which (in common with System Dynamics Modelling) may be regarded as a special aspect or branch of the Theory of Dynamical Systems (see 5 below). It entails the mathematical theory of feedback control systems and optimal control, much used by engineers, but so far has little direct relevance to archaeological problems.

(4) *System Dynamics Modelling:* The approach pioneered by Forrester and his colleagues of expressing the behavior of a complex system by a large number of equations of state and of using the computer to calculate the successive values through time of all relevant parameters by means of these equations, hence achieving a simulation; and the

(5) *Theory of Dynamical Systems:* The broad undertaking of mathematicians to create a theory for all systems that evolve according to a dynamical law. These are generally described either by differential equations or by difference equations, whose solutions may be studied by qualitative as well as quantitative methods. Although there are as yet no explicit archaeological formulations using this framework, the methods are of such power and relevance that significant progress is to be anticipated.

Let it be at once acknowledged, as Salmon (1978) has rightly stressed, that there is no single body of explicit formulations called Systems Theory which is ready and available for application to elucidate the behavior of humans or cultures. On the other hand, there is already, at this early stage, a good deal of useful experience available.

Systems Thinking constitutes in my view the most important advance in archaeology in recent years. It implies the use of series of concepts that are now becoming familiar and, one may hope, through that familiarity, are emerging as something more than mere jargon expressions. Among these important notions are: closed system, open system, subsystem, input, output, trajectory, negative feedback, positive feedback, homeostasis, stable and unstable equilibrium, steady state, state variable, flow rate, morphogenesis, transformation, exogeneous and endogeneous inputs, variety, equifinality, and so forth.

The value of such an approach and such terms is simply that, for the first time, they offer a framework and a language for the analysis of complex entities, such as societies, organizations, or cultures, in a manner that allows a direct and simple treatment without denying the difficulties inherent in such a task.

The underlying ideas are obvious enough, like most good ideas, when one has acquired a familiarity with them. But to measure the gain, it is sufficient to make comparison with the level of explanation which preceded their introduction. In archaeology, this often amounted to little more than a bald narrative of a sequence of events, often given a false coherence in the light of a diffusionist interpretation. If anyone doubts the value of systems thinking, let him make comparison with almost any purported explanations in the archaeological literature offered prior to 1960 (although every archaeologist could compile his own short list of honorable exceptions).

Systemic ideas were introduced to archaeology by Binford (1962) and set out with great coherence by Clarke (1968); they have already inspired a number of studies (Flannery 1968; Renfrew 1972; F. Plog 1974). No well-organized body of theory is implied, although it is not necessarily excluded. Rather, systems thinking is simply an approach to the world within one intuitional framework, which implies the exclusion of others that are incompatible with it. Such a framework is, of course, implicit within both General Systems Theory and System Dynamics modelling and is common to simulation in general.

General Systems Theory, originated by von Bertalanffy (see von Bertalanffy 1950), is concerned with the formal correspondence of general principles in the behavior of systems, irrespective of the kind of relations or forces between the components. As such, it goes far beyond the scope of the anthropologist or archaeologist, although patterns may indeed be observed in cultural systems which are common to those of other kinds. Exponential growth and logistic growth are well-known examples (Hamblin, Jacobsen, and Miller 1973).

A similar although more restricted intention underlies the work of a number of anthropologists who seek to make general statements about the behavior of sociocultural systems (see Flannery 1972; Rathje 1975; Gall and Saxe 1977; Athens 1977; Cherry 1978; Renfrew 1979). The concern here is limited, of course, to systems composed of human societies, but with this limitation, the aim is, indeed, very general.

It would be a mistake to claim that very much has yet been achieved along this path but a still graver one to deny the importance of the undertaking, for the aim here is close to that to which Binford (1968a:27) many years ago aspired: "Our ultimate goal is the formulation of laws of cultural dynamics." Today this need not be read as implying that the formulation will be in a strictly Hempelian lawlike form, nor indeed in any anatomization of a system into specific subsystems. That the goal is as yet dimly perceived does not make it any the less real. To dismiss General Systems Theory on the grounds that it does not measure up to some a priori concept of "theory" risks discarding the conceptual baby with the philosophical bath water.

Mathematical Systems Theory is a well-developed field, where the behavior of precisely defined control systems is subjected to rigorous analysis. Like System Dynamics modelling, it may be seen as a special branch of the Theory of Dynamical Systems. Here the consideration centers on the input and output of a conversional device which lies between them—often a control mechanism. The distinction between Mathematical Systems Theory and the Theory of Dynamical Systems is lucidly expressed by Berlinski (1976:110) in writing of the former:

> The fundamental systems here are much like dynamical systems. The method by which engineering objects are classified, moreover, mirrors the organization of the theory of differential equations. But it would be a mistake to dismiss the differences between engineering and dynamical systems: engineering is preeminently a concern for the relationship between inputs and outputs, while the mathematical focus of the theory of dynamical systems is on the equations themselves and the models in which they are satisfied.

Usually feedback control is employed, and often optimization procedures to minimize total expenditure or energy, or to operate in least time. Such work can trace its origins back to the same interest in cybernetics (Wiener 1948; W. R. Ashby 1956) which is ancestral to much current systems thinking. But it appears to have little to offer archaeology at present, its explicitly formulated problems are not our problems, and few of ours can ever hope to be given definitive formal solutions in this way.

A comparable formulation has nonetheless been attempted in the study of political science by Easton (1965), and the same schema of the archaeologist's culture systems as a "black box" was set out by Leach (1973:765–66). The archaeological or anthropological cases are much less rigorously defined, however, than those of the control engineer, and for this reason are more profitably discussed within the more general framework of the Theory of Dynamical Systems.

System Dynamics Modelling involves a particular approach to the problems of dynamical systems devised by Forrester (1961, 1969, 1971).

Dynamic behavior simply means behavior analyzed with time as ·an important variable. There can be many kinds of dynamical systems models, all of them giving explicit formulations for the behavior of a system through time. System Dynamics models represent a subset of this general field of dynamical systems models, whereby a real and rather complex system is modelled by a complicated structure rich in feedback loops. The components are accumulations or reservoirs, measured by a level (state) variable, between which there is activity measured by a rate (flow) variable. An equation is written for each component of the system stating (predicting) its level or rate at the next point in time in terms of the present levels or rates of all the other components. The computer uses these numerous equations to calculate the values for all these state and flow variables at the next point in time, given the initial values. Then it proceeds to do the same again for the next time point, and so, by a series of iterations, the values of all the variables of the system are simulated.

The model discussed above by Zubrow (Chapter 6) is a good example of this kind, displaying the rather complicated "spaghetti-and-meat-balls" network of flows and interrelations common to such constructions. Despite their apparent complexity, they certainly produce clear results.

The construction of such a model does not necessarily imply any remarkably original theoretical insights. It can be simply a systematic and painstakingly explicit analysis of a familiar if rather complicated situation. But Forrester (1973) has effectively made the point that the behavior of such complex systems is often counter-intuitive. The whole is greater than its parts. The value of technique as a research tool lies precisely in this counterintuitive behavior.

The Theory of Dynamical Systems is a general approach to the problem of change that, in a sense, subsumes the more specific concerns of Mathematical Systems Theory and System Dynamics modelling as defined above but is not limited by the specific assumptions and concerns which serve to define them more closely. It entails the attempt, by specifying the influences causing short-term changes, to derive the long-term behavior of the system, and involves the use of difference equations or differential equations.

The state of the system is the smallest collection of numbers that must be specified in order to predict uniquely the system's behavior: the variables in question are related by means of a set of differential equations. The solutions of the equations allow, or would allow, the prediction of the future behavior of the system. But the solutions of many sets of differential equations cannot be found quantitatively, and it is the *qualitative* study of the differential solutions and their properties, interpreted geometrically, which often proves enlightening.

The approach, and its archaeological potential, has been lucidly set out by Cooke (1979), and considered by Berlinski (1976:47–51), as a preliminary to his critique of System Dynamics modelling undertaken by Forrester and Meadows. The mathematical literature, which extends back a century to the pioneering work of Poincaré, is extensive (see Chillingworth 1976). Yet despite its technical difficulty for the nonmathematician, some aspects of this approach are accessible to archaeologists: the use of phase portraits to illustrate the geometrical properties of trajectories is clear and illuminating at a general level. In this way, one is brought to grips with such fundamental notions as equilibrium, stability, periodic and recurrent motions, attractors, bifurcation, and other important ideas to which the mathematics naturally gives rise.

Living systems, including culture systems, exhibit such modes of behavior and properties as these, and the opportunities offered by Dynamical Systems Theory to examine such behavior in the most abstract way possible is valuable. It leads naturally to the preoccupations of mathematical biologists such as Rosen (1979) or Waddington (1977), with which archaeologists are discovering much in common. Catastrophe theory, for example, may be regarded as a branch of the Theory of Dynamical Systems. Important concepts arising from this approach, such as the notion of the chreod and of the epigenetic landscape (Waddington 1977:103–14), will be found highly relevant to the long-term behavior of human societies.

Archaeological applications have hardly yet been developed, but in the adjacent field of ecology, the elegant investigation of the predator-prey relationship through the Volterra-Lotka equations (Maynard-Smith 1974:19–27) suggests how fruitful this general approach can be in practical cases. Equations of comparable form are now being used as models of interaction between two human groups rather than between two species (Cooke and Freedman n.d.), and other explorations using similar approaches are sure to follow.

It seems noteworthy that the pessimism of Berlinski (1976) concerning existing systems analysis in the social, political, and biological sciences does not appear to be directed either toward Dynamical Systems Theory or its application in ecology. My own optimism is based, on the one hand, on the appropriateness of systems thinking for the expression of archaeological problems and, on the other, on the apparent suitability of Dynamical Systems Theory for investigating relationships expressed in systems terms. Nonetheless a gap remains to be bridged: either archaeologists must learn more mathematics (and the right kind of mathematics) or mathematicians must prove willing to immerse themselves in the theoretical preoccupations of modern archaeology.

From the above, it will be seen that the "systemic approach" can mean a number of different things, and that these should be carefully distinguished. Of course, the term "system" can be defined in a multitude of different ways, but its chief value in archaeology is in its applicability to the very elaborate complex of interactions which any sociocultural entity represents, which can always be subdivided into a number of subsystems, each meriting analysis in its own right. It is this very complexity which makes the systems approach, with its own flexibility and ability to cope with elaboration, so useful.

This may not be the occasion on which to take issue in detail with what I feel are the problems arising from Salmon's treatment of this general topic. One feature is the apparent equation of mathematical models in general with systems theory in particular. Mathematical Systems Theory is one very specific and perhaps rather minor branch of mathematics. To say of the whole general class of mathematical models used to describe the real world, as exemplified by the simple Gas Law $PV = RT$, "the classification of such models is thus an important part of Mathematical Systems Theory" (Salmon 1978:179), may introduce a confusion. The treatment of mathematical models in general is certainly provocative: "Mathematical models, even when they fit, do not in and of themselves constitute satisfactory explanations" (1978:182). My main objection to such a statement is not so much that it is questionable (as I believe) but that it has little specific bearing upon the role of systems theory as such in archaeology.

THE NATURE OF SIMULATION

Simulations differ in procedure and purpose. Only a few of them fall within the class of System Dynamics models, including the example set out by Zubrow (Chapter 6) and the instance presented to us by

Sabloff (Hosler, Sabloff, and Runge 1977). Many simulations—particularly those of high complexity—are nonetheless approached within the intuitional framework of systems thinking, but this is certainly not a precondition for a simulation study.

The whole field of simulation, in archaeology and beyond, was thoroughly reviewed in Aldenderfer's Chapter 2, the first such comprehensive survey, and only a few comments are required here.

First, it may be useful to distinguish between two classes of simulation, although many examples fall within both. In the first class, the *output* alone represents the simulation, while the procedures used to obtain it do not set out to mimic those of the real world. The output is thus a *simulacrum*, a representation of reality produced by the simulation. Interest focuses upon the relationship, the goodness of fit, between the simulacrum and the real data set which is being simulated.

An example of such a simulation is the XTENT model (Renfrew and Level 1979), by which the computer draws a political map, for instance of modern Europe, plotting in the notional boundaries, given only the location and size of the major cities, without information as to their territorial affiliation. The output is a map, the simulacrum which is to be compared with the real map (or, in archaeological cases, to be used as an approximation to a political map). But the procedures used to reach the conclusion do not follow the real course of events in time; this is not a dynamical model.

In the second class of model, it is not the final state, the terminal output at the last time point, which particularly interests us, but the sequence of events in time. The successive sequence of events experienced by the model is supposed to mirror those experienced in the real world: the real trajectory is *mimicked* by that of the model. Moreover the very computations undertaken in the course of the simulation correspond, at least notionally, to real activities. As Bell said in discussion: "Every transformation in the computer is also going on out there in the world." Such is certainly the case for all System Dynamics models, including Zubrow's (Chapter 6) and Aldenderfer's ABSIM simulation (Chapter 4).

It is arguable, therefore, that any simulation, to qualify as such, must produce as output a pattern representing the real world at a given point in time (that is, a simulacrum). Otherwise it must mimic the world by undergoing a series of operations, each of which has a real-world analog and by producing a series of values representing the

292

trajectory through time of one or more state variables of the system.

Procedures which do not show one or the other (or both) of these features may well require a great elaboration of calculations to reach a final output value, but they are computations, not simulations.

During the discussion of Cordell's Wetherill Mesa analysis (Cordell 1975, Chapter 5), the interesting methodological question was introduced as to whether the procedure used is, in the strict sense, a simulation. Low raised the point, suggesting that it might rather be seen as a procedure for *calculating* abandonments. The input is a time series, employing the dendroclimatic data of Fritts and others, and Cordell formulated rules by which the suitability for settlement of different areas of land in the study region could be assessed given the varying climatic data, hence allowing quantitative data for abandonment to be predicted. Sabloff, replying to Low, argued on the other hand that this should be regarded as simulation, since a real process is being replicated.

The discussion proved illuminating, focusing on the presence or absence of feedback within the model, feedback being seen by some as an essential ingredient of a simulation model. It was pointed out that if the past system-state has any bearing on the present system-state, then feedback is operating. Models which are completely input-driven need not have any feedback component. But a continuous trajectory—a feature of all living systems—is not possible without feedback.

The other notable feature of the Wetherhill Mesa case is its extraordinary success rate. The predictions for inhabited sites with consecutive occupations, for successive phase transitions, compared with those observed in the field, were respectively: 98.6 percent, 96.6 percent, 90.0 percent, and 100.0 percent. In this sense, it must surely be one of the most successful predictive models in the history of archaeology.

The same question of status, with respect to simulation, was raised in relation to some of Day's economic analyses (Chapter 7). In some cases, although successive system states could be computed graphically by iteration, the terminal state of the system was directly predicted by the analysis as much as by the iteration procedure. The question is perhaps ultimately a verbal one, and interest focused on the power of this approach to clarify issues and make predictions in a manner which raised no objections from the "substantivist" anthropologists present.

In common with recent work by Reidhead (1976) and Keene (1979), Day's work appears to transcend the rather arid debate between "formalist" and "substantivist" economic anthropologists and may prove the forerunner to the general (and long overdue) application of formal economic models to early societies. The application advocated by Day of recursive programming—that is to say, successive optimization procedures employing feedback—offers a very appropriate model both for the process of human learning and development at the individual level, and of the developing adjustment of a culture system to its environment. Recursive programming could clearly be used to simulate the developing subsistence and economic strategies of the community or culture against a background of environmental change, both directional and stochastic. Moreover, with its emphasis on cognitive aspects, on the process of 'learning' which a system undergoes as it adapts, the approach goes beyond rigidly deterministic models.

Three very different objectives were evident among the simulations discussed. The first, exemplified by Cordell's work, was the desire to obtain output data that would closely match the data collected in the field for the real case. The object of the simulation here is to offer a test to the underlying assumptions and theory, from which the algorithm for the simulation has been derived. As Cooke concisely pointed out, the sequence of operation in such cases is always: concept ⟶ theory ⟶ algorithm ⟶ simulation run ⟶ output ⟶ test.

It should be stressed that many simulations involve the use of a stochastic process. In this way, a rather elaborate body of data can be generated, using very simple underlying rules together with the stochastic input. This was not a feature of Cordell's model as expounded, but the procedure is seen in most models where spatial pattern is generated. At the end of the simulation, the output is usually compared with the real data.

Aldenderfer's Aboriginal Simulation (ABSIM) model (Chapter 4) avowedly had a different objective. His ultimate aim was to generate data which could then be used to test taxonomic methods upon which he was working. Here is an unusual case where the output is to be used, in its own right, for further procedures, rather than to be tested against real data, as is more often the case.

For us, however, the ABSIM model had a different interest, and the taxonomic procedures for the investigation of which it is was originally designed were neither presented nor discussed. Instead, interest focused upon a third use of simulation studies: simulation as a heuristic exercise. Here the desire to simulate the processes of lithic assemblage formation led to a very careful formal analysis of the factors involved, in a manner more explicit and precise than had hitherto been undertaken. There is no doubt that the discipline imposed by constructing a simulation procedure, such as can form the basis for a satisfactory algorithm, brings to light interesting hidden problems which remain hidden in less painstaking investigations. As an aid to clear thought about processes—whether formation processes or culture processes of other kinds—the construction of a simulation has considerable heuristic value.

The fourth function of a simulation, discussed in the next section, is more open-ended than these, which are concerned chiefly (a) with testing the further implications of a number of initial assumptions; (b) with investigating these assumptions more deeply; or simply (c) with generating data for other purposes. The framework can, however, be considerably broader.

THE SIMULATOR AS DEMIURGE

PRODUCER: And where's the script?
FATHER: It is in us, sir. *(The* ACTORS *laugh.)* The drama is in us. We are the drama and we are impatient to act it—so fiercely does our inner passion urge us on. . . .

Once the characters are alive . . . Once they are standing truly alive before their author . . . He does nothing but allow the words and gestures they suggest to him . . . And he must want them to be what they want themselves to be. When a character is born he immediately acquires such an independence . . . Even of his own author . . . That everyone can imagine him a whole host of situations in which his author never thought of placing him . . . They can even imagine his acquiring, sometimes, a significance that the author never thought of giving him.

—Luigi Pirandello,
Six Characters in Search of an Author (1954:11, 58)

It is one thing to make certain assumptions, posit certain relationships, and construct a device that will follow these and explore their implications. That, as discussed in the preceding section, implies working within a well-defined frame of reference. It is quite another undertaking to seize upon certain ideas as component parts, to fit them together without any clear notion of exactly where they may lead, and to use the simulation as a means of exploration toward lands as yet uncharted. In this sense, the simulator is like an inventor, creating a device about whose behavior and properties he is far from certain. He does not know where his brainchild may lead him: possibly in directions remote from his expectation.

Perhaps the most exciting moment in simulation modelling is when the machine is ready for lift-off. As the system proceeds through its dynamic trajectory, it can develop modes of behavior which in Forrester's term are "counter-intuitive" (Forrester 1973), and wander off, like the utensils bewitched by the Sorcerer's Apprentice or like Count Frankenstein's monster, into unexpected system states.

Zubrow's interesting chapter (6) catches something of this spirit. He has employed Forrester's *Urban Dynamics* model without any very thoroughgoing scrutiny of the underlying theory or assumptions. Instead, he has taken considerable care that the equations for each component should be modified so as to be as appropriate as possible to ancient Rome, and he has gone to some trouble to provide suitable input data. Then it is a case of "Chocks away, and clear for take-off."

Zubrow terms his simulation a heuristic device, but I am not sure that this is the correct term. For the task here is not one simply of clarification or illumination or instruction. The exercise is more one of exploration than of elucidation, and the simulator is the inventor of an exploratory mechanism that goes ahead to fashion a simulacrum of the sensible world in the light of his ideas; Zubrow has (like Count Frankenstein) almost the status of demiurge.

The machine which he has created can, indeed, appear to have a life of its own, and thus it is not at all surprising that the simulator should find himself able to fashion and fit together certain components without being able to see where their interactions may lead them. Something of the same feeling of creating the components and then letting them get on with it was expressed by the playwright Pirandello in the construction of his comedy *Six Characters in Search of an Author*. The characters, created by him, had their own logic of behavior, and the scenario was conceived as the playing out by these characters of their roles, with consequences which, although perhaps in a sense implicit within them, could not be or were not foreseen at the outset.

There is a genuine feeling of creation here. And the nub is this very quality of unexpectedness and unpredictability. For, as in any real and

296

original act of creation, the qualities and potential of the product are not obvious or completely specified at the moment of formation; rather, they remain to be realized during the effective lifespan of the created object.

One point of great interest here is the methodological one. The simulator is not simply testing a hypothesis—in Zubrow's case, he avowedly was not taking explicit theoretical statements as his starting point. On the contrary, the procedure is to construct a system and see what happens. Yet this is not just building a device for its own sake: the exercise remains a simulation i that comparison with the real world is intended. The model becomes a successful one precisely when its behavior in some respects resembles that of the real world.

In an interesting way, the usual systematic procedures, as set out in standard works on scientific method, are here reversed. In this case, the sequence is not to proceed from theory to deduction, to comparison with real data, to refutation or validation. When the fit between output (simulacrum) and real data is not a good one, the mismatch will not lead to automatic rejection of the generating model but rather to modifications in its structure, to produce a more closely comparable output. (It remains nonetheless true that if, after repeated improvements and modifications, the model is still not able to produce an output adequately resembling reality, it will probably be discarded.)

In many ways, here the activity is more akin to experiment ("Research and Development") than to the testing of preexisting hypotheses. The model is being used as an exploratory device, and although there must still be underlying equations of state, they need not necessarily be exhaustively considered, nor even explicitly known, before the simulation is undertaken.

This view of the simulator in a creative role, rather than simply as a researcher using simulation in a highly controlled way to test the implications of preexisting and carefully formulated hypotheses, may seem a shade imaginative. No doubt there is a risk of exaggerating the apparent autonomy in the behavior of the simulation. The behavior, it will be argued, is always implicit in the equations of state which govern the behavior of the system which has been constructed, even if these equations have not been fully analyzed at the outset.

Nonetheless, the methodological point made above and at the beginning of this chapter does have a certain validity. System dynamics modelling, and no doubt certain other simulation procedures, do make it possible for the model to be logically (and in reality) prior to the theory.

As an example, I should like to refer to a simulation exercise undertaken some years ago by Cooke and myself, with the assistance of Level (Cooke and Renfrew 1979). The starting point was a systemic model concerned with the emergence and development of early Aegean civilization (Renfrew 1972). Subsystem interactions, involving seven subsystems, were summarized in matrix form. When all these interactions were positive, the simulation showed the system as a whole to grow and develop with increasing rapidity. When a number of these interactions were now given negative value (implying both negative feedback and some continuing depletions in the system), the system in some cases, after a period of initial growth, suffered drastic collapse, in the manner to which we have become accustomed from Forrester's *Urban Dynamics* studies, and more particularly from the World Model popularized by the Club of Rome (Meadows et al. 1972).

Since the initial values which we were using, as well as most of the matrix coefficients, were highly hypothetical, we did not take this as an unduly adverse judgment on the viability of the Aegean culture system in the past or subsequently. Instead, we reduced the number of subsystems in order to reach some clearer understanding of what was causing the long-term instability of the system. It proved effectively impossible, using the model, to simulate a behavior for the system which would have long-term stability. Subsequent formal analysis by Cooke showed that there were in fact only a very few equilibrium states for the system, other than those where the coefficients were either zero or infinitely large. In practice these were unstable states, since any small perturbation—which is inevitable as a result of "noise" in a simulation procedure—results in a departure from the equilibrium and either a collapse or an "explosion" (move toward infinite values) for the system. Oscillatory behavior, however, is possible.

Here, then, is a case where behavior unexpected by us emerged from the simulation. Further analysis was able to give explicit theoretical understanding of that behavior.

Two further points of interest emerged here. In the first place, the experience led us to ask to what extent the unstable behavior of the *Limits to Growth* model (Meadows et al. 1972) is a behavior mode specific to that particular model—quite independent of the specific initial values used as input. If it should prove to have the inherently unstable behavior shown analytically by Cooke to be a property of our own model, much of the discussion surrounding it, and certainly all the effort which has gone into the appropriate estimation of suitable initial values for the state variables, could be seen to be misplaced. The world may indeed be doomed to end, but the matter is not further illuminated by choosing for the world a model whose only terminal state is collapse. It follows that with any model it is important to test the full range of its behavior modes, with a wide range of different estimates for the parameters involved, before imagining that it is simulating anything but its own behavior.

The second point arises from this. At what stage is it appropriate to imagine such a model as simulating more than its own behavior? The simulator is, of course, quite at liberty to give names to certain variables in his equation: "Let x_1 indicate population density, x_2 the rate of inflow of labor to the city, and so forth." But at precisely what point should these instructions be regarded as reasonable, and when should it be felt plausible that the model is making statements about the real world, or bearing on the real world? Zubrow has tellingly spoken of "the willing suspension of disbelief." When the model can produce so great a richness of behavior that it is, in many ways, an effective simulation of the real world, there are now philosophical/methodological problems to be considered, indeed perhaps a new chapter to be written in the philosophy of science. The theatrical metaphor is not inappropriate, and there is an uncomfortable analogy between the simulator-demiurge and the dramaturge.

LONG TERM CHANGE: EVOLUTIONARY MACHINES?

The archaeologist has the opportunity to concern himself with long-term change, and hence with problems that only rarely confront many of those undertaking simulation in other disciplines. The consideration of long-term change, indeed, soon highlights the shortcomings of any explanatory model where the range of behavior is in some ways predetermined at the outset. I have recently made this point elsewhere (Renfrew 1979:37), and reproduce a table (Table 10.1) intended to show that working *within* such a model is not enough; a way must be found to generate changes in structure. This would appear to be one of the current limitations of most dynamical systems modelling.

It is, however, a point addressed by Day in his discussion of meta-

TABLE 10.1
THE DIFFICULTY OF MODELLING LONG-TERM CHANGE

Approach	Short-term change	Long-term growth: Morphogenesis
Game theory	Different actual moves, different constraints	Different strategies, different utilities, different rules
System dynamics	Change in values for flow and state variables, and for constraints in model equations of state	Change in components of system, new feedback loops, new equations of state
Directed graphs	Transition to successive states	Radical changes in transition probabilities/times/costs. Possible addition of new states
Interaction matrix	Changing strengths of interaction between variables	Introduction of new variables

adaptation "in which rules of behavior or the population of agents, or both, are variables" (Chapter 7). The problem is to explain structural changes taking place within the system that result in patterns of growth which are more than simply change in scale. Ideally we should like to see the model itself *generate* precisely these changes in its own structure. It is not enough simply to state thresholds beyond which different behavior modes will take place, for it is inherent in the process of evolution, whether in the sphere of natural organisms or of human societies, that new, emergent properties are seen, that epigenesis (Waddington 1977:110) takes place in the course of the unfolding through time, and that thresholds are defined, not externally, but by the developing system itself.

At this point, it is necessary to correct a serious misconception that substantially mars a previous Advanced Seminar volume (Hill 1977a). There, it is repeatedly asserted that the origin of changes must be sought *outside* the system in question. Thus Hill (1977b:76) states:

No system can change in itself; change can only be instigated by outside sources. If a system is in equilibrium it will remain so unless inputs (or lack of inputs) from outside the system disturb the equilibrium. Of course, the individuals in a social system may consciously realize that change is necessary; but the reason the change is necessary lies in the relationship of the system with its environment.

Otherwise, why would change occur at all? In Buckley's approach, why would not the negotiation process eventually lead to stable equilibrium? Why do further "tensions" arise? Where do

300

they come from? Buckley claims that they are inherent in the system—but this is no answer; it begs the question.

The same point is made with great emphasis by Saxe (1977:116): "The processes that result in systemic change for all systems are and must be initiated by extra-systemic variables."

Of course Hill and Saxe are correct that changes external to the system—and Saxe emphasizes rightly the effect of the arrival of Europeans on eighteenth- and nineteenth-century Hawaii—can be of determining significance, an important trigger to the developments which subsequently take place. But it cannot be too firmly stressed that change within a system can only be understood in terms of the internal structure of that system. Sometimes an exogenously determined alteration in certain variables may be seen as the "cause" without which change would not have occurred. But in other cases, no such striking environmental alteration is necessary.

Hill's discussion of "equilibrium" here may be misleading. It is a matter for discussion whether any human cultural system is ever, from the standpoint of the long-term, in equilibrium; long-term processes of change are probably always taking place, whether or not they are of great significance for the future trajectory of the system. And the significance of such changes, often small in themselves, may not be easy to assess. Sanders, during discussion in this same volume, pointed out that population growth can be seen in some cases as a source of change internal to the system, but Saxe (1977:289), in a reply which is incomprehensible to me, pronounced it external. A rather different view is presented by Perlman (1977) later in that volume, but nowhere is this unfortunate conclusion explicitly rebutted.

Archaeology has already faced this problem in recent years with the rejection of diffusionist explanations (Renfrew 1973; Binford 1968b). To define the system so that the source of change is always external to it is not merely to "beg the question," but to reduce all explanation to the status of a will o' the wisp, something which eludes our grasp. It "has the effect of relegating to the wings all the action of the prehistoric drama" (Childe 1956:154).

If the source of change is indeed seen as external to the system, it may be necessary to redefine the limits of the system so that the source can be included within it. In practice, however, what is ultimately of significance is not the possible origin of a change in an altered environmental variable, such as decline in rainfall. We seek to understand why and how this particular external change has long-term effects upon the structure (and hence upon the future trajectory) of the system, when other changes do not. Until we see this as the nub of the problem, the question has not been effectively posed at all.

This point has been well made in a recent paper by Bell and Senge (1980): "A minimum standard for acceptance of many system dynamics models is generating the empirical behavior of interest with *no exogenous time series inputs*." Most real cases will indeed have such inputs, but to place the whole weight of the explanation upon them, as those cited above have sought to do, seems to defeat much of the object of the exercise.

The usefulness of systemic simulations for modelling long-term change is likely to depend upon their effectiveness for modelling changes in structure rather than simply changes in rate and level in an existing structure. And here it may be worth speculating whether or not the approach may usefully be linked with others which have been employed in the discussion of morphogenesis. Here I am thinking, for instance, of Catastrophe Theory (Thom 1975; Renfrew 1978), where the focus is upon qualitative change, rather than on precise quantitative modelling.

The Catastrophe Theory approach encourages one to consider the global dynamics of the system and to think of the whole series of stable states which it may occupy. Some insight may thus be gained into its range of possible behaviors, without concerning ourselves at a detailed quantitative level with the values of all the variables in the system. This can bring out in a helpful way that, while the values of variables which we may consider external to the system (which will be numbered among the control variables) are of crucial relevance in determining at just what point certain changes may take place, the nature of those changes is governed by the global topology of the system itself.

Of course, the special strength of system dynamics modelling is that it allows one to work simultaneously at the detailed, quantitative level and to follow the broad, qualitative trends of the developing behavior as it occurs. In some cases, however, other approaches may help one to see the forest for the trees.

This whole problem of the emergence of form is one which has fascinated mathematical biologists for many decades (Thompson 1942; Thom 1975; Waddington 1977), and I believe that their approach has much to offer us (Rosen 1979). To say that is not to overlook the

302

numerous pitfalls in applying to cultural evolution some of the concepts of Darwinian evolution in a mechanistic way. Burnham (1973) has analyzed the circularities that lurk in the application of the concept of "adaptation" to human societies, and the Darwinian notion of monogenesis, which is of great value to the taxonomic paleontologists, has been positively misleading when applied to archaeology (Renfrew 1979). But there, in the workings of evolution, we can indeed view the genesis of structure, as it unfolds before our eyes. The models now being used to simulate this process will be of great relevance to us.

It is here that simulation may be of special value. If we can adequately simulate the structure and behavior of an organism or organization, we should be able to see it survive or decline, grow or change along a series of different life histories or trajectories. What will happen if certain changes take place in the structure of the system, changes which we may regard as the analogue of genetic mutations? Under what circumstances along the time trajectory will these minor "mutations" bring about an evolutionary change of greater significance, a transformation to a new organizational form? In this sense we might be able to view our system simulations as evolutionary machines, plotting out for us different evolutionary paths, and exploring within a relatively short time in the laboratory possibilities which in reality would take centuries or millennia to realize.

In order to reach new structures, however, we must overcome the ultimately deterministic nature of·most present system simulations. The system must be enabled to modify itself in ways both initially unforeseen and unpredictable. This implies, referring to Table 10.1, that the system itself must be allowed to generate new feedback loops and new components in a way which is not completely determined at the outset. Perhaps this means introducing a stochastic element, on analogy with mutation. Sometimes that will lead to dysfunction, and the system may not survive. In some cases competition between coexisting systems will lead to some sort of Darwinian "survival of the fittest," but in others the system will have no competitor. Unfortunately, we have no obvious way of deciding now which possible "mutation" is likely to occur and survive.

In some ways, there is little that is new in this notion of human societies and their operation being simulated by evolutionary machines. But in most existing simulations, the level of determinacy is so high that, given comparable initial conditions and similar external conditions along the trajectory, the final states are likely to be much the same. This is not the way to allow interesting new structures to emerge. We may, instead, find it fruitful to create system simulations which have the property of producing the unexpected.

Such a turn of events has intrigued many of those who have written of automata, from Mary Shelley to Arthur Clarke, and, in a different field, has disquieted those who are alert to the potentialities of re-combinant DNA. It is perhaps time that, within the framework of our simulations, we should attempt to harness the unexpected in order to generate truly emergent properties. We are, however, dealing with human, not molecular, interactions, and the analogy with DNA must not be stretched too far.

These problems are usefully discussed within a rather different framework by Day in Chapter 7 under the heading "Meta-adaptation." In the discussion following the presentation of his paper, we began to consider some of the devices by which human societies have success-fully countered disequilibrium. These are innovations, such as the introduction of coinage, for instance, or of the limited liability company, or of currencies of account, which result in the long run in major changes in society which we can regard as structural changes.

One of the most promising features of the adaptive economics framework which Day proposes is the manner in which the development of 'disequilibrium mechanisms' may be approached. For it is very clear that what may originate as a mechanism simply to restore equilibrium may develop until it represents a significant structural change in the system, a major innovation in the unfolding development and growth process. This, then, is an aspect of the adaptive economics approach which will repay further exploration. Nor need the use of the term *economics* here inhibit the application of comparable ideas to other aspects of the culture system such as social structure. The underlying notion is a perfectly general one.

Some evolutionary changes in human societies, just as in living organisms, may be regarded as an increasingly effective *mapping* of the environment. Thus the development of the eye can, with the wisdom of hindsight, be seen as a positive adaptive response—a suc-cessful innovation in the mapping of an environment rich in electro-magnetic radiation of the appropriate wavelengths. An analogous case in human culture might be the tapping of atomic energy, or within the archaeological time range the "invention" of metallurgy. Such inventions, which simply imply the new exploitation of a preexisting (although not hitherto perceived) environment, may be regarded as an improvement in the mapping effected by the human society. It may be that, in cases where we as simulators already possess the relevant "map," an effective simulation of the mapping activity of past societies could be possible. (If we do not possess the relevant map—as in the case of controlled thermonuclear reactions—the simulation will not be so easy.)

These, however, are cases where the developments are ultimately determined by the structure of the environment, although in a different and perhaps more subtle sense than that of Hill and Saxe. More problematical, and, at the present stage of in our understanding of human societies, more interesting, are the evolutionary changes within the structure of society, where the society is adjusting to essentially human problems. Many human social institutions are of this kind—all of the wide range of hierarchical structures, the various devices for controlling and processing information, the different types of exchange and the devices for facilitating it. When we have constructed simulations which can begin to come up with new structures of this kind—although not necessarily with just those devices which societies known to us have produced, then we shall be at a new and more productive stage of modelling.

These are mere speculations at the moment. Yet many of the necessary ingredients are already available. For all the participants at the Advanced Seminar, it was an impressive experience to see how a skilled systems analyst could break a given problem down and express it in system dynamics terms. Low undertook this task for Cordell's Wetherill Mesa case, setting out in a logical analysis the loops and flows required to express fully the proposed insights into the causes of settlement abandonment. The next stage, which he could clearly have accomplished without difficulty, would be to write the necessary equations and proceed to a full simulation in the Forrester manner.

Already, then, it is possible to give an analytical account of the detailed behavior of specified aspects of a culture system, which will include predictions about its future behavior, at least over the short term. Such predictions are possible because we have an explicit understanding of the structure of the system, whose behavior is thus, in a

305

sense, determined, although it may not be known to us until the implications of the structure are explored by simulation.

The next stage must be to explore the future behavior and the future structural evolution of systems whose evolution is not uniquely determined by their present form, but which have themselves the potential for generating emergent properties.

NOTE

1. I should like to express my thanks for useful critical comment on an earlier draft of this chapter from Day and for some important and helpful suggestions from Cooke.

References

ABE, MASATOSHI, R. H. DAY, J. P. NELSON, AND W. K. TABB
1978   "Behavioral, Suboptimizing Models of Industrial Production, Investment and Techno- $\mathcal{G}^{\mathfrak{I}}$
       logical Change," in *Modelling Economic Change: The Recursive Programming Approach*,
       eds. R. H. Day and A. Cigno (Amsterdam: North-Holland Publishing Co.).
ABEL, LELAND J.
1955   "San Juan Red Ware, Mesa Verde Gray Ware, Mesa Verde White Ware, and San Juan
       White Ware," in *Ceramic Series* 3B (Flagstaff: Museum of Northern Arizona).
ADAMS, R. M., AND H. J. NISSEN
1972   *The Uruk Countryside: The Natural Setting of Urban Society* (Chicago: The University
       of Chicago Press).
AKERMAN, KIM
1974   "Spearmaking Sites in the Western Desert, Western Australia," *Mankind* 9:310– 13.
ALDENDERFER, MARK S.
1977   "The Computer Simulation of Assemblage Formation Processes: The Evaluation of
       Multivariate Statistical Methods in Archaeological Research" (Ph.D. dissertation, Penn-
       sylvania State University).
ALDENDERFER, MARK S., AND ROGER BLASHFIELD
1978   "Cluster Analysis and Archaeological Classification," *American Antiquity* 43:502– 5.
ALLAN, WILLIAM C., ALAN OSBORN, WILLIAM J. CHASKO, AND DAVID E.
STUART
1975   "An Archeological Survey: Road Construction Rights-of-Way Block II Navajo Indian
       Irrigation Project," in *Archeological Reports, Cultural Resource Management Projects,
       Working Draft Series*, no. 1, eds. Frank J. Broilo and David E. Stuart (Albuquerque:
       Office of Contract Archeology, University of New Mexico).
AMMERMAN, ALBERT J., AND MARCUS FELDMAN
1974   "On the Making of an Assemblage," *American Antiquity* 39:610– 19.

REFERENCES

AMMERMAN, A. J., D. P. GIFFORD, AND A. VOORIPS
1979   "Towards an Evaluation of Sampling Strategies: Simulated Excavations of a Kenyan Pastoralist Site," in *Simulation Studies in Archaeology*, ed. Ian Hodder (New York: Cambridge University Press).

ANDREWS, D. F., R. GNANADESIKAN, AND J. L. WARNER
1973   "Methods for Assessing Multivariate Normality," in *Multivariate Analysis III*, ed. P. R. Krishnaiah (New York: Academic Press).

AOKI, M.
1967   *Optimizing of Stochastic Systems* (New York: Academic Press).
1977   "Adaptive Control Theory: Survey and Potential Application to Decision Processes," paper presented at the Stochastic Control Workshop, AIDS National Meeting, Chicago.

ARNOLD, J.
1963   "Climate of the Wiluna-Meekatharra Area," *CSIRO Australian Land Research Series* 7:71–92.

ASHBY, L. D.
1964   *Regional Change in the National Economy*, Staff Working Papers No. 7 (Washington, D. C.: U.S. Department of Commerce).

ASHBY, W. R.
1956   *An Introduction to Cybernetics* (London: Methuen).
1967   "The Set Theory of Mechanism and Homeostasis," in *Automation Theory and Learning Systems*, ed. D. J. Stewart (Washington, D. C.: Thompson Book Co.).

ATHENS, J. S.
1977   "Theory Building and the Study of Evolutionary Process in Complex Societies," in *For Theory Building in Archaeology*, ed. L. R. Binford (New York: Academic Press).

BACON, SIR FRANCIS
1960   *The New Organum and Related Writings*, ed. F. H. Anderson (Indianapolis: Bobbs-Merrill Co.).

BALFOUR, H. R.
1951   "A Native Tool Kit from the Kimberley District, Western Australia," *Mankind* 4:273–74.

BALSDON, J. P. V. B.
1963   *Roman Woman* (New York: John Day Co.).

BASEDOW, HERBERT
1904   "Anthropological Notes Made on the South Australian Government Northwest Prospecting Expedition," *Transactions of the Royal Society of South Australia* 28:12–51.

BATTY, M.
1972   "Dynamic Simulation of an Urban System," in *Patterns and Processes in Urban and Regional Systems*, ed. A. G. Wilson (London: Pion Ltd.).

BAYARD, D. T.
1969   "Science, Theory and Reality in the 'New' Archaeology," *American Antiquity* 34:376–84.

BAZOVSKY, IGOR
1961   *Reliability Theory and Practice* (Englewood Cliffs: Prentice-Hall).

BEARD, J.
1968   "Drought Effects in the Gibson Desert," *Journal of the Royal Society of Western Australia* 51:39–50.
1969   "The Natural Regions of the Deserts of Western Australia," *Journal of Ecology* 47:671–711.

BELL, JAMES A., AND JAMES F. BELL
1980   "System Dynamics and Scientific Method," in *Elements of the System Dynamics Method*, ed. Jorgen Randers (Cambridge: MIT Press).

BELL, JAMES A., AND PETER M. SENGE
1980   "Methods for Enhancing Objectivity in System Dynamics Models," *Management Science* (in press).

308

References

BELLMAN, RICHARD E.
1961   *Adaptive Control Processes: A Guided Tour* (Princeton: Princeton University Press).
BELLMAN, RICHARD E., AND KENNETH L. COOKE
1963   *Differential-Difference Equations* (New York: Academic Press).
BENDER, E. A.
✓✓1978   *An Introduction to Mathematical Modeling* (New York: Wiley–Interscience).
BENNET, R. J., AND R. J. CHORLEY
1978   *Environmental Systems* (Princeton: Princeton University Press).
BERGER, EDWARD, HARVEY BOULAY, AND BETTY ZISK
1970   "Simulation and the City: A Critical Overview," *Simulation and Games* 1:411–29.
BERLINSKI, DAVID
1976   *On Systems Analysis* (Cambridge: M.I.T. Press).
BERNDT, R.
1959   "The Concept of the 'Tribe' in the Western Desert of Australia," *Oceania* 30:81–107.
1970   *The Sacred Site: the Western Arnhem Land Example,* Australian Aboriginal Studies, no. 29 (Canberra: Australian Institute of Aboriginal Studies).
BERTALANFFY, L. VON
✓✓ 1950   "An Outline of General System Theory," *British Journal of the Philosophy of Science* 1:134–65.
BINFORD, L. R.
1962   "Archaeology as Anthropology," *American Antiquity* 28:217–25.
1968a   "Archaeological Perspectives," in *New Perspectives in Archaeology*, eds. S. R. Binford and L. R. Binford (Chicago: Aldine).
1968b   "Some Comments on Historical Versus Processual Archaeology," *Southwestern Journal of Anthropology* 24:267–76.
1972a   *An Archaeological Perspective* (New York: Seminar Press).
1972b   "Contemporary Model Building, Paradigms and Lower Paleolithic Research," in *Models in Archaeology*, ed. David Clarke (London: Methuen).
1973   "Interassemblage Variability—the Mousterian and the 'Functional Model'," in *Explanation of Culture Change*, ed. Colin Renfrew (London: Duckworth).
1976   "Forty-seven Trips—A Case Study in the Character of Some Formation in Processes of the Archaeological Record," in *Contributions to Anthropology: The Interior Peoples of Northern Alaska*, ed. E. S. Hall. Archaeological Survey Paper, no. 49 (Ottawa: National Museum of Canada).
1977   "General Introduction," in *For Theory Building Archaeology*, ed. L. R. Binford (New York: Academic Press).
1978   "Dimensional Analysis of Behavior and Site Structure: Learning from an Eskimo Hunting Stand," *American Antiquity* 43:330–61.
BINFORD, L. R. (ED.)
1977   *For Theory Building in Archaeology* (New York: Academic Press).
BINFORD, L. R., AND J. BERTRAM
1977   "Bone Frequencies and Attritional Processes," in *For Theory Building in Archaeology*, ed. L. R. Binford (New York: Academic Press).
BINFORD, L. R., AND S. BINFORD
1966   "A Preliminary Analysis of Functional Variability in the Mousterian of Levallois Facies," in *Recent Studies in Paleoanthropology*, eds. J. D. Clarke and F. C. Howell (*American Anthropologist* Special Publications).
BLALOCK, H.
1971   *Causal Inference in Non-experimental Research* (Chapel Hill: University of North Carolina Press).
BLASHFIELD, ROGER K., AND MARK S. ALDENDERFER
1978   "The Literature on Cluster Analysis," *Multivariate Behavioral Research* 13:271–95.

BLASHFIELD, R. K., M. S. ALDENDERFER, AND L. C. MOREY
In Press "Cluster Analysis Literature on Validation," in *Clustering Social Data*, ed. H. Hudson (San Francisco: Jossey-Bass).

BLEVINS, BYRON B., AND CAROL JOINER
1977 "The Archeological Survey of Tijeras Canyon," in *Archeological Report No. 18* (Albuquerque: USDA Forest Service, Southwestern Regional Office).

BONESS, NEIL
1971 "Desert Adze to Woodland Adze: A Study of Available Ethnographic Data to Determine the Functions of Stone Tools in Selected Environmental Areas" (B. A. thesis, University of Sydney).

BOULDING, K. E.
1972 "Toward the Development of a Cultural Economics," *Social Science Quarterly* 53:267–83.

BOX, G. E. P.
1960 "Fitting Empirical Data," *Annals of the New York Academy of Sciences* 86:792–816.

BRETERNITZ, DAVID A., ARTHUR H. ROHN, JR., AND ELIZABETH A. MORRIS
1974 "Prehistoric Ceramics of the Mesa Verde Region," in *Ceramic Series* 5 (Flagstaff: Museum of Northern Arizona).

BRITTING, K. R., AND J. G. TRUMP
1973 "The Parameters Sensitivity Issue in Urban Dynamics," in *Proceedings of the 1973 Summer Computer Simulation Conference*, vol. 2 (La Jolla: Simulation Councils, Inc.).

BRONSTEIN, NANCY
1977 "Report on a Replicative Experiment in the Manufacture and Use of Western Desert Micro-Adzes," in *Puntutjarpa Rockshelter and the Australian Desert Culture*, ed. Richard Gould. Anthropological Papers of the American Museum of Natural History, no. 54 (New York: American Museum of Natural History).

BRUES, ALICE M.
1963 "Stochastic Tests of Selection in ABO Blood Groups," *American Journal of Physical Anthropology* 21:287–99.

BURNHAM, P.
1973 "The Explanatory Value of the Concept of Adaptation in Studies of Culture Change," in *The Explanation of Culture Change*, ed. C. Renfrew (London: Duckworth).

BUXTON, J. N.
1968 *Simulation Programming Languages* (Amsterdam: North-Holland Publishing Company).

CALE, WILLIAM G., AND P. L. ODELL
1979 "Concerning Aggregation in Ecosystem Modeling," in *Theoretical Systems Ecology*, ed. Efraim Halfon (New York: Academic Press).

CANON, W. B.
1939 *The Wisdom of the Body*, rev. ed. (New York: W. W. Norton and Co.).

CASWELL, HAL
1976 "The Validation Problem," in *Systems Analysis and Simulation in Ecology*, vol. 4, ed. B. Patten (New York: Academic Press).

CAVALLI-SFORZA, L. L., AND G. ZEI
1967 "Experiments with an Artificial Population," in *Proceedings of the Third Congress of Human Genetics*, eds. J. F. Crow and J. V. Neel (Baltimore: Johns Hopkins Press).

CHANDLER, T., AND G. FOX
1974 *3000 Years of Urban Growth* (New York: Academic Press).

CHAPMAN, T.
1970 "Optimization of a Rainfall-Runoff Model for an Arid-Zone Cachement," *International Association of Scientific Hydrology Publications* 96:127–44.

310

References

CHENERY, HOLLIS B.
1952   "Overcapacity and the Accelerator Principle," *Econometrica* 20:1–28.
CHERRY, J.
1978   "Generalisation and the Archaeology of the State," in *Social Organisation and Settlement*, eds. D. Green, C. Heselgrove, and M. Spriggs (British Archaeological Reports International Series vol. 47, pt. 2).
CHILDE, V. GORDON
1951   *Social Evolution* (London: Watts and Co.).
1956   *Piecing Together the Past* (London: Routledge and Kegan Paul).
CHILLINGWORTH, D. R. J.
1976   *Differential Topology with a View to Applications* (London: Pitman Publishing).
CHIPPENDALE, G. M.
1968   "The Plants Grazed by Red Kangaroos, *Megeleia Rufa* (Desmarest), in Central Australia," *Proceedings of the Linnean Society of New South Wales* 93:98–110.
CLARKE, D. L.
1968   *Analytical Archaeology* (London: Methuen).
1972   "Models and Paradigms in Contemporary Archaeology," in *Models in Archaeology*, ed. D. L. Clarke (London: Methuen).
CLELAND, J. B., AND T. HARVEY JOHNSON
1933   "The Ecology of the Aborigines of Central Australia," *Transactions of the Royal Society of South Australia* 57:113–24.
1938   "Notes on the Native Names and Uses of Plants in the Musgrave Ranges Region," *Oceania* 8:208–15,328–42.
CLELAND, J. B., AND N. B. TINDALE
1954   "The Ecological Surroundings of the Ngalia Natives in Central Australia and Native Names and Uses of Plants," *Transactions of the Royal Society of South Australia* 77:81–86.
1959   "Native Names and Uses of Plants at Haast Bluff, Central Australia," *Transactions of the Royal Society of South Australia* 82:132–40.
COMMONS, JOHN R.
1924   *The Legal Foundations of Capitalism* (New York: Macmillan Co.).
CONWAY, R. W.
1963   "Some Tactical Problems in Digital Simulation," *Management Science* 10:47–61.
CONWAY, R. W., B. M. JOHNSON, AND W. L. MAXWELL
1959   "Some Problems of Digital Systems Simulation," *Management Science* 6:92–110.
COOKE, KENNETH L.
1979   "Mathematical Approaches to Culture Change," in *Transformations: Mathematical Approaches to Culture Change*, eds. C. Renfrew and K. L. Cooke (New York: Academic Press).
COOKE, K. L., AND H. I. FREEDMAN
n.d.   "A Model for the Adoption of a Technological Innovation," in preparation.
COOKE, K. L., AND C. RENFREW
1979   "An Experiment on the Simulation of Culture Change," in *Transformations: Mathematical Approaches to Culture Change*, eds. C. Renfrew and K. L. Cooke (New York: Academic Press).
COOPER, W. W.
1951   "A Proposal for Extending the Theory of the Firm," *Quarterly Journal of Economics* 65:87–109.
CORDELL, LINDA S.
1972   "Settlement Pattern Changes at Wetherill Mesa, Colorado: A Test Case for Computer Simulation in Archaeology" (Ph.D. dissertation, University of California, Santa Barbara).

311

1975 "Predicting Site Abandonment at Wetherill Mesa," *The Kiva* 40:189–201.

1977a "Cultural Evolution: An Overview of Theory," paper presented at the Annual Meeting of the American Anthropological Association, Houston.

1977b "Late Anasazi Farming and Hunting Strategies: One Example of a Problem in Congruence," *American Antiquity* 42:449–61.

1979a *A Cultural Resources Overview of the Middle Rio Grande Valley* (Albuquerque USDA Forest Service, Southwestern Regional Office).

1979b "Prehistory: Eastern Anasazi," *Handbook of North American Indians*, The Southwest, vol. 9 (Washington, D. C.: Smithsonian Institution).

CORDELL, LINDA S., AND FRED PLOG

1979 "Escaping the Confines of Normative Thought: a Re-evaluation of Puebloan Prehistory," *American Antiquity* 40:1–28.

CRAIN, W. MARK, AND ROBERT D. TOLLISON

n.d. "The Convergence of Satisficing to Marginalism: An Empirical Tact," Center for Study of Public Choice, Virginia Polytechnic Institute and State University, Blacksburg, Virginia.

CRECINE, J. P.

1964 "TOMM: Time Oriented Metropolitan Model," *C.R.P. Technical Bulletin*, no. 6 (Pittsburgh: Consad Research Corp.).

1968 "A Dynamic Model of Urban Structure," The Rand Corporation, Santa Monica, Calif.

1969 "Spatial Location Decisions in Urban Structure: A Time Oriented Model," *Discussion Paper no. 4.* (Ann Arbor: The Institute of Public Policy Studies, University of Michigan).

CROSBIE, R. E.

✓✓ 1977 "Simulation—Is It Worth It?" in *Simulation of Systems*, ed. L. Dekker. Proceedings of the 8th AICA Conference (Amsterdam: North-Holland Publishing Co.).

CULBERT, T. P. (ED.)

1973 *The Classic Maya Collapse* (Albuquerque: University of New Mexico Press, School of American Research Advanced Seminar Series).

CYERT, RICHARD M., AND JAMES G. MARCH

1963 *A Behavioral Theory of the Firm* (Englewood Cliffs: Prentice–Hall).

DANIEL, C., AND F. WOOD

1971 *Fitting Equations to Data* (New York: Wiley-Interscience).

DARLINGTON, C. D.

1969 *The Evolution of Man and Society* (New York: Simon and Schuster).

DAVID, NICHOLAS

1972 "On the Lifespan of Potters, Type Frequencies, the Archaeological Inference," *American Antiquity* 37:141–42.

DAVID, NICHOLAS, AND HILKE HENNING

1972 *The Ethnography of Pottery: A Fulani Case in Archaeological Perspective*, McCaleb Module in Anthropology 21 (Reading: Addison Wesley).

DAVIDSON, D., S. RICHTER, AND A. ROGERS

1976 "A Simulation Program for the Analysis of Archaeological Distributions," *Newsletter of Computer Archaeology* 11:1–10.

DAWKINS, RICHARD

1976 *The Selfish Gene* (New York: Oxford University Press).

DAY, RICHARD H.

✓ 1967 "Profits, Learning and the Convergence of Satisficing to Marginalism," *Quarterly Journal of Economics* 81:302–11.

✓ 1975 "Adaptive Processes and Economic Theory," in *Adaptive Economic Models*, eds. R. H. Day and T. Groves (New York: Academic Press).

312

References

1978   "Adaptive Economic Theory and Modelling, a Review," in *Contemporary Issues in Natural Resource Economics*, ed. E. N. Castle. Resources for the Future, reprint 152.

1980   "The Emergence of Chaos from Classical Economic Growth," *Department of Economics Working Paper*, no. 8014 (Los Angeles: University of Southern California).

DAY, RICHARD H., AND A. CIGNO
1978   *Modelling Economic Change: The Recursive Programming Approach* (Amsterdam: North-Holland Publishing Co.).

DAY, RICHARD H., AND T. GROVES (EDS.)
1975   *Adaptive Economic Models* (New York: Academic Press).

DAY, RICHARD H., AND EVAN F. KOENIG
1974   "Malthusia: Population and Economic Growth in the Pre-Industrial State," *Social Systems Research Institute, University of Wisconsin–Madison Workshop Series* no. 7144.

DAY, RICHARD H., AND INDERJIT SINGH
1977   *Economic Development as an Adaptive Process: The Green Revolution in the Indian Punjab* (Cambridge: Cambridge University Press).

DEAN, JEFFREY S.
1978   "An Evaluation of the Initial SARG Research Design," in *Investigations of the Southwestern Anthropological Research Group, Proceedings of the 1976 Conference*, eds. Robert C. Euler and George J. Gumerman (Flagstaff: Museum of Northern Arizona Press).

DEWIT, C. T., AND J. GOUDRIAAN
1978   *Simulation of Ecological Processes* (New York: Halsted Press).

DITTERT, A. E., JR.
1959   "Cultural Change in the Cebolleta Mesa Region, Central Western New Mexico" (Ph.D. dissertation, University of Arizona).

DORAN, JAMES
1970   "Systems Theory, Computer Simulations, and Archaeology," *World Archaeology* I: 289–98.

DRIVER, RODNEY D.
1977   *Ordinary and Delay Differential Equations* (New York: Springer–Verlag).

DUBES, RICHARD, AND ANIL K. JAIN
1977   *Models and Methods in Cluster Validity*. Technical Report TR-77-05, Department of Computer Science (Lansing: College of Engineering, Michigan State University).

DUCKSTEIN, L., M. FOGEL, AND C. KISSEL
1972   "A Stochastic Model of Runoff-Producing Rainfall for Summer-Type Storms," *Water Resources Research* 8:410–21.

DUTTON, J. M., AND W. G. BRIGGS
1971   "Simulation Model Construction," in *Computer Simulation of Human Behavior*, eds. J. M. Dutton and W. H. Starbuck (New York: John Wiley and Sons).

DYKE, BENNETT
1977   "On the Appropriate Use of Simulation," paper presented at the 42nd Annual Meeting of the Society for American Archaeology, New Orleans.

DYKE, BENNETT, AND JEAN W. MACCLUER (EDS.)
1974   *Computer Simulation in Human Population Studies* (New York: Academic Press).

EASTON, DAVID
1965   *A Systems Analysis of Political Life* (New York: John Wiley and Sons).

EDDY, FRANK W.
1966   *Prehistory in the Navajo Reservoir District, Northwestern New Mexico*, Papers in Anthropology 15 (Santa Fe: Museum of New Mexico).

REFERENCES

EIGHMY, JEFFREY L.

1979 "Logistic Trends in Southwest Population Growth," in *Transformations: Mathematical Approaches to Culture Change*, eds. C. Renfrew and K. L. Cooke (New York: Academic Press).

EMSHOFF, J. R., AND R. L. SISSON

1970 *Design and Use of Computer Simulation Models* (New York: MacMillan).

ERASMUS, J. C.

1965 "Monument Building: Some Field Experiments," *Southwestern Journal of Anthropology*, 21:4:277–301.

ERDMAN, J. A., C. L. DOUGLASS, AND J. W. MARR

1969 *Environment of Mesa Verde, Colorado*. Archaeological Research Series 7-B (Washington, D.C.: National Park Service).

EULER, ROBERT G., AND S. M. CHANDLER

1978 "Aspects of Prehistoric Settlement Patterns in Grand Canyon," in *Investigations of the Southwestern Anthropological Research Group, the Proceedings of the 1976 Conference*, eds. R. C. Euler and G. J. Gumerman (Flagstaff: Museum of Northern Arizona).

FAIRBRIDGE, R.

1968 "The Hydrology of Scott, Cooper, Bentley, and Talbot 1/250000 Sheets," *Western Australia Geological Survey Records 1968/6* (Perth).

FEL'DBAUM, A. A.

1965 *Optimal Control Systems* (New York: Academic Press).

FISHMAN, GEORGE S.

1973 *Concepts and Methods in Discrete Event Digital Simulation* (New York: Wiley-Interscience).

1978 *Principles of Discrete Event Simulation* (New York: Wiley-Interscience).

FITZPATRICK, E., AND A. KRISHNAN

1967 "A First-Order Markov Model for Assessing Rainfall Discontinuity in Central Australia," *Archivs Meteorologika, Geophysika, Bioklimatologike B* 15:242–59.

FITZPATRICK, E. A., R. O. SLAYTER, AND A. I. KRISHNAN

1967 "Incidence and Duration of Periods of Plant Growth in Central Australia as Estimated From Climatic Data," *Agricultural Meteorology* 4:389–404.

FLANNERY, KENT V.

1968 "The Olmec and the Valley of the Oaxaca," in *Dumbarton Oaks Conference on the Olmec*, ed. E. P. Benson (Washington, D. C.: Dumbarton Oaks).

1972 "The Cultural Evolution of Civilizations," *Annual Review of Ecology and Systematics* 3:399–425.

1973 "Archaeology with a Capital S," in *Research and Theory in Current Archaeology*, ed. C. L. Redman (New York: John Wiley).

FLANNERY, K. V. (ED.)

1976 *The Mesoamerican Village* (New York: Academic Press).

FLANNERY, K. V., AND H. T. WRIGHT

1966 "Faunal Remains from Hut Soundings at Eridu, Iraq," *Sumer* 22:61–63.

FOGEL, M., AND L. DUCKSTEIN

1969 "Point Rainfall Frequencies in Convective Storms," *Water Resources Research* 5:1229–37.

FORRESTER, JAY W.

1961 *Industrial Dynamics* (Cambridge: M.I.T. Press).

1966 "Modelling the Dynamic Processes of Corporate Growth," *Proceedings of the IBM Scientific Computing Symposium on Simulation Models and Gaming* (White Plains: IBM Data Processing Division).

1968 *Principles of Systems* (Cambridge: M.I.T. Press).

1969 *Urban Dynamics* (Cambridge: M.I.T. Press).

1971 *World Dynamics* (Cambridge: M.I.T. Press).

References

1973 "Understanding the Counterintuitive Behaviour of Social Systems," in *Towards Global Equilibrium: Collected Papers*, eds. D. L. Meadows and D. H. Meadows (Cambridge: Wright-Allen).

FORRESTER, JAY W., N. J. MASS, AND C. J. RYAN
1976 "The System Dynamics National Model: Understanding Socio-Economic Behavior and Policy Alternatives," *Technological Forecasting and Social Change* 9:51–68.

FORRESTER, JAY W., AND PETER M. SENGE
1979 "Tests for Building Confidence in System Dynamics Models," *Management Science* (in press).

FRANK, T.
1962 *An Economic History of Rome*, 2d Ed. (New York: Cooper Square Publishing).

FREIDEL, DAVID A.
1979 "Culture Areas and Interaction Spheres: Contrasting Approaches to the Emergence of Civilization in Maya Lowlands," *American Antiquity* 44:36–55.

FRISCH, RAGNAR
1933 "Propagation Problems and Impulse Problems in Dynamic Economics," in *Economic Essays in Honor of Gustav Cassell* (London: George Allen & Unwin).

FRITTS, HAROLD C., DAVID G. SMITH, AND MARVIN A. STOKES
1965 "The Biological Model for Paleoclimatic Interpretation of Mesa Verde Tree-Ring Series," in *Contributions of the Wetherill Mesa Archaeological Project*, ed. D. Osborne. Memoirs of the Society for American Archaeology, 19.

GALL, P. L., AND SAXE, A.A.
1977 "The Ecological Evolution of Culture: The State as Predator in Succession Theory," in *Exchange Systems in Prehistory*, eds. T. K. Earle and J. Ericson (New York: Academic Press).

GALLAGHER, JAMES
1972 "A Preliminary Report on Archaeological Research Near Lake Zuai," *Annales D'Ethiopie* 9:13–18.

GELZER, MATHIAS
1969 *The Roman Nobility*, tr. R. Seiger (New York: Oxford University Press).

GENTILLI, J.
1971 *Climates of Australia and New Zealand*, World Survey of Climatology 13, series ed., H. Landsberg (Amsterdam: Elsiever Publishing Company).

GIBBS, W.
1969 "Meteorology and Climatology," in *Arid Lands of Australia*, eds. R. Slayter and R. Perry (Canberra: Australia National University Press).

GILMOUR, PETER
1973 "A General Validation Procedure for Computer Simulation Models," *Australian Computer Journal* 5:127–31.

GLASSOW, MICHAEL A.
1972 "Changes in the Adaptations of Southwestern Basketmakers: A Systems Perspective," in *Contemporary Archaeology*, ed. M. P. Leone (Carbondale: Southern Illinois University Press).

GOLDHAMER, H., AND H. SPEIER
1957 "The Role of Operational Gaming in Operations Research," *Journal of Operations Research Society of America* 5:1–27.

GOODALL, D.
1969 "Simulating the Grazing Situation," in *Concepts and Models of Biomathematics*, ed. F. Heinmets (New York: Marcel Dekker).

GOODE, TERRY M.
1977 "Explanation, Expansion and the Aims of Historians: Toward an Alternative Account of Historical Explanation," *Philosophy of the Social Sciences* 7:367–84.

315

GOODMAN, MICHAEL R.
1974   *Study Notes in System Dynamics* (Cambridge: M.I.T. Press).
GOODWIN, RICHARD
1948   "Secular and Cyclical Aspects of the Multiplier and Accelerator," in *Income, Employment and Public Policy: Essays in Honor of Alvin Hansen* (New York: W. W. Norton and Co.).
GOODYEAR, ALBERT C., L. MARK RAAB, AND TIMOTHY C. KLINGER
1978   "The Status of Archaeological Research Design in Cultural Resource Management," *American Antiquity* 43:159– 73.
GORDON, C.
1969   *System Simulation* (Englewood Cliffs: Prentice-Hall).
GOULD, RICHARD A.
n.d.   Unpublished Field Notes (manuscript).
1967   "Notes on Hunting, Butchering and Sharing of Game Among the Ngatatjara and Their Neighbors in the West Australian Desert," *Kroeber Anthropological Society* 36:41– 66.
1968   "Living Archaeology: The Ngatatjara of Western Australia," *Southwestern Journal of Anthropology* 24:101– 22.
1969   "Subsistence Behavior Among the Western Desert Aborigines of Australia," *Oceania* 39:253– 74.
1970   "Spears and Spearthrowers of the Western Desert Aborigines of Australia," *American Museum Novitiates* 2403 (New York: American Museum of Natural History).
1971   "The Archaeologist as Ethnographer: A Case from the Western Desert of Australia," *World Archaeology* 3:143– 77.
1978   "The Anthropology of Human Residues," *American Anthropologist* 80:815– 35.
GRAUPE, DANIEL
✓✓ 1976   *Identification of Systems*, 2d rev. ed. (Huntington: Krieger).
GROSS, A. J., AND V. A. CLARK
1975   *Survival Distributions: Reliability Applications in the Biomedical Sciences* (New York: John Wiley and Sons).
GUETZKOW, H.
1959   "A Use of Simulation in the Study of International Relations," *Behavioral Sciences* 4:183– 91.
HALL, C. S., AND J. W. DAY, JR.
1977   "Systems and Models: Terms and Basic Principles," in *Ecosystem Modelling in Theory and Practice*, eds. C. S. Hall and J. W. Day, Jr. (New York: John Wiley and Sons).
HALL, E. T., JR.
1944   "Early Stockaded Settlements in the Governador, New Mexico," *Columbia University Studies in Archeology and Ethnology*, vol. 2, pt. 2 (New York: Columbia University Press).
HAMBLIN, R. L., R. B. JACOBSEN, AND J. L. L. MILLER
1973   *A Mathematical Theory of Social Change* (New York: John Wiley).
HAMBURG, J. R., AND R. H. SHARKEY
1961   *Land Use Forecast*, REP 3.26.10. (Chicago: Chicago Area Transportation Study).
HAMMEL, E. A.
1976   "The Matri-lateral Implications of the Structural Cross-Cousin Marriage," in *Demographic Anthropology: Quantitative Approaches*, ed. E. Zubrow (Albuquerque: The University of New Mexico Press, School of American Research Advanced Seminar Series).
HAMMERSLEY, J. M., AND D. C. HANDSCOMB
1964   *Monte Carlo Methods* (New York: John Wiley).

316

References

HANSON, W. G.
1960   "Land Use Forecasting for Transportation Planning," *Highway Research Board* 253: 145–51 (Washington, D. C.: Highway Research Board).

HATCH, JAMES W.
1976   "'Change' Versus 'Noise' in Ceramic Frequency Seriation," paper presented at the 41st Annual Meeting of the Society for American Archaeology, St. Louis.

HAYDEN, BRIAN
1978   "Snarks in Archaeology of Inter-assemblage Variability in Lithics (a View from the Antipodes)," in *Lithics and Subsistence: The Analysis of Stone Tool Use in Prehistoric Economies*, ed. D. D. Davis, Publications in Anthropology, no. 20 (Nashville: Vanderbilt University).

HAYES, ALDEN C.
1964   *The Archeological Survey of Wetherill Mesa*. Archeological Research Series 7-A (Washington, D. C.: National Park Service).

HEMPEL, CARL
1966   *Philosophy of Natural Science* (Englewood Cliffs: Prentice-Hall, Inc.).

HILL, JAMES N.
1977a   "Discussion," in *Explanation of Prehistoric Change*, ed. James N. Hill (Albuquerque: University of New Mexico Press, School of American Research Advanced Seminar Series).

1977b   "Systems Theory and the Explanation of Change," in *Explanation of Prehistoric Change*, ed. J. N. Hill (Albuquerque: University of New Mexico Press, School of American Research Advanced Seminar Series).

HILL, JAMES N. (ED.)
1977   *Explanation of Prehistoric Change* (Albuquerque: University of New Mexico Press, School of American Research Advanced Seminar Series).

HILL, IAN
1976   "Australian Aboriginal Stone Tool Terminology and the Ethnographic Evidence" (B.A. Honors Thesis, University of Queensland).

HIRSCH, MORRIS W., AND STEPHEN SMALE
1974   *Differential Equations, Dynamical Systems and Linear Algebra* (New York: Academic Press).

HODDER, IAN (ED.)
1978   *Simulation Studies in Archaeology* (Cambridge: Cambridge University Press).

HOLE, FRANK, AND ROBERT F. HEIZER
1973   *An Introduction to Prehistoric Archaeology*, 3d ed. (New York: Holt, Rinehart, and Winston).

HOSLER, D. H., J. A. SABLOFF, AND D. RUNGE
1977   "Simulation Model Development: A Case Study of the Classic Maya Collapse," in *Social Process in Maya Prehistory*, ed. N. Hammond (London: Academic Press).

HOUSE, PETER, AND JOHN MCLEOD
1977   *Large-Scale Models for Policy Evaluation* (New York: Wiley-Interscience).

HOWE, R. M.
1977   "Tools for Continuous System Simulation: Hardware and Software," in *Simulation of Systems*, ed. L. Dekker. Proceedings of the 8th AICA Conference (Amsterdam:North-Holland Publishing Company).

HOWELL, NANCY, AND VICTOR A. LEHOTAY
1978   "AMBUSH: A Computer Program for Stochastic Microsimulation of Small Human Populations," *American Anthropologist* 80:905–22.

HUDSON, N.
1971   *Soil Conservation* (Ithaca: Cornell University Press).

HUSLER, J., AND F. FOSBERG
1977   "Chemical Analyses of Anasazi Fields in White Rock Canyon" (Unpublished man-
        uscript on file, Office of Contract Archeology, University of New Mexico, Albu-
        querque).
INNIS, GEORGE S.
✓ 1973   "Simulation of Ill-defined Systems, Some Problems and Progress," *Simulation* 19(6),
        Center Section.
1974   "Dynamic Analysis in 'Soft Science' Studies: In Defense of Difference Equations," in
        Mathematical Problems in Biology, ed. P. Vander Driessche (Berlin: Springer-Verlag).
✓ 1978   "Objectives and Structure for a Grassland Simulation Model," in *Grassland Simulation*
        Model, ed. G. Innis (New York: Springer-Verlag).
INNIS, GEORGE S. (ED.)
1978   *Grassland Simulation Model* (New York: Springer-Verlag).
INNIS, GEORGE, STEWART SCHLESINGER, AND RICHARD SYLVESTER
✓ 1977   "Model Certification—Varying Views from Different Specialties," in 1977 *Summer*
        Computer Simulation Conference (La Jolla: Simulation Councils, Inc.).
IRWIN, N. A., AND D. BRAND
1965   "Planning and Forecasting Metropolitan Development," *Traffic Quarterly* 19:520–40.
ISARD, W., T. W. LANGFORD, AND E. ROMANOFF
1966–   *Philadelphia Regional Input-Output Study: Working Papers*, vols. 1–4 (Philadelphia:
68   Regional Science Research Institute).
JAQUARD, A., AND H. LERIDON
✓ 1974   "Simulating Human Reproduction: How Complicated Should a Model Be?" in *Com-*
        puter Simulation in Human Population Studies, eds. Bennett Dyke and Jean MacCluer
        (New York: Academic Press).
JOACHIM, M.
1976   *Hunter-Gatherer Subsistence and Settlement: A Predictive Model* (New York: Academic
        Press).
JOHNSON, T. HARVEY, AND J. B. CLELAND
1943   "Native Names and Uses of Plants in the North-Eastern Corner of Australia," *Transac-*
        tions of the Royal Society of South Australia 67:149–73.
JONES, A. M. H.
1974   *The Roman Economy*, ed. P. A. Brunt (Oxford: Basil Blackwell).
JONES, RICHARD DUNCAN
1974   *The Economy of the Roman Empire, Quantitative Studies* (New York: Cambridge
        University Press).
JUDGE, W. J.
1976   "The Development of a Complex Cultural Ecosystem in the Chaco Basin, New Mexi-
        co," paper presented at the First Conference on Scientific Research in the National
        Parks, New Orleans.
KAHN, H.
1965   *On Escalation* (New York: Praeger).
KAPLAN, ABRAHAM
1964   *The Conduct of Inquiry* (San Francisco: Chandler Publishing Company).
KARPLUS, WALTER
1977   "The Spectrum of Mathematical Modeling and Systems Simulation," in *Simulation of*
        Systems, ed. L. Dekker. Proceedings of the 8th AICA Conference (Amsterdam: North-
        Holland Publishing Company).
KAY, I. M.
1972   "Digital Discrete Simulation Languages: A Discussion and Inventory," in *Progress in*
        Simulation, eds. K. Gohring, N. Swain, and R. Sauder (New York: Grodon and
        Breach).

References

KAY, I. M., T. M. KISIO, AND D. VAN HOUWELING
1975   "GPSS/SIMSCRIPT: The Dominant Simulation Languages," in *Eighth Annual Simulation Symposium*, eds. W. Stow, C. Miglierina, and W. Coxon (Tampa: Annual Simulation Symposium).

KEENE, A. S.
1979   "Economic Optimisation Models and the Study of Hunter-Gatherer Subsistence-Settlement Systems," in *Transformations: Mathematical to Culture Change*, eds. C. Renfrew and K. L. Cooke (New York: Academic Press).

KENDALL, P. G.
1974   "Hunting Quanta," in *The Place of Astronomy in the Ancient World*, ed. F. R. Hodson (London: Royal Society).

KENYON, K. M.
1957   *Digging up Jericho* (New York: Praeger).

KIVIAT, P. J.
1967   "Development of Discrete Simulation Languages," *Simulation* 8:65–70.

KLEIJNEN, J. P. C.
1974   *Statistical Techniques in Simulation*, pt. 1 (New York: Marcel Dekker).
1977   "Discrete Simulation: Types, Applications, and Problems," in *Simulation of Systems*, ed. L. Dekker (Amsterdam: North-Holland Publishing Company).

KLEINE, H.
1971   "A Second Survey of Users' Views of Discrete Simulation Languages," *Simulation* 17:89–93.

KNUTH, F.
1973   *The Art of Computer Programming* (Reading: Addison Wesley).

LAKATOS, IMRE
1970   "Falsification and the Methodology of Scientific Research Programs," in *Criticism and the Growth of Knowledge*, eds. I. Lakatos and A. Musgrave (Cambridge: Cambridge University Press).

LAMBERG-KARLOVSKY, C. C.
1971   *Excavations at Tepe Yahya, Iran, 1967–69*, American School of Prehistoric Research Bulletins, no. 27 (Cambridge: Harvard University, Peabody Museum).

LEACH, E. R.
1973   "Concluding Address," in *The Explanation of Culture Change: Models in Prehistory*, ed. C. Renfrew (London: Duckworth).

LEHMAN, R. S.
1977   *Computer Simulation and Modeling: An Introduction* (Hillsdale: Lawrence Erlbaum Associates).

LEVINS, RICHARD
1977   "The Search for the Macroscopic in Ecosystems," in *New Directions in the Analysis of Ecological Systems*, ed. G. Innis (La Jolla: Simulation Councils, Inc.).

LEWIS, P., A. GOODMAN, AND J. MILLER
1969   "A Pseudo-random Number Generator for the System/360," *IBM System Journal* 8: 136–46.

LEWONTIN, R. C.
1968   "The Concept of Evolution," in *International Encyclopedia of the Social Sciences* 5:202–7.

LI, C.
1975   *Path Analysis—A Primer* (Pacific Grove: Boxwood Press).

LIMP, W. FREDERICK
1978   "Optimization Theory and Subsistence Change: Implications for Prehistoric Settlement Analysis," paper presented at the 43rd Annual Meeting of the Society for American Archaeology, Tucson, Arizona.

319

LORENZ, EDWARD H.
1963   "Deterministic Nonperiodic Flow," *Journal of Atmospheric Sciences* 20:78– 89.
LOVE, J. R. B.
1944   "A Primitive Method of Making a Wooden Dish by Native Women of the Musgrave
Ranges, South Australia," *Transactions of the Royal Society of South Australia* 66:215– 9.
LOW, GILBERT W.
1979   "The Multiplier-Accelerator Model of Business Cycles Interpreted from a System Dynamics Perspective," *Management Science* (in press).
LOWRY, I. S.
1964   *A Model of Metropolis*, no. RM 4035RC (Santa Monica: Rand Corporation).
MACCLUER, JEAN W.
1973   "Computer Simulation in Anthropology and Human Genetics," in *Methods and Theo-
ries in Anthropological Genetics*, eds. M. H. Crawford and P. L. Workman (Albuquerque: University of New Mexico Press, School of American Research Advanced Seminar
Series).
MACLAREN, M.
1912   "Notes on Desert Water in Western Australia Gnamma Holes and Night Wells,"
Geological Magazine N.S. 9:301– 4.
MACNEISH, R. S.
1961   "The First Annual Report of the Tehuacan Archaeological-Botanical Project," *Project
Reports*, no. 1 (Andover: Peabody Foundation).
MAHER, J. V.
1967   "Drought Assessment by Statistical Analysis of Rainfall," paper presented at the Austra-
lian– New Zealand Association for the Advancement of Science Symposium on Drought,
Melbourne.
MAISEL, H., AND G. GNUGNOLI
1977   *Simulation of Discrete Stochastic Systems* (Chicago: Science Research Associates, Inc.).
MAKRIDAKIS, S., AND C. FAUCHEUX
1973   "Stability Properties of General Systems," in *General Systems* 18:3– 12.
MALTHUS, THOMAS R.
1817   *An Essay on the Principle of Population*, Irwin Classics in Economics, 1963 reprint
(Homewood: Richard D. Irwin, Inc.).
MANKIN, J. B., R. V. O'NEILL, H. H. SHUGART, AND B. W. RUST
1975   "Importance of Validation in Ecosystem Analysis," in *New Directions in the Analysis of*
Ecological Systems, ed. G. Innis (La Jolla: Simulation Councils, Inc.).
MARCH, JAMES G., AND HERBERT A. SIMON
1958   *Organizations* (New York: John Wiley and Sons).
MARTIN, F. F.
1968   *Computer Modeling and Simulation* (New York: John Wiley and Sons).
MARTIN, J.
1973   "On the Estimation of the Sizes of Local Groups in a Hunting/Gathering Environment," *American Anthropologist* 75:1448– 68.
MARTIN, PAUL S., AND FRED PLOG
1973   *The Archaeology of Arizona* (Garden City: Doubleday Natural History Press).
MASS, NATHANIEL J.
1975   *Economic Cycles: An Analysis of Underlying Causes* (Cambridge: M.I.T. Press).
MASS, NATHANIEL, AND PETER SENGE
1978   "Alternative Tests for the Selection of Model Variables," *Systems, Man, and Cybernetics*, IEEE 8:450– 60.
MATSON, R.
1975   "SAMSIM: A Sampling Simulation Program," *Newsletter of Computer Archaeology* 11:1– 4.

References

MATSON, R. G., AND W. D. LIPE
1975   "Regional Sampling: A Case Study of Cedar Mesa, Utah," in *Sampling in Archaeology*, ed. J. W. Mueller (Tucson: University of Arizona Press).

MAY, ROBERT M.
1974   "Biological Populations with Non-overlapping Generations: Stable Points, Stable Cycles, and Chaos," *Science* 186:654–57.

MAY, ROBERT M., AND GEORGE F. OSTER
✓ 1976   "Bifurcations and Dynamic Complexity in Simple Ecological Models," *American Naturalist* 110:573–99.

MAYNARD-SMITH, J.
1974   *Models in Ecology* (Cambridge: Cambridge University Press).

MCLEOD, J.
1973a   "Simulation: From Art to Science for Society," *Simulation* 21(6), Center Section.
1973b   "Simulation Today—From Fuzz to Fact," *Simulation* 20(3), Center Section.
1977   "Panel Comments," in *New Directions in the Analysis of Ecological Systems*, pt. 2, ed. G. Innis (La Jolla: Simulation Councils, Inc.).

MEADOWS, D. H., D. MEADOWS, J. RANDERS, AND W. BEHRENS III
1972   *The Limits to Growth, A Report for the Club of Rome's Project on the Predicament of Mankind* (New York: Universe Books).

MIHRAM, G. ARTHUR
1972a   *Simulation: Statistical Foundations and Methodology* (New York: Academic Press).
✓ 1972b   "Some Practical Aspects of the Verification and Validation of Simulation Models," *Operations Research Quarterly* 23:17–19.

MILLER, D. R.
1974   "Model Validation Through Sensitivity Analysis," in *Proceedings of the 1974 Summer Computer Simulation Conference*, vol. 2 (La Jolla: Simulation Councils, Inc.).

MILLIGAN, GLENN W.
1978   *An Examination of the Effect of Six Types of Error Perturbation on Fifteen Clustering Algorithms*, Working Paper Series, WPS 78–79, College of Administrative Science (Columbus: The Ohio State University).

MILLON, RENE
1967   "Teotihuacan," *Scientific American* 216(6):38–48.

MIZE, J. H., AND J. G. COX
1968   *Essentials of Simulation* (Englewood Cliffs: Prentice-Hall).

MOORE, DAN
1978   "Simulation Languages for the Archaeologist," in *Simulation Studies in Archaeology*, ed. Ian Hodder (Cambridge: Cambridge University Press).

MORGENTHALER, G. W.
1961   "The Theory and Application of Simulation in Operations Research," in *Progress in Operations Research*, ed. R. Ackoff (New York: John Wiley).

MORTENSEN, P.
1972   "Seasonal Camps and Early Villages in the Zygros," in *Man, Settlement, and Urbanism*, eds. P. Ucko, R. Tringham, and G. W. Dimbleby (London: Duckworth).

MOTT, J.
1972   "Germination Studies on Some Annual Species from an Arid Region of Western Australia," *Journal of Ecology* 60:293–304.

MOUNTFORD, CHARLES
1941   "An Unrecorded Method of Manufacturing Wooden Implements by Simple Stone Tools," *Transactions of the Royal Society of South Australia* 65:312–16.

MUELLER, J. H., AND K. F. SCHUESSLER
1969   *Statistical Reasoning in Sociology* (Boston: Houghton Mifflin).

321

REFERENCES

MUELLER, J. W.
1974   "The Use of Sampling in Archaeological Survey," *Society for American Archaeology, Memoirs*, no. 28.

MUNTON, R. J. C.
1973   "Systems Analysis: A Comment," in *The Explanation of Culture Change*, ed. C. Renfrew (London: Duckworth).

NAUTA, DOEDE
1972   *The Meaning of Information* (The Hague: Mouton).

NAYLOR, T. H.
✓ 1973   "Simulation and Validation," in *Proceedings of the 6th IFORS International Conference on Operations Research* (Amsterdam: North-Holland Publishing Company).

NAYLOR, T. H., J. BALINFFY, D. BURDICK, AND K. CHU
1966   *Computer Simulation Techniques* (New York: John Wiley).

NAYLOR, T. H., AND J. FINGER
1967   "Verification of Computer Simulation Models," *Management Science* 14:92–101.

NAYLOR, T. H., K. WERTZ, AND T. H. WONNACOTT
1969   "Spectral Analysis by Simulation Experiments with Economic Models," *Econometrica* 37:333–52.

NOLAN, R. L.
✓ 1972   "Verification/Validation of Computer Simulation Models," in *Proceedings of the 1972 Summer Computer Simulation Conference* (La Jolla: Simulation Councils, Inc.).

NOY-MEIR, I.
1972   "Desert Ecosystems: Environment and Producers," *Annual Review of Ecology and Systematics* 4:25–51.
1974   "Desert Ecosystems: Higher Trophic Levels," *Annual Review of Ecology and Systematics* 5:195–214.

ORLOB, G. T.
1975   "Present Problems and Future Prospects of Ecological Modeling," in *Ecological Modeling in a Resource Management Framework*, ed. C. S. Russell (Baltimore: John Hopkins University Press).

OSBORNE, DOUGLAS
1965   "Introduction," in *Contributions of the Wetherill Mesa Archaeological Project*, ed. D. Osborne. Memoirs of the Society for American Archaeology, 19.

OVERTON, W. S.
1977   "A Strategy of Model Construction," in *Ecosystem Modelling in Theory and Practice*, eds. C. Hall and J. W. Day, Jr. (New York: John Wiley and Sons).

PATTEN, BERNARD
1969   "Ecological Systems Analysis and Fisheries Science," *Transactions of the American Fisheries Society* 98:570–81.
1976   *Systems Analysis and Simulation in Ecology*, vol. 4 (New York: Academic Press).
(ed.)

PATTEN, BERNARD, R. ROSSERMAN, J. FINN, AND W. COLE
1976   "Propagation of Cause in Ecosystems," in *Systems Analysis and Simulation*, vol. 4, ed. B. Patten (New York: Academic Press).

PERLMAN, M. L.
1977   "Comments on Explanation and on Stability and Change," in *Explanation of Prehistoric Change*, ed. J. N. Hill (Albuquerque: University of New Mexico Press, School of American Research Advanced Seminar Series).

PERROT, J.
1966   "Le Gisement Natrufien De Mallaha (Eynan), Israel," *L'Anthropologie* 7:437–84.

PHILLIPS, D. C.
1976   *Holistic Thought in Social Science* (Stanford: Stanford University Press).

322

References

PIRANDELLO, L.
1954   *Six Characters in Search of an Author*, trans. F. May (original Italian in 1921, London: Heinemann).

PLATT, J.
1964   "Strong Inference," *Science* 146:347– 53.

PLOG, FRED
1974   *The Study of Prehistoric Change* (New York: Academic Press).
1975   "Systems Theory in Archaeology Research," *Annual Review of Anthropology* 4:207– 24.
1977a   "Systems Theory and Simulation: The Case of Hawaiian Warfare and Redistribution," in *Explanation of Prehistoric Culture Change*, ed. James N. Hill (Albuquerque: University of New Mexico Press, School of American Research Advanced Seminar Series).
1977b   "Explaining Change," in *Explanation of Prehistoric Change*, ed. James N. Hill (Albuquerque: University of New Mexico Press, School of American Research Advanced Seminar Series).
1978   "The Keresan Bridge: An Ecological and Archeological Account," in *Social Archeology: Beyond Subsistence and Dating*, eds. C. L. Redman, M. J. Berman, E. V. Curtin, W. T. Langhorne, N. M. Versaggi, and J. C. Wanser (New York: Academic Press).
1979   "The Western Anasazi," in *Handbook of North American Indians*, vol. 9, *The Southwest* (Washington, D. C.: Smithsonian Institution).

PLOG, FRED, R. EFFLAND, AND D. F. GREEN
1978   "Inferences Using the SARG Data Bank," in *Investigations of the Southwestern Research Group, the Proceedings of the 1976 Conference*, eds. R. C. Euler and G. J. Gumerman (Flagstaff: Museum of Northern Arizona).

PLOG, STEPHEN
1976   "Relative Efficiencies of Sampling Techniques for Archaeological Surveys," in *The Early Mesoamerican Village*, ed. Kent Flannery (New York: Academic Press).
1977   "A Multivariate Approach to the Explanation of Ceramic Design Variation" (Ph.D. dissertation, University of Michigan).

PLOG, S., F. PLOG, AND W. WAIT
1978   "Decision Making in Modern Surveys," in *Advances in Archaeological Method and Theory*, vol. 1, ed. M. B. Schiffer (New York: Academic Press).

POPPER, KARL R.
1959   *The Logic of Scientific Discovery* (New York: Harper and Row).
1965   *Conjectures and Refutations: The Growth of Scientific Knowledge* (New York: Harper and Row).

RAMAGE, E. A.
1977   "An Agricultural Stratification of the Cochiti Study Area," in *Archeological Investigations in Cochiti Reservoir, New Mexico, Vol. 1: A Survey of Regional Variability*, eds. J. V. Biella and R. C. Chapman (Albuquerque: Office of Contract Archeology, University of New Mexico).

RANDERS, JORGEN
1973   "Conceptualizing Dynamic Models of Social Systems: Lessons from a Study of Social Change" (Ph.D. dissertation, M.I.T.).

RAPPAPORT, ROY
1968   *Pigs for the Ancestors: Ritual in the Ecology of a New Guinea People* (New Haven: Yale University Press).

RASER, JOHN R.
1969   *Simulation and Society* (Boston: Allyn and Bacon).

RATHJE, W.
1971   "The Origin and Development of The Lowland Classic Maya Civilization," *American Antiquity* 36(3):275– 85.

1973   "Classic Maya Development and Denouement: A Research Design," in *The Classic Maya Collapse*, ed. T. P. Culbert (Albuquerque: University of New Mexico Press, School of American Research Advanced Seminar Series).

1975   "The Last Tango in Mayapan: A Tentative Trajectory of Production-Distribution Systems," in *Ancient Civilization and Trade*, eds. J. A. Sabloff and C. C. Lamberg-Karlovsky (Albuquerque: University of New Mexico Press, School of American Research Advanced Seminar Series).

RAUP, DAVID M.

1977   "Probabilistic Models in Evolutionary Paleobiology," *American Scientist* 65:50–57.

REDMAN, CHARLES L.

1973   "Research and Theory in Current Archaeology: An Introduction," in *Research and Theory in Current Archaeology*, ed. Charles L. Redman (New York: John Wiley).

1978   *The Rise of Civilization: From Early Farmers to Urban Society in the Ancient Near East* (San Francisco: W. H. Freeman, Inc.).

REHER, CHARLES A.

1975   "Archeological Survey of 16 Anaconda Company Proposed Exploration Well Sites," in *Archeological Reports, Cultural Resource Management Projects, Working Draft Series* 2, eds. Frank J. Broilo and David E. Stuart (Albuquerque: Office of Contract Archeology, University of New Mexico).

REIDHEAD, V. A.

1976   "Optimization and Food Procurement at the Prehistoric Leonard Haag Site, Southwest Indiana: A Linear Programming Approach" (Ph.D. dissertation, Indiana University).

REITMAN, JULIAN

✓✓ 1971   *Computer Simulation Applications* (New York: Wiley-Interscience).

RENFREW, COLIN

1972   *The Emergence of Civilization: The Cyclades and the Aegean in the Third Millennium B.C.* (London: Methuen).

1973   "Review of *Explanation in Archaeology: An Explicitly Scientific Approach*, by Patty Jo Watson, Steven A. LeBlanc, and Charles L. Redman," *American Anthropologist* 75: 1928–30.

1978   "Trajectory Discontinuity and Morphogenesis: The Implications of Catastrophe Theory for Archaeology," *American Antiquity* 43:203–44.

1979   "Transformations," in *Transformations: Mathematical Approaches to Culture Change*, eds. C. Renfrew and K. L. Cooke (New York: Academic Press).

RENFREW, COLIN, AND E. LEVEL

1979   "Exploring Dominance: Predicting Polities from Centres," in *Transformations: Mathematical Approaches to Culture Change*, eds. C. Renfrew and K. L. Cooke (New York: Academic Press).

RICHARDS, F. M., ET AL.

1973   "A Validation Procedure for Discrete Digital Simulation Models," *Proceedings of the 1973 Summer Computer Simulation Conference* (La Jolla: Simulation Councils, Inc.).

RICK, JOHN W.

1976   "Downslope Movement and Archaeological Intrasite Spatial Analysis," *American Antiquity* 41:133–44.

ROHN, ARTHUR H.

1977   *Cultural Change and Continuity on Chapin Mesa* (Lawrence: The Regents Press of Kansas).

ROSE, MICHAEL R., AND R. HARMSEN

1978   "Using Sensitivity Analysis to Simplify Ecosystem Models: A Case Study," *Simulation* 31:15–26.

References

ROSEN, ROBERT
1979   "Morphogenesis in Biological and Social Systems," in *Transformations: Mathematical Approaches to Culture Change*, eds. C. Renfrew and K. L. Cooke (New York: Academic Press).

ROSS, M.
1969   "An Integrated Approach to the Ecology of Arid Australia," *Proceedings of the Ecological Society of Australia* 4:67–81.

ROSTOVRZEFF, M.
1957   *The Social and Economic History of the Roman Empire*, vols. 1 and 2 (New York: Oxford University Press).

RUPPE, R. J.
1966   "The Archaeological Survey: A Defense," *American Antiquity* 31:313–33.

RUSSELL, C. S.
1975   *Ecological Modeling in a Resource Management Framework* (Baltimore: Johns Hopkins University Press).

SABLOFF, JEREMY A.
1973   "Major Themes in the Past: Hypotheses of the Maya Collapse," in *The Classic Maya Collapse*, ed. T. P. Culbert (Albuquerque: University of New Mexico Press, School of American Research Advanced Seminar Series).

SABLOFF, JEREMY A., THOMAS W. BEALE, AND ANTHONY M. KURLAND, JR.
1973   "Recent Developments in Archaeology," *The Annals of the American Academy of Political and Social Science* 408:113–18.

SALMON, M. H.
1978   "What Can Systems Theory Do for Archaeology?" *American Antiquity* 43:174–83.

SAMUELSON, P. A.
1947   *Foundations of Economic Analysis* (Cambridge: Harvard University Press).

SANDERS, W. T.
1968   "Hydraulic Agriculture, Economic Symbiosis and Evolution of States in Central Mexico," in *Anthropological Archaeology in the Americas* (Washington, D.C.: Anthropological Society of Washington).

SAXE, A. A.
1977   "On the Origin of Evolutionary Processes: State Formation in the Sandwich Islands," in *Explanation of Prehistoric Change*, ed. J. N. Hill (Albuquerque: University of New Mexico Press, School of American Research Advanced Seminar Series).

SCHIFFER, MICHAEL
1975a   "Behavioral Chain Analysis: Activities and the Use of Space," *Fieldiana Anthropology* 65:103–19.

1975b   "The Effects of Occupation Span on Site Content," in *The Cache River Archaeological Project: An Experiment in Contract Archaeology*, eds. M. Schiffer and J. House, Arkansas Archaeological Survey Research Series 8.

1975c   "Factors as 'Tool Kits': Evaluating Multivariate Analyses in Archaeology," *Plains Anthropologist* 20:61–70.

1976   *Behavioral Archaeology* (New York: Academic Press).

SCHOPF, THOMAS J. M., DAVID M. RAUP, STEPHEN J. GOULD, AND DANIEL S. SIMBERLOFF
1975   "Genomic versus Morphologic Rates of Evolution: Influence of Morphologic Complexity," *Paleobiology* 1:63–70.

SCHRANK, W. E., AND C. C. HOLT
1967   "Critique of 'Verification of Computer Simulation Models'," *Management Science* 17:104–6.

REFERENCES

SHAH, B. V.

1974 "On Mathematics of Population Simulation Models," in *Computer Simulation in Human Population Studies*, eds. Bennett Dyke and Jean MacCluer (New York: Academic Press).

SHANAN, L., M. EVENARI, AND N. TADMOR

1967 "Rainfall Patterns in the Central Negev Desert," *Israeli Journal of Exploration* 17:163–84.

SHANNON, R. E., AND M. M. WYATT

1973 "Discrete Simulation Languages Users Survey Revisited," *Simulation* 19:26.

SHANTZIS, S. B., AND W. W. BEHRENS

1973 "Population Control Mechanisms in a Primitive Agricultural Society," in *Toward Global Equilibrium*, eds. D. L. Meadows and D. H. Meadows (Cambridge: M.I.T. Press).

SHARON, D.

1970 "Areal Patterns of Rainfall in a Small Watershed," *International Association of Scientific Hydrological Publications* 96:3–11.

1972 "The Spottiness of Rainfall in a Desert Area," *Journal of Hydrology* 17:161–75.

SHOEMAKER, CHRISTINE

1977 "Mathematical Construction of Ecological Models," in *Ecosystem Modeling in Theory and Practice*, eds. C. Hall and J. W. Day, Jr. (New York: Wiley-Interscience).

SHUBIK, MARTIN B.

1959 *Strategy and Market Structure* (New York: Wiley).

SIMON, H. A.

1952 "Application of Servomechanism Theory to Production Control," *Econometrica* 20: 247–68.

SINGH, INDERJIT, AND RICHARD H. DAY

1975 "Microeconometric Chronicle of the Green Revolution," *Economic Development and Cultural Change* 23:661–86.

SKOLNICK, M., AND C. CANNINGS

1974 "Simulation of Small Human Populations," in *Computer Simulations in Human Population Studies*, eds. Bennett Dyke and J. W. MacCluer (New York: Academic Press).

SLAYTER, R.

1962 "Climate of the Alice Springs Area," *CSIRO Australian Land Research Series* 8:109–28.

SMITH, P. E. L.

1975 "Ganj Dareh Tepe," *Journal of Iran* 13:178–80.

SMITH, VERNON L.

1975 "The Primitive Hunter Culture, Pleistocene Extinction, and the Rise of Agriculture," *Journal of Political Economy* 83:727–55.

SOLECKI, R.

1959 "Early Man in Cave and Village at Shanidar, Kurdistan, Iraq," *Transactions of the New York Academy of Science* 21:712.

STEINHORST, R. K., W. H. HUNT, G. INNIS, AND K. P. HAYDOCK

1978 "Sensitivity Analyses of the ELM Model," in *Grassland Simulation Model*, ed. G. Innis (New York: Springer-Verlag).

STEWARD, JULIAN H.

1938 *Basin Plateau Aboriginal Sociopolitical Groups*, Bureau of American Ethnology, Bulletin 120 (Washington, D. C.: U. S. Government Printing Office).

1956 "Cultural Evolution," *Scientific American* 194:69–80.

STITELER, W. M. II

1974 "Computer Generation of Random Variates," in *Computer Simulation in Human Population Studies*, eds. Bennett Dyke and Jean W. MacCluer (New York: Academic Press).

References

STOCKING, GEORGE W. JR. (ED.)

1974   *The Shaping of American Anthropology, 1883–1911: A Franz Boas Reader* (New York: Basic Books).

STOUFFER, S. A.

1940   "Intervening Opportunities," *American Sociological Review* 5 (6).

STRUEVER, STUART, AND GAIL L. HOUART

1972   "An Analysis of the Hopewell Interaction Sphere," in *Social Exchange and Interaction*, ed. E. N. Wilmsen, Anthropological Papers of the Museum of Anthropology, University of Michigan, no. 46.

SYSTEM DYNAMICS GROUP

1979   *System Dynamics Newsletter* (published annually) (Cambridge: System Dynamics Group, M.I.T.).

TALBOT, H. W. B.

1910   *Geological Observations in the Country Between Wiluna, Hall's Creek and Tanami*, Geological Survey of Western Australia, Bulletin 39 (Perth: Government Printer).

1912   *Geological Investigations in Parts of the North Coolgardie and East Murchison Goldfields*, Geological Survey of Western Australia, Bulletin 45 (Perth: Government Printer).

TALBOT, H. W. B., AND E. DE C. CLARKE

1917   *A Geological Reconnaissance of the Country Between Laverton and the South Australian Border*, Geological Survey of Western Australia, Bulletin 75 (Perth: Government Printer).

THOM, R.

1975   *Structural Stability and Morphogenesis* (Reading: Benjamin).

THOMAS, DAVID H.

1972   "A Computer Simulation Model of Great Basin Shoshonean Settlement Patterns," in *Models in Archaeology*, ed. D. Clarke (London: Methuen).

THOMPSON, D'ARCY W.

1942   *On Growth and Form*, 2d ed. (Cambridge: Cambridge University Press).

THOMSON, DAVID F.

1964   "Some Wood and Stone Implements of The Bindibu Tribe of Central Australia," *Proceedings of the Prehistoric Society* 17:400–22.

1974   *Bindibu Country* (Melbourne: Nelson).

TINDALE, NORMAN

1965   "Stone Implement Making Among the Nakako, Ngadajars, and Pitjandjara of the Great Western Desert," *Records of the South Australian Museum* 15:131–64.

1972   "The Pitjandjara," in *Hunter-gatherers Today*, ed. M. Bicchieri (New York: Holt, Rinehart, and Winston).

TOCHER, K. D.

1963   *The Art of Simulation* (Princeton: Van Nostrand).

TRINGHAM, RUTH

1978   "Experimentation, Ethnoarchaeology, and the Leapfrogs in Archaeological Methodology," in *Explorations in Ethnoarchaeology*, ed. Richard A. Gould (Albuquerque: University of New Mexico Press, School of American Research Advanced Seminar Series).

TSOKOS, C.

1972   *Probability Distributions: An Introduction to Probability and Its Applications* (Belmont: Duxbury Press).

TUCKER, T. G.

1928   *Life in the Roman World of Nero and St. Paul* (New York: McMillan Co.).

327

TWIDALE, C., AND E. CORBIN
1963   "Gnammas," *Revue de Geomorphologie dynamique* 1-2-3:1–20.

USHER, M. B.
1972   "Developments in the Leslie Matrix Model," in *Mathematical Models in Ecology*, ed. J. N. R. Jeffers (Oxford: Blackwell Scientific Publications).

VAN FOERSTER, H.
1966   "The Number of Man," *Report 130, Biological Computer Laboratory* (Urbana: University of Illinois).

VAN HORN, R. L.
✓ 1971   "Validation of Simulation Results," *Management Science* 17:247–58.

VOORIPS, A., D. GIFFORD, AND A. J. AMMERMAN
1978   "Toward an Evaluation of Sampling Strategies: Simulated Excavations Using Stratified Sampling Designs," in *Sampling in Contemporary British Archaeology*, eds. J. F. Cherry, C. Gamble, and S. Shennan. British Archaeological Reports, British Series, no. 50.

✓✓ WADDINGTON, C. H.
1977   *Tools for Thought* (St. Albans: Paladin).

WARD, RICHARD E.
1977   "An Approach to Validation Through Evolutionary Model Building," in *Proceedings of the 1977 Summer Computer Simulation Conference* (La Jolla: Simulation Councils, Inc.).

✓✓ WATSON, PATTY JO, STEVEN A. LEBLANC, AND CHARLES L. REDMAN
1971   *Explanation in Archaeology: An Explicitly Scientific Approach* (New York: Columbia University Press).

WEIBULL, W.
1951   "A Statistical Distribution of Wide Applicability," *Journal of Applied Mathematics* 18:293–97.

WHITE, J. PETER, AND DAVID H. THOMAS
1972   "What Mean These Stones? Ethnotaxonomic Models and Archaeological Interpretation in New Guinea Highlands," in *Models in Archaeology*, ed. D. Clarke (London: Methuen).

WIENER, N.
1948   *Cybernetics* (Cambridge: M.I.T. Press).

WILDESEN, LESLIE E.
1973   "A Quantitative Model of Archaeological Site Formation" (Ph.D. dissertation, Washington State University).

WILLEY, GORDON R., AND JEREMY A. SABLOFF
1974   *A History of American Archaeology* (San Francisco: W. H. Freeman Co.).
1980   *A History of American Archaeology*, 2d ed. (San Francisco: W. H. Freeman Co.).

WINKWORTH, R. E.
1967   "The Composition of Several Arid Spinifex Grasslands of Central Australia in Relation to Rainfall, Soil Water Relations, and Nutrients," *Australia Journal of Botany* 15:107–30.

WINTER, S. G.
1964   "Economic Natural Selection and the Theory of the Firm," *Yale Economic Essays* 4:225–72.
✓ 1971   "Satisficing, Selection and the Innovating Remnant," *Quarterly Journal of Economics* 85:237–61.

WOOD, J. J., AND R. G. MATSON
1973   "Two Models of Sociocultural Systems and Their Implications for the Archaeological Study of Change," in *The Explanation of Culture Change*, ed. C. Renfrew (London: Duckworth).

328

References

WOOD, W. RAYMOND, AND DONALD LEE JOHNSON
1978   "Survey of Disturbance Processes in Archaeological Site Formation," in *Advances in Archaeological Method and Theory*, vol. 1, ed. M. B. Schiffer (New York: Academic Press).
WOODMANSEE, R. G.
✓ 1978   "Critique and Analyses of the Grassland Ecosystem Model ELM," in *Grassland Simulation Model*, ed. G. Innis (New York: Springer-Verlag).
WYMAN, F. P.
1974   "Special Purpose Simulation Languages for Population Studies," in *Computer Simulation in Human Population Studies*, eds. Bennett Dyke and Jean MacCluer (New York: Academic Press).
WYNNE-EDWARDS, V.
1962   *Animal Dispersion in Relation to Social Behavior* (New York: Hafner Publishing Co.).
ZEIGLER, BERNARD
1976a   *Theory of Modelling and Simulation* (New York: John Wiley and Sons).
✓ 1976b   "The Aggregation Problem," in *Systems Analysis and Simulation in Ecology*, ed. B. Patten (New York: Academic Press).
ZIMMERMAN, L. J.
1977   *Prehistoric Locational Behavior: A Computer Simulation*, Report 10, Office of the State Archeologist (Iowa City: University of Iowa).
ZUBROW, EZRA B. W.
1973   "Adequacy Criteria and Prediction in Archeological Models," in *Research and Theory in Current Archeology*, ed. C. L. Redman (New York: John Wiley and Sons).
1975   *Prehistoric Carrying Capacity: A Model* (Menlo Park: Cummings).

Index

Abe, Masatoshi, 217
Aboriginal: adaptations to the desert, 83;
assemblage, 102; informants, 102;
populations, 89, 92, 98; subsistence, 96;
subsistence and settlement technology, 83
Aboriginal Simulation. *See* ABSIM
Aborigine, 89, 97, 102, 107
ABSIM (Aboriginal Simulation), 48, 68, 69,
70, 74, 83, 85–92, 94–98, 99–100, 102,
104–5, 107–11, 113–14, 116, 117*n*7,
292, 294; basic assumptions, 97; critique
of, 245; population movement
implemented in, 98; validation of, 99;
critique of, 294
Ackmen Phase, 125, 133–35, 137
activity: areas, 110; frequency, 81; set, 81,
82; type, 81
Adams, Robert McC., 149
adaptation, 213–15, 217, 219–21, 225,
303. *See also* cultural adaptation
adapting: economic systems, 190, 223, 224;
processes, 225; systems, 213
adaptive, 214, 217, 219; behavior, 190, 222;
control model, 219; decision-makers, 224;
economic models, 212, 220, 226, 304;
mechanism, 254; motivated behavior, 216;
programming, 219–20; systems, 246
Advanced Seminar. *See* School of American
Research Advanced Seminar
Aegean civilization, 298
aggregation, 29, 279–81; defined, 29
agriculture, 190–92, 194–95, 200, 246;
technology of, 279

agriculturalists, 116*n*3
Akerman, Kim, 100
Aldenderfer, Mark S., 8, 13, 113, 242, 245,
251, 255–56, 259, 271–72, 292, 294
ALGOL: general-purpose computer language, 34
Ali Kosh, 149
Ammerman, Albert J., 75, 76, 80
analog computer, 18. *See also* computer
analytical model: defined, 15. *See also*
conceptual model
Anasazi, 122–26, 138–41, 276–77, 281;
habitations, 127; model, 138; settlement
pattern 136, 138; sites, 127–28; 130, 274;
Southwest, 127, 133–35
ANOVA, 46; function of, 39; when used, 45
anthropologist, 201, 287
APL: general-purpose computer language, 34
archaeological: assemblages, 75; data, 72;
record, 76; theory building, 6
The Archaeology of Arizona, 276
The Art of Computer Programming, 147
artifact set: components of, 78, 82
assemblage formation, 85, 114, 116*n* 4, 256;
model of, 77, 114; process of, 73, 75–76,
83, 109, 113
assemblage variability. *See* variability
Askili Huyuk, 149
asymptotic behavior: of equations, 238
Athens, 257
attractors, 290
Augustan period, 170, 172
Australia, 94–95, 99; biologists, 96; deserts

331

Index

FORTRAN IV, 86, 152, 156, 158, 164
Freidel, David A., 182
Frisch, Ragnar, 257
Fritts, Harold C., 293
Fulani, 102–3
functionalist approaches, 4; argument, 70; patterning, 70
fuzzy: defined, 19; conceptual model, 19–22, 29; law, 19, 27–38, 46–47

gaming technique, 48, 48n1
gamma, 103–4
GASP: special-purpose language, 34
gathering, 191
geography, 92
general assemblage formation model, 78, 94. *See also* conceptual model
general linear model, 46. *See also* conceptual model
general model. *See* conceptual model
general-purpose language, 34–36; examples of, 34; when used, 34
general systems theory (GST), 6, 260–61, 285, 287–88
genetic: drift, 122; inheritance, 139; modelling, 120; theory, 139
Gibson Desert, Australia, 96
Giles Weather Station, 92, 95
GNP, 258
goal, 254; of the system, 253, 264; goal-seeking, 254–56
Goodall, D., 95
Goode, Terry M., 63n3
Goodman, Michael R., 263
Goodwin, Richard, 215
Gould, Richard A., 92, 98, 100, 102–5, 108
Governador, 134
GPSS: special-purpose simulation language, 34–35
Grand Canyon sites, 129
graph theory, 28
gravity models, 148. *See also* conceptual model
Great Basin environment, 83
Green, D. F., 130
growth models, 148. *See also* conceptual model

Hall, A. D., 261
hard science, 18
Harmsen, R., 238–39, 242, 247n1
Hatch, James W., 102–3, 117n10
Hayden, Brian, 74
Hayes, Alden C., 133, 275

Hempel, Carl, 53–54, 58, 60–62, 63n3; Hempelian law, 287
Hempel-Oppenheim Covering Law, 285
heuristic: defined, 266; device, 5
Hill, Ian, 100
Hill, James N., 138, 252–54, 257, 262, 264, 300–301, 305
historical sources, 101
Hodder, Ian, 6
holist view, 4, 260
Holt, C. C., 43
homeostatic, 222, 224, 278; mechanisms, 201, 254, 264; rule, 216
homeostsis, 202, 215, 224, 252–53, 286; in the general sense, 215, 221, 252; in the specific sense, 215, 252, 254
Hopewell, 4
Hopi, 279–80
Hosler, Dorothy H., 163, 252, 258, 268, 273
Houart, Gail, 4
House, Peter, 13, 20, 41–42
Howell, Nancy, 91
Hume, D., 188
hunter-gatherers, 81–85, 99, 116n3, 256; societies, 7, 90
hunting, 191–94, 246; efficiency, 194
hybrid computer, 18. *See also* computers
hypothesis, 281; construction, 7, 25–26, 68; guiding experimentation, 44; testing, 5, 39

IBM 370/168, 86
IBM assembly language, 87
imitation, 146
Imperial Rome. *See* Rome
IMSL subroutines, 86
inductive analysis, 52–53; technique, 62; theory, 53; view, 52–53, 62
inference, 39
initial conditions, 225
Innis, George S., 16, 19, 25, 30, 42
input: changes, 44; -output models, 148; values, 44
insensitivity, 270
instability, 186–90, 254, 264, 298
integral calculus. *See* calculus
interassemblage variability, 70
internal, 265, 301; approach, 260; causal structure, 260; components, 259; decision mechanisms, 258, 264; feedback, 258, 261, 264–65, 277; perspective, 256–60, 264, 279; structure, 137, 301. *See also* endogenous
INTERNATIONAL, 188n1
intervening opportunity models, 148
Iron Law, 198, 200–201

Index

Mize, J. H., 23
model, 76; building, 5; definition, 14; goals, 23; numerical, 15; rejection, 42; utility, 41; validation, 29, 40. *See also* conceptual model, recursive programming model
modelling process, 23, 26, 164
modes of behavior, 238
monogenesis, 303
monopsony, 196, 198; defined, 227
Monte Carlo simulation, 14
Moore, Dan, 35–36, 90
morphogenesis, 225, 286, 302
Mortensen, P., 149
Mountford, Charles, 100
Mousterian assemblage, 70
multidimensional scaling, 70
multiple regression, 46, 114
multivariate methods, 4, 48, 70–72, 75, 113; normal mixtures, 116n2
mutations, 303

NATIONAL, 188n1
National Model, 268
natural growth function, 192
natural selection, 121
Navajo Reservoir District, 134, 141n1
Naylor, T. H., 13, 45
negative feedback, 201, 215, 224, 252–56, 263, 278, 286, 298; loop, 254–55, 267–68, 273; mechanism, 216; structure, 263. *See also* feedback
neoclassical economics, 196
Neumann, John von, 14
new archaeology, 3–4, 6, 259
New Guinea, 116n3
Newton, Isaac, 61–62, 63n2, 140
Newtonian physics, 46, 139
Newton's Laws of Motion, 59
New York Metropolitan Regional Study, 188n1
Ngatatjara, 100
Ngatjara, 100
Nissen, Hans, 149
noise, 115, 117n5; defined, 120; in ABSIM, 114
nonnormal multivariate distribution forms, 116n2
normal, 103–4
n-transforms, 74, 110
Nyatunyatjara, 100

observability, theory of, 246
occupation span: defined, 81
Ocos, 149
Odell, P. L., 29
one-cycle structures, 182

open system, 286
optimal, 214, 217–19, 227n9, 264; decisions, 218–19; environmental fitneess, 212; performance, 227n9; strategy, 219
optimization problems, 216–19, 288, 294
optimizing calculations, 207, 209, 214, 216–20, 224, 246
ordering archaeological data, 5
originality, 146
origin of urban society, 149
oscillation, 238
Oster, George F., 234
output, 292; utility, 20–22, 32, 48, 49n2; validity, 21, 47; variables, 38, 45, 86–87

parameters, 44, 76, 179, 182, 192, 270; defined, 16, 77; parametric test, 40
Park Service investigations, 132
parsimony, 146
partial-data problems, 5
partial differential equations. *See* equations. *See also* differential equations
pastoralism, 195
patterned regularity, 121
pdf (probability density function), 30–31, 87, 102–3; defined, 87
periodic motion, 290
Perlman, M. L., 301
Perrot, J., 149
pessimal performance, 227n9
phase diagram, 194, 198
phase portraits, 290
Phillips, D. C., 261
philosophy of science, 39, 42, 283, 299; validation in, 42–43
physics, 140
Piedra Phase, 125
Pirandello, Luigi, 295–96
Pitjandjara, 100
Plato, 160
Plato's Republic, 160
Pleistocene, 207, 217
PL/I, 34, 88; problems of use, 36
Plog, Fred, 7, 12, 68, 127, 130, 267–68, 276–77, 279, 281
Poincaré, Henri, 290
POLIMETRIC, 148
Pompeii, 144
Popper, Karl R., 53, 58, 61, 64n6
Popperian falsification, 284
population growth, 42
positivist model, 43
positive feedback, 252, 254–55, 258, 263, 280, 286; link, 280; loop, 263, 280; mechanisms, 254; structure, 263, 280
PRAND, 87

Index

Smith, Vernon L., 149, 191, 217
Social Darwinist doctrine, 212
Society for Computer Simulation, 247n1
soft science, 18, 23
Solecki, Ralph, 149
Southwestern archaeological sequence, 122
spatial location, 81; structure, 232
special-purpose simulation language: 34–36
spectral analysis, 39, 45
stability, 187, 290; stable state, 286, 302
"Stability Properties of General Systems," 186
state (of the system), 212, 286, 289
state-determined dynamics models, 122, 190, 226, 256, 270. See also conceptual model
state variables, 150, 152, 185, 195, 207, 246, 250, 264, 286, 289, 293. See also variable
statistical: criteria, 60; relations, 60–63
Steward, Julian H., 83
stochastic, 86, 91, 94, 144, 294, 303; components, 33, 39, 87, 91; model, 30–31, 37, 45, 87; process, 91, 219, 294; simulation, 33, 147; variables, 31–32
Stocking, George, 63n1
strong inference, 43
student's t-test, 39
strategies, 146
Struever, Stuart, 4
suboptimization, 217–219, 264
subroutine, 88, 114
subsistence activity, 88
substantivist anthropologist, 293
Susa, 149
Sylvester, Richard, 16, 42
system, 76; defined, 251, 261; behavior, 264; boundaries, 27–28, 69, 74, 139, 256, 270; identification, 246; level, 162; rates, 162; stability, 186; state, 202, 213
system dynamics, 15, 31, 39, 56, 140, 236, 239, 243, 251, 255–65, 270–73, 275–76, 281, 283, 285, 287–90, 297, 302, 305; group, 282n1; model, 5–6, 138, 140, 202, 261, 270, 272, 286, 291–92, 302; National Model, 267; theory, 7–8
systems analysis, 5–6
"Systems Theory and the Explanation of Change," 252
systems thinking, 5, 54, 285; theory, 12

table functions, 157–58
Tasaday, 116n3
task site, 92
tâtonnement, 222, 227n10
technological diffusion, 207

teleological, 253
Teotihuacan, 149
Tepe Yahya, 149
theoretical model, 16, 71. See also conceptual model
theory, 23; construction, 39; middle-range, 7
Theory of Dynamical Systems, 288–90
Thomas, David H., 83
Thompson, D'Arcy W., 164
Thomson, David F., 100
Tijeras Canyon, 128
time constant, 236; -dependent factors, 135; series analysis, 39, 45
Tindale, Norman, 100
tinkering, 49n3
TOMM (Time-Oriented Metropolitan Model), 148
TOMII, 148
TOMMIII, 148
tool kit, 70, 73, 102, 113
transformation, 286
transient data, 49n4
tree-ring chronology, 124
trend models, 148. See also conceptual models
Tsembaga, 202
"2001," 304

Ulam, S. M., 14
universal statement, 59–62
unobservable relations, 61–62
unstable equilibrium, 286. See also equilibrium
urban dynamics, 143, 245; model, 47; studies, 298
Urban Dynamics, 148, 152, 163–64, 252, 265, 296
urban revolution, 161
Uruk, 149
useful mode, 20, 28; defined, 41
use-life, 80, 117n5, 256; of a tool, 78
Usher, M. B., 114
US/IBP Grassland Biome Project, 25
utility, of models,. See useful model

validation, 32, 38–45, 47, 71–73, 83, 105, 232, 242–47, 258–59, 264–65, 271–73, 297; defined, 242; phase, 100
value changes, 44; mechanisms, 57
variable, 46, 76, 78, 82; action, 250–51; assemblage, 91; defined, 77; random, 33; rate, 251, 274; types, 16, 44, 82, 162. See also descriptive variables, state variables
verification, 32, 36–37, 88, 284
village agriculturalists, 7
Volterra-Lotka equations, 290

339